Guide to
Network Cabling
Fundamentals

Beth Verity

THOMSON

COURSE TECHNOLOGY

Australia • Canada • Mexico • Singapore • Spain • United Kingdom • United States

THOMSON

COURSE TECHNOLOGY

Guide to Network Cabling Fundamentals

by Beth Verity

Acquisitions Editor:
Will Pitkin

Product Manager:
Karen Lyons

Development Editor:
Dan Seiter

Associate Product Manager:
Tim Gleeson

Editorial Assistant:
Nick Lombardi

Marketing Manager:
Jason Sakos

Production Editor:
Christine Gatliffe

Cover Design:
Steve Deschene

Compositor:
GEX Publishing

For permission to use material from text or product, contact us by
Tel (800) 730-2214
Fax (800) 730-2215
www.thomsonrights.com

Disclaimer
Course Technology reserves the right to revise this publication and make changes from time to time in its conte without notice.

ISBN 0-619-12012-6

TABLE OF
Contents

Preface

Welcome to *Guide to Network Cabling Fundamentals!* This book covers telecommunications and network cabling concepts using real-world, interactive examples and hands-on projects that introduce you to the tools of the trade. The book also includes information about the standards and codes that govern cable installation in commercial buildings, guidelines for designing effective telecommunications networks, and instructions for creating comprehensive system documentation.

Guide to Network Cabling Fundamentals offers in-depth coverage of cable types and topologies to help you select the right ones for any application. Throughout the book, review questions reinforce the concepts introduced in each chapter, while detailed projects provide firsthand experience in designing and installing telecommunications systems, using installation and testing tools, and creating network documentation. These involved, scenario-based assignments prepare you for situations you will face in real life, and require independent work to demonstrate what you have learned.

The Intended Audience

This book serves both entry-level students and information systems professionals who want to learn standardized cabling practices. It prepares readers to take an active role in designing and installing a network infrastructure that meets customer needs. Students who work their way through the entire book should be well equipped to install standards-compliant, scalable networks, and should be well prepared for the BICSI Installer, Level 1 Certification exam.

Chapter 1, "Introduction to Network Cabling," discusses the origins of cabling standards in the wake of deregulation, which resulted in mass confusion and substandard workmanship. The chapter also identifies standards organizations, popular network systems, the Open Systems Interconnection (OSI) reference model for networking, and IEEE Project 802. The chapter then covers the development of networking technology, with an emphasis on structured cabling systems. The chapter concludes with an overview of common types of cable, an introduction to topology, a comparison of cable media, and an introduction of the importance of cable documentation.

Chapter 2, "Grounding and Bonding," covers the codes and standards that apply to grounding and bonding requirements for commercial buildings. The chapter explores grounding and bonding components in detail. You will also find coverage of grounding systems, as well as cable protection and equipment grounding practices, including primary and secondary protection for telecommunications circuits. The chapter ends by emphasizing how documentation benefits you and your network.

Chapter 3, "Cables and the Cabling Infrastructure," compares various cable types and their unique characteristics. The chapter also discusses popular network topologies, when and how to use them, and the advantages and disadvantages of each. You will also find a detailed discussion of network design techniques. The chapter concludes by describing the network components you need to document.

Chapter 4, "Installing Cables and Supporting Structures," begins by discussing structured cabling in general, and horizontal cabling and horizontal pathways in particular. The text describes common types of pathways and the types of cable you can use in them. You will also find detailed guidelines for installing and terminating cables, and for effective cable management.

Chapter 5, "Backbone and Horizontal Distribution Systems," covers the two primary distribution systems in cabling networks. The sections on backbone distribution discuss interbuilding and intrabuilding backbones, appropriate topologies, and guidelines for selecting backbone distribution media and connecting hardware. The sections on horizontal distribution discuss general design guidelines, work area components, and horizontal cross-connects. The chapter concludes with detailed sections on documenting cable plants and equipment rooms.

Chapter 6, "Cable Termination and Splicing," provides in-depth information about cable preparation and termination procedures, the color code and wiring schemes, and the locations where cables are terminated, such as demarcation points, equipment rooms, telecommunications rooms, and work areas. Also included are detailed figures and descriptions of the tools of the trade. The chapter concludes by explaining how to document your network hardware.

Chapter 7, "Firestopping and Comprehensive Fire Prevention Systems," tackles one of the most important sets of codes and regulations—fire protection. This chapter discusses the components of a comprehensive fire protection system, and describes popular firestopping products and materials, complete with guidelines for their proper selection and installation. The final section discusses how to document network addressing, network changes, and logging procedures in your documentation manual.

Chapter 8, "Testing and Troubleshooting," covers the different types of required testing for all cable systems. It includes a detailed discussion of certification tests, complete with acceptable pass/fail parameters. The chapter introduces you to a series of general techniques and methods for troubleshooting problems, and includes descriptions of many useful testing and troubleshooting tools. The final section of the chapter is a discussion about managing your documentation manual.

Appendix A provides mapping to the exam objectives for BICSI Installer, Level 1 Certification.

Features

To ensure a successful learning experience, this book includes the following pedagogical features:

- **Chapter objectives** — Each chapter begins with a list of the concepts to be mastered within the chapter. This list provides a quick reference to the chapter's contents, and can serve as a useful study aid.

- **Illustrations and tables** — Numerous illustrations of equipment, diagrams, and tools help you visualize cable setup, theories, concepts, and identification. Tables provide details and comparisons of both practical and theoretical information, and permit a quick review of topics.

- **End-of-chapter material** — This material includes many features to reinforce the concepts covered in the chapter. The chapter summary reviews important ideas, the key terms define new concepts introduced in the chapter, and the review questions test your knowledge of important concepts. The hands-on projects help you apply what you learned in the chapter, and the case projects take you through real-world scenarios.

Text and Graphic Conventions

Where appropriate, additional information and exercises are included to help you better understand the chapter discussions. Several types of icons throughout the book alert you to additional materials:

The Note icon indicates additional, helpful material that relates to the main discussion.

NOTE

Each hands-on project is preceded by the Hands-on icon and a description of the exercise.

HANDS-ON PROJECTS

Special icons mark the case projects in each chapter.

CASE PROJECTS

Instructor's Materials

The following supplemental materials are available when this book is used in a classroom setting. All of these supplements are provided to the instructor on a single CD.

Electronic Instructor's Manual. This manual accompanies the textbook and includes the following material:

- Additional instructional material to assist in class preparation, including suggestions for classroom activities, discussion topics, and additional projects

- Solutions to all end-of-chapter materials, including review questions, hands-on projects, and case projects

- Examples of forms that students can use while planning, installing, testing, troubleshooting, and documenting a network

ExamView®. This textbook is accompanied by ExamView, a powerful testing software package that allows instructors to create and administer printed, computer (LAN-based), and Internet exams. ExamView includes hundreds of questions that correspond to topics covered in this text, enabling students to generate detailed study guides that include page references for further review. The computer-based and Internet testing components allow students to take exams at their computers, and save the instructor time by grading each exam automatically.

PowerPoint presentations. This book comes with Microsoft PowerPoint slides for each chapter. They can be used as a teaching aid for classroom presentation, made available to students on the network for chapter review, or be printed for classroom distribution. Instructors, please feel free to add your own slides for additional topics you introduce to the class.

ACKNOWLEDGMENTS

Writing this book has been quite an experience—sometimes frustrating, sometimes exhausting, but always fulfilling and exciting, and most of all a remarkable learning opportunity.

Writing a book doesn't involve just an author and a subject. It requires a great publisher, numerous editors, teamwork, support, guidance, and constant encouragement. First, I want to thank Course Technology for the chance to write a new and useful network-cabling textbook. To Will Pitkin, my acquisitions editor, and to Laura Hildebrand, my first product manager, thank you for your support and encouragement and especially for your confidence in me.

I offer special thanks to Karen Lyons, my product manager, whose patience and understanding never wavered, even when I missed deadlines. Karen, you gave me constant encouragement, and you always seemed to know when I needed it most. I have truly enjoyed and appreciated the opportunity to work with you.

More thanks go to Dan Seiter, my development editor, who fine-tuned my work into the polished book before you. Dan's patience, concern, and attention to detail are just a few reasons I was lucky to have had him for an editor. Dan, I am grateful for your support, encouragement, and guidance; you helped me through some rough times and taught me a lot.

To the peer reviewers and technical reviewer, who checked my work every step of the way, thank you for ensuring its accuracy and helping to make the book more user-friendly.

To Devra Kunin, my copyeditor, thank you for making my writing more literate and keeping it free from errors. To Christine Gatliffe, my production editor, thank you for ensuring that the final drafts were ready for production. To GEX, thanks for your attention to detail and for helping me provide clear and accurate figures.

I want to give special thanks to some very special people. Mom, thanks for believing in me and loving me, no matter what. Artie, thanks for being proud of your big sister. Sibby, thank you for being there; your extra help and support are always appreciated. Danny, thanks for all your help, especially late at night. To my kids, AJ, Kyra, and Tommy, thanks for your support, love, and understanding. To my four loving and incredible cats, Hazel, George, Sister, and Fred, thanks for making me leave my desk often enough to maintain some balance in all of this.

Finally, I want to thank my partner, Liz, for reading and re-reading drafts, helping with review questions, projects, and case projects, for staying up with me all hours of the day and night, reminding me to eat and take breaks, and for making sure I didn't have to worry about household chores. Your contributions were, and continue to be, immeasurable and inexpressible.

DEDICATION

To those who are gone—Dad, Mary, and Tish—but not forgotten. You loved me, you supported me, you believed in me.

Read This Before You Begin

To the User

This book is intended to be read in sequence from the beginning. Each chapter builds upon the preceding chapters to provide a solid understanding of network cabling types, characteristics, standards, design guidelines, installation, testing, and troubleshooting. Readers are also encouraged to investigate the many online and printed sources of additional information cited throughout the book.

To the Instructor

When setting up a classroom lab, make sure that each workstation has a computer with Windows 98, 98 SE, or 2000 Professional. In addition, make sure that each computer has Visio installed, along with Internet access; students will use both in the hands-on projects and case projects throughout the book. These projects will also require students to use hand tools, testing and troubleshooting equipment, a supply of all major types of cable, and various terminating hardware.

Visit Our World Wide Web Site

Additional materials might be available for your course on the World Wide Web. Go to the Course Technology Web site, *www.course.com*, and then search periodically using this book title for more details.

Readers are also encouraged to e-mail comments, questions, and suggestions about this book to the author at *bverity516@hotmail.com*.

Coping with Change on the Web

Eventually, all the Web-based resources we mention in this book will become stale or be replaced by newer information. In some cases, the outdated URLs lead you to their replacements; in other cases, the URLs will lead nowhere, leaving you with the dreaded 404 error message, "File not found."

When this happens, please do not give up! Most large or complex Web sites offer search engines to help you find what you need. The more focused you can make your search request, the more likely you are to find useful information. For instance, you can search the string "Cat 5 cable" to find data about the subject in general, but if you are looking for information about certification testing for Cat 5 cable, you can find it more quickly using a search string such as "TSB-67".

Finally, do not be afraid to use general search engines such as *www.search.com*, *www.whatis.com*, *www.about.com*, or *www.google.com* to find related information.

LAB REQUIREMENTS

Use the following hardware, software, and other tools to perform the projects at the end of the chapters:

- Pentium II 300-MHz CPU or higher
- 128 MB of RAM
- 2-GB hard disk, with at least 1 GB of storage available
- CD-ROM drive
- Windows 98, 98 SE, 2000 Professional, or 2002
- Internet Explorer 5.5 or other Web browser
- Visio diagramming software
- Internet access
- Hand tools, as described in Chapter 6
- A good supply of all types of cable
- Testing and troubleshooting equipment, as described in Chapter 8
- A variety of connecting and termination hardware

1

INTRODUCTION TO NETWORK CABLING

After reading this chapter and completing the exercises, you will be able to:

♦ Understand the need for certification and registration in telecommunications

♦ Summarize the history of standardization efforts

♦ Explain networking specifications and communications

♦ Understand the major developments in network technology

♦ Determine which type of network cable to use

♦ Define cabling documentation

As network technology continues to mature, the demand to connect more people to networks also continues to grow. Because the foundation of any network is its cabling, the demand for trained network cable specialists is growing as well. Networking and its related equipment have become more complex; a good network cable specialist now needs a comprehensive understanding of cabling as it relates to network access methods and network management. Specialists must also understand how different forms of cabling compare in terms of reliability, transmission speeds, and serviceability.

In addition to teaching concepts and theory, this book provides a practical, hands-on approach to the installation of all types of cable. The labs throughout this book provide you with experience working with a variety of termination devices, patch panels, cable media, connectors, splices, and relevant test equipment.

This chapter introduces you to the origins of cabling standards, standards organizations, and popular network cable systems. You will learn some of the standards required by industry and be introduced to structured cabling practices.

THE NEED FOR CERTIFICATION AND REGISTRATION IN TELECOMMUNICATIONS

The worldwide deregulation of the telecommunications industry began with the divestiture of AT&T in 1984. This divestiture resulted in the breakup of the Bell systems, and eventually to the establishment of standardization. AT&T was required by judicial decree to sell its local operating companies and restrict itself to providing long-distance telephone service and manufacturing and selling telephone products.

Divestiture caused mass confusion and problems for customers, manufacturers, long-distance carriers, and **service providers (SP)**, companies that provide telecommunications services for other companies. After deregulation, anyone could design, install, and maintain telephone systems, giving rise to many fly-by-night companies whose names became synonymous with shoddy work.

To add to the confusion, computer technology was maturing, and more organizations were installing computer systems. Each system required its own unique cable and connectors, and customers were displeased that their wiring needs changed each time their computer platform changed. In the past, local telephone companies had always looked after basic cabling needs, and companies that used mainframes had relied on their vendors to install the appropriate cable for their system. These practices didn't work anymore, and many customers who had been victimized by bad installations began seeking certified industry professionals.

BICSI Certifications and Registrations

In the wake of deregulation, one of the only organizations providing standards in telecommunications was the **Building Industry Consulting Service (BICS)**. AT&T and Bell Canada created BICS in the late 1960s, and it became responsible for identifying construction projects during the planning stage and working with architects, contractors, and engineers to create a project design. The design included all the pathway elements used in telecommunications cabling, such as raceways, equipment ducts, and **conduits**, the pipes that carry cable through a ceiling, wall, or floor. BICS worked with building contractors to implement the design, and helped operating companies install the necessary infrastructure (wires, cables, and termination hardware) to provide telephone facilities for commercial buildings.

In 1974, **Building Industry Consulting Services International (BICSI)** was founded to serve telecommunications consultants around the world. BICSI, a non-profit organization, began publishing its manuals to share standards-based design, installation guidelines, and methods that were accepted by the telecommunications industry. As the association grew, its programs and interests expanded to cover the broad spectrum of voice, data, and video technologies. BICSI offers courses, conferences, publications, and registration programs for cabling distribution designers and installers.

BICSI has established registration programs that provide a level of assurance to the industry and to consumers that a person is proficient in a designated area. Candidates for these registrations are required to pass rigorous exams and keep their knowledge current through continuing education. Some of the professional registration programs offered by BICSI are:

- **Registered Communications Distribution Designer (RCDD)** — RCDDs demonstrate proficiency in the design, integration, and implementation of telecommunications transport systems and related infrastructure components.

- **RCDD/LAN specialist** — In addition to their RCDD foundation, these specialists demonstrate proficiency with **local area networks (LANs)** and internetworking design. A LAN is a network of computers and other devices confined to one building, or even one office.

- **Installer, Level 1; Installer, Level 2; and technician** — Installers and technicians demonstrate their proficiency in conducting site surveys and pulling wire, cable, and optical fiber to the highest level of specification. This three-level career advancement program is designed to meet the diverse needs of the industry.

STANDARDIZATION BODIES

Standards are specifications that guarantee a minimum level of performance. As defined in the *Telecommunications Industry Association Engineering Manual*, a standard is "a document that establishes engineering and technical requirements for processes, procedures, practices, and methods that have been decreed by authority or adopted by consensus. Standards may also be established for selection, application, and design criteria for material." Standards are used to quantify and qualify a given material or component. Because of the wide array of available hardware and software, standards are especially important in telecommunications.

Standardization of cabling systems was nonexistent until 1985, when the Computer Communications Industry Association (CCIA) approached the Electronics Industry Association (EIA) about developing cabling standards. The associations agreed that standards were required for voice and data communications designed for commercial and residential use. EIA assigned the task of developing cabling standards to a committee called TR-41.

Subcommittees and work groups were established to deal with the wide-ranging issues involved in developing cabling standards for commercial and residential buildings. In 1991 TR-41 split into two committees: TR-41 was still responsible for User Premise Equipment standards, but a new engineering committee, designated as TR-42, was now responsible for User Premise Telecommunications Cabling Infrastructure standards. TR-42 was charged with ensuring that the standards remained as an open system in support of voice, data, video, building control, and other low-voltage, **power-limited applications**. These applications use a circuit that limits power (generally to 50 volts and under) to the external wiring in the event of an overload condition.

Several more organizations have evolved within the telecommunications industry to set and oversee standards. You should become familiar with the following groups, which set standards referenced by manuals, articles, and books:

- **International Organization for Standardization (ISO)** — Headquartered in Geneva, Switzerland, the ISO is a collection of standards organizations that represents 130 countries. Its goal is to establish international technological standards that facilitate the global exchange of information. In addition to information processing and communications, ISO's authority applies to the fields of textiles, packaging, distribution of goods, energy, shipbuilding, banking, and financial services. Only about 500 of the ISO's nearly 12,000 standards apply to computer products and functions.

- **American National Standards Institute (ANSI)** — ANSI has more than 1000 representatives from industry and government, who together determine standards for the electronics industry and other fields. ANSI also represents the United States in setting international standards. ANSI does not dictate that manufacturers comply with its standards, but asks them to comply voluntarily. This compliance assures potential customers that systems are reliable and can be integrated with an existing infrastructure. To earn ANSI's approval, new electronic equipment and methods must undergo rigorous testing.

- **Electronic Industries Alliance (EIA)** — This trade organization has representatives from electronics manufacturing firms across the United States. EIA began as the Radio Manufacturers Association (RMA) in 1924; it has evolved to include manufacturers of televisions, semiconductors, computers, and networking devices. EIA not only sets standards for its members, it helps write ANSI standards and lobbies for legislation that favors the growth of the computer and electronics industries.

- **Telecommunications Industry Association (TIA)** — A subgroup of EIA, TIA is best known for developing cabling standards used in the design and installation of structured cabling systems that support a wide range of applications.

- **International Telecommunication Union (ITU)** — The ITU is a specialized United Nations agency that regulates international telecommunications, including radio and TV frequencies, satellite and telephony specifications, networking infrastructures, and tariffs applied to global communications. The ITU began as the Comité Consultatif International Télégraphique et Téléphonique (CCITT). You may still see references to CCITT standards in some manuals and texts.

- **Institute of Electrical and Electronics Engineers (IEEE)** — The IEEE is an international society of engineering professionals that promotes development and education in electrical engineering and computer science. IEEE establishes its own standards for the electronics and computer industries and contributes to the work of other standards-setting bodies such as ANSI. IEEE technical papers and standards are highly respected in the networking profession.

Codes and Regulations

In addition to standards, telecommunications professionals must understand and follow numerous codes and regulations in everyday business. From distribution design to final installation, the telecommunications field encompasses a variety of industries, each governed by its own rules.

A **code** is a body of law that is enforced by a local jurisdictional agency and systematically interpreted by the courts. A code's general purpose is to safeguard people and property from hazards, and to ensure the quality of construction. Codes and standards encompass almost all aspects of the building and construction industry. All installation methods and electrical products must conform to local electrical codes, building codes, fire codes, and other safety codes. However, these codes do not ensure that a system will function correctly or guarantee a minimum level of performance.

For example, the **National Electrical Code® (NEC)** is one of the most thorough and widely adopted sets of electrical safety requirements in the United States. The NEC is issued to minimize the risk of electrical shock, fires, and explosions. If state, municipal, or local codes are more restrictive than the NEC's, then the most restrictive code takes precedence.

A **regulation** reflects a local authority's ability to enforce codes and standards to regulate the building and construction industry. For example, service providers are regulated by the Federal Communications Commission (FCC) and state public service or public utility commissions.

NETWORKING SPECIFICATIONS AND COMMUNICATIONS

Besides the necessary hardware and software, sets of rules were needed to enable truly networked computer communications. The IEEE and the ISO both responded by creating specifications that standardized network communications.

Developed in 1980, the IEEE's "Project 802" standardized the physical elements of a network and addressed networking specifications as they apply to connectivity, networking media, encryption, emerging technologies, and **error-checking algorithms**, the process used in a frame to check for errors in data transmission. Meanwhile, in the early 1980s the ISO began work on a universal set of specifications that would enable computer platforms across the world to communicate openly. The result was a helpful model for understanding and developing computer communications, called the **Open Systems Interconnection (OSI) model**. The IEEE 802 standards were developed before the

ISO standardized its OSI model, but the 802 standards can be applied to the layers of the OSI model.

The IEEE 802 standards are listed in Table 1-1, and the OSI model is summarized in Table 1-2.

Table 1-1   IEEE 802 standards

Standard	Name	Explanation
802.1	Internetworking	Covers routing, bridging, and internetwork communications
802.2	Logical Link Control	Relates to error and flow control over data frames
802.3	Ethernet LAN	Covers all forms of Ethernet media and interfaces
802.4	Token Bus LAN	Covers all forms of Token Bus media and interfaces
802.5	Token Ring LAN	Covers all forms of Token Ring media and interfaces
802.6	Metropolitan Area Network (MAN)	Covers MAN technologies, addressing, and services
802.7	Broadband Technical Advisory Group	Covers broadband networking media, interfaces, and other equipment
802.8	Fiber-Optic Technical Advisory Group	Covers use of fiber-optic media and technologies for various networking types
802.9	Integrated Voice/Data Networks	Covers integration of voice and data traffic over a single network medium
802.10	Network Security	Covers network access controls, encryption, certification, and other security topics
802.11	Wireless Networks	Covers standards for wireless networking for different broadcast frequencies and usage techniques
802.12	High-Speed Networking	Covers a variety of 100-Mbps-plus technologies, including 100BASEVG-AnyLAN

The OSI model divides network architecture into seven layers, as shown in Table 1-2. Each layer has its own set of functions, and interacts with the layers directly above and below it. The OSI model is a theoretical representation of what happens between two nodes (computers) on a network.

Table 1-2 OSI model and layer functions

Layer Number, Function, and Interaction	Layer Name
Layer 7 — Provides services directly to applications. The applications can vary, but they include electronic messaging.	Application
Layer 6 — Formats the data to provide a common interface for applications. This can include encryption services.	Presentation
Layer 5 — Establishes end connections between two nodes. Services include establishing whether a connection can be set at full- or half-duplex, although duplex is actually handled at Layer 4.	Session
Layer 4 — Handles general data delivery, whether connection-oriented or connectionless. Includes full- or half-duplex, flow control, and error recovery services.	Transport
Layer 3 — Establishes the connection between two nodes through addressing. It includes routing and relaying of data through an internetwork.	Network
Layer 2 — Frames data and handles flow control. Specifies the topology and provides hardware addressing.	Data Link
Layer 1 — Transmits the raw bitstream (data), electrical signaling, and hardware interface.	Physical

IEEE 802 defined many rules for how networks should transfer data. These rules, or **protocols**, are primarily directed at the two lowest layers of the OSI model—the Physical and Data Link layers. These layers are sometimes referred to jointly as the hardware level (Figure 1-1), because hardware and software work together at these layers to specify how data is handled by Ethernet and Token Ring networks. These layers also dictate how electrical signals are amplified and transmitted over the wire.

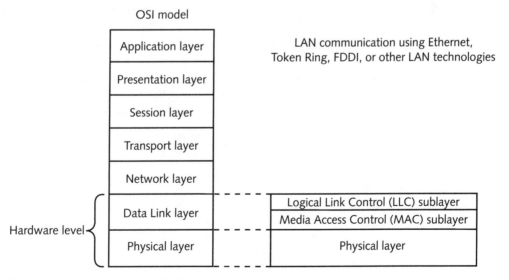

Figure 1-1 OSI model and LAN communications

The Physical layer defines the actual mechanical specifications and electrical data bitstream, the data transmission rate, the maximum distance, and the physical connectors. The Data Link layer consists of two sublayers. The upper level is the Logical Link Control (LLC), which provides a common interface and supplies reliability and flow control services. The lower level is the Media Access Control (MAC), which appends the physical address of the destination computer onto the frame. The physical address of every computer is a unique number that is hard-coded onto the **network interface card (NIC)** by the manufacturer. This card enables a user **workstation** to communicate with the network and other computers. Additional information on the OSI model and the services provided by each layer is shown in Figure 1-2.

Layer	Equipment and Functions	Data Format	Service Provided
Application	Interface	Messages	The service that identifies the message and processes it
Presentation	Translation and encryption	Messages	Message is presented to correct service; data translated as necessary
Session	Remote procedural calls (RPCs), error checking	Messages	Establishes connection dialog; provides reliable delivery of user requests to appropriate network service
Transport	Reliability, error checking	Segments	Logical WAN definition, error checking to ensure message is delivered correctly
Network	Software (logical) address, routers	Datagrams	Provides internetworking pathway for WAN communications
Data Link	Hardware (physical) address, bridges, intelligent hubs, NICs, error checking	Frames	Provides pathway for message to travel on
Physical	Pins, RS232, wires, cards, volts, cables, repeaters, hubs	Bits	Provides pathway for message to travel on

The Application, Presentation, and Session layers provide the vehicle for delivering network services.

The Transport and Network layers provide the logical pathway for communications among LANs.

The Data Link and Physical layers provide the transmission media and protocols for local network communications. Due to the physical nature of these layers, they rely on cabling boundaries for station-to-station communications.

Figure 1-2   Detailed OSI model

DEVELOPMENT OF NETWORK TECHNOLOGY

The original **Ethernet** was developed in the 1970s by Xerox Corporation as an experimental coaxial cable network with a data rate of 3 **megabits per second (Mbps)**. The network used the **Carrier Sense Multiple Access/Collision Detection (CSMA/CD)** protocol for LANs, which allows nodes to listen for traffic on the network before sending data.

The success of this project attracted the attention of Digital Equipment Corporation and Intel, who joined forces with Xerox to develop the 10-Mbps Ethernet Version 1.0 specification in 1980. As the holder of the Ethernet trademark, Xerox established and published the standards. Ethernet uses a thick, usually yellow, coaxial backbone cable known as "Thick Ethernet," "ThickNet," or 10Base5. The "10" refers to the data speed of 10 Mbps. The "Base" refers to **baseband**, which means it uses all of its bandwidth for each transmission. The "5" is short for 500, which refers to the maximum cable length of 500 m.

The original IEEE 802.3 standard was closely based on the Ethernet Version 1.0 specification. The draft standard was approved by the IEEE 802.3 working group in 1983 and published as an official standard in 1985. Since then, a number of supplements to the standard have been defined to take advantage of improvements in technology and support additional network media and higher data rates. The first type of cable used was a thin coaxial backbone cable known as "Thin Ethernet," "ThinNet," or 10Base2. The "10" and "Base" are the same as in 10Base5 above, and the "2" refers to the maximum cable length of 185 m.

In 1984, IBM introduced **Token Ring**, which was able to transmit data at 4 Mbps. This networking technology employs a ring topology using a token to allow data transmission, and is still the primary LAN technology used by IBM today. The IEEE 802.5 standard is almost identical to the Token Ring network, and completely compatible with it. Token Ring uses a thick, shielded twisted-pair cable and a special data connector developed by IBM called an IDC (IBM data connector) or UDC (universal data connector).

At the same time, numerous other networks were in use, and each used different types of cable and connectors. As the market for network communications continued to grow and the technology advanced, it became clear that a standard was needed. Three of the organizations discussed earlier—ANSI, TIA, and EIA—stepped in to fill the void.

Structured Cabling and ANSI/EIA/TIA-568-A

The TR-41 and TR-42 work groups developed the first telecommunications cabling standard, ANSI/EIA/TIA-568, which continues to evolve as network speeds increase and cable improves. The ANSI/EIA/TIA-568 Commercial Building Wiring Standard gave birth to the **structured cabling** system, whose primary focus was uniform, enterprise-wide, multivendor cabling. Structured cabling suggests how telecommunications media can best be installed to maximize performance and minimize upkeep.

Structured cabling divides the infrastructure into six subsystems that are then integrated to provide consistent, reliable networks. There are several advantages to using a structured cabling system:

- **Consistency** — A structured cabling system uses the same cabling for data, voice, and video.

- **Support for multivendor equipment** — A standards-based system supports numerous applications and hardware for all vendors.

- **Simplified additions, moves, and changes** — The system is designed to support any changes within it.

- **Simplified troubleshooting** — The wiring scheme makes it difficult for a single problem to bring down the network. Problems are easier to isolate and repair.

- **Support for new applications** — Structured cabling systems support new applications such as multimedia and video conferencing with little or no upgrade difficulty.

The ANSI/EIA/TIA-568-A standard identifies the six subsystems of the building infrastructure. The primary focus of this standard is to provide specifications and guidance for the installation of telecommunications cabling systems and components in commercial buildings.

The six sublayers are:

- **Entrance facility** — The place where the **telecommunications service** enters a building. This service is the cabling from the local service provider. If applicable, the entrance facility is where backbone pathways link with other buildings. It is also the place where the building's internal wiring begins. The division between the telecommunications service cabling and the building's internal cabling is the **demarcation point (d-mark)**.

- **Equipment room(s)** — The location of telecommunications equipment common to building occupants. This common equipment can include large telephone systems called **private branch exchanges (PBXs)**, servers, and mainframes. The cabling in this room usually connects to telecommunications rooms.

- **Telecommunications room (TR)** — Also known as the telecommunications closet, the TR is the space within the building that provides the common access point between the backbone and horizontal cabling. The TR houses the telecommunications cabling equipment, mechanical terminations, and **cross-connect** wiring, a group of connections used to mechanically terminate and administer building wiring.

- **Backbone pathways and cabling** — A backbone is essentially a network of networks. Backbone cabling provides interconnection among telecommunications rooms, equipment rooms, and entrance facilities. The backbone cabling consists of the feeder field of the horizontal cross-connect, **intrabuilding** and **interbuilding** cabling (which runs within the same building and between buildings, respectively), and the main and intermediate cross-connects. Distance limitations for backbones are application-dependent. In Table 1-3 the distance limits are based on voice and data transmission for unshielded twisted-pair cable (UTP) and data transmission for fiber.

Table 1-3   Backbone distance limits

Cable Type	Maximum Backbone Distance
100-ohm UTP (24 or 22 **American Wire Gauge**, or **AWG**)	800 m (voice specification) 90 m (data specification)
Single-mode fiber (independent of speed)	3000 m (data specification)
Multimode fiber (independent of speed)	2000 m (data specification)

- **Horizontal pathways and cabling** — The wiring that connects workstations to the TR. These pathways must be able to handle all types of cable. The pathways that are recognized by the ANSI/EIA/TIA-569 standard include underfloor duct, access floors, conduit, ceiling pathways, perimeter raceways, cable trays, and wire trays. The maximum allowable distance for horizontal cabling is 100 m (Figure 1-3). This span includes 90 m to connect the work-area jack on the wall to the TR, plus a maximum of 3 m to connect a workstation to the jack on the wall, and a maximum of 6 m for patch cords or cross-connects at the horizontal cross-connect.

- **Work area** — An area where building occupants use telecommunications devices. The work area includes **patch cables** that connect network or telecommunications devices to data jacks on the wall.

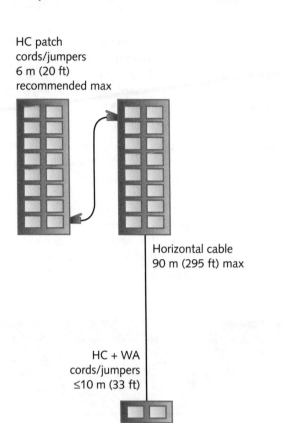

HC patch
cords/jumpers
6 m (20 ft)
recommended max

Horizontal cable
90 m (295 ft) max

HC + WA
cords/jumpers
≤10 m (33 ft)

WA patch cords
3 m (10 ft)
assumed max

HC = horizontal cable
WA = work area

Figure 1-3   Horizontal cross-connect and maximum distances

NETWORK CABLES

A **cable** is the medium that provides the physical foundation for data transmission. Several types of cable are commonly used. Some networks use only one type of cable, while others employ several cable types in the same network. The type of cable you

1

choose depends on the size of the network, the protocol(s) being used, and the network's physical layout, or **topology**.

To develop a successful network, you must understand the different types of cable you can use, and how each relates to other aspects of the network. The following sections explain your options.

Twisted-Pair Cable

Twisted-pair cable is the most common form of cabling used on LANs today. It is relatively inexpensive, flexible, easy to install, and capable of spanning a significant distance before additional equipment is required. Twisted-pair cable can accommodate several different topologies, but is most often implemented in a **star topology**, in which every node is connected through a central device. Twisted-pair cable can also handle the faster networking transmission rates in use today. This cable is available in unshielded, shielded, and screened forms.

Unshielded Twisted-Pair

Unshielded twisted-pair (UTP) cable comes in a variety of grades, from voice grade to extremely high-speed grade. The cable contains color-coded pairs of insulated copper wires inside a plastic jacket, as shown in Figure 1-4. Each pair has a different number of twists per inch, depending on the grade, to help eliminate interference from adjacent pairs, adjacent cables, and other electrical devices. The more twists per inch a pair of wires has, the more resistant it will be to all forms of noise.

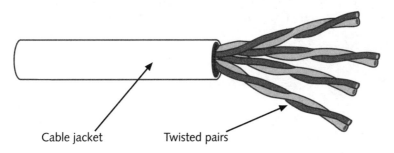

Cable jacket   Twisted pairs

Figure 1-4   Unshielded twisted-pair cable

UTP cable has been designated as 10BaseT. The "10" represents its minimum transmission rate of 10 Mbps. The "Base" refers to baseband, which means that UTP uses all of its bandwidth for each transmission. The "T" represents UTP.

Table 1-4 lists the various grades of UTP, along with its cable transmission speeds and specifications provided by the ANSI/EIA/TIA UTP standard.

Table 1-4   ANSI/EIA/TIA UTP specifications by category

Cable Category	Data Rate	Bandwidth	Application
Category 1 (CAT1)	20 Kbps		Analog voice, doorbell wiring
Category 2 (CAT2)	4 Mbps	1 MHz	Voice
Category 3 (CAT3)	10 Mbps	16 MHz	Voice and data on 10BaseT Ethernet
Category 4 (CAT4)	16 Mbps	20 MHz	Token Ring and 10BaseT Ethernet
Category 5 (CAT5)	100 Mbps	100 MHz	100BaseT Ethernet, 10BaseT Ethernet, ATM
Enhanced CAT5	1.2 Gbps	200 MHz	Same as CAT5, Gigabit Ethernet
Category 6 (CAT6)	2.4 Gbps	250 MHz	Same as Enhanced CAT5, but better performance
Category 7 (CAT7)	Unknown at this time	600 MHz	Same as Enhanced CAT5; standard was still in testing at press time

Shielded Twisted-Pair

Shielded twisted-pair (STP) cable consists of insulated wire pairs that are surrounded by a metallic shielding such as foil (Figure 1-5). If the wire is properly grounded, the shielding acts as an antenna, converting noise into current. The effectiveness of the shield depends on the environmental noise to which the STP is subjected, the grounding mechanism, and the material, thickness, symmetry, and consistency of the shielding.

STP is more expensive than UTP. On the other hand, shielded cable provides better immunity to **electromagnetic interference (EMI)** and **radio frequency interference (RFI)**. EMI is the noise generated when stray electromagnetic fields induce currents in electrical conductors, and RFI is interference caused by electrical devices or broadcast signals.

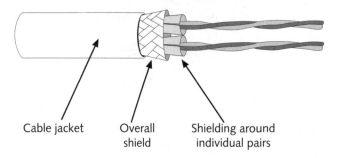

Cable jacket   Overall   Shielding around
                    shield   individual pairs

Figure 1-5   Shielded twisted-pair cable

Screened Twisted-Pair

Screened twisted-pair (ScTP) cable is commonly used in Europe, but has recently received more attention in North America as various organizations attempted to harmonize their telecommunications cabling standards. ScTP specifications are based on those for UTP cabling, but there are notable differences. For example, the maximum distance for a horizontal ScTP cable is 98 m. Also, the size of its screen makes ScTP unable to fit into a standard modular plug, so stranded 26 AWG must be used instead of the standard 24 AWG. Finally, when ScTP is installed correctly, its immunity to radio frequency fields is superior to that of UTP.

Coaxial Cable

Coaxial cable (coax) was the foundation for Ethernet networks in the 1980s and remained a popular transmission medium for many years. Coax comes in several types, but they are all similar in their construction: a central copper core is surrounded by an insulator, a braided metal shielding, and an outer cover called the sheath or jacket (Figure 1-6). Because of its construction, coax has a high immunity to interference from EMI and RFI.

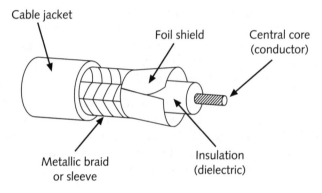

Figure 1-6   Coaxial cable

Fiber-Optic Cable

Fiber-optic cable (fiber) contains one or more glass fibers in its core, surrounded by a layer of glass called cladding. The glass and cladding are covered by layers of plastic, also referred to as the buffer coating. Buffer coatings are available in two basic designs: loose-tube and tight-tube. Loose-tube buffer has an inner diameter that is much larger than the fiber. The interior of the buffer tube is filled with a gel that protects the fiber. Tight-tube buffer is a direct extrusion of plastic over the fiber. The buffer coating is covered by a braiding of Kevlar®, which in turn is covered by a plastic jacket (Figure 1-7). Data is transmitted by a pulsing light sent from a laser or light-emitting diode (LED) through the core. The cladding acts as a mirror, reflecting the light back to the core in patterns that vary depending on the transmission mode. The reflection allows the fiber to bend around corners without diminishing the integrity of the signal. Fiber can reliably transmit data at rates as high as 1 Gbps, and because it transmits light rather than electrical signals, it is immune to EMI and RFI.

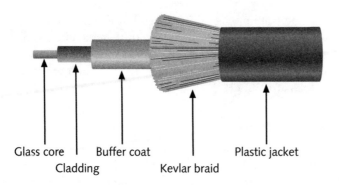

Glass core   Buffer coat   Plastic jacket
          Cladding   Kevlar braid

Figure 1-7   Optical fiber

Fiber can transmit signals over much longer distances and carry information at significantly greater speeds than coax or twisted-pair cable. Thus, fiber can expand a company's communications to include video conferencing and other interactive services. The biggest drawback to fiber is its cost and the associated costs of its connectors, patch panels, jumper cables, testers, and network interface cards. Fiber is also more difficult to install and modify than other cabling, and it can only transmit in one direction at a time unless each cable contains two strands—one to send data and one to receive it.

Fiber comes in two categories: single-mode and multimode. Single-mode fiber carries a single wave of light at a time, to transmit data from one end of the cable to the other. Data can travel faster and farther on single-mode fiber, but the cost is extremely high. Multimode fiber can transmit multiple waves of light simultaneously over one or more fibers, and is the type of fiber used by most data networks.

Comparing Cable Media

Before choosing the type of cable you will use, you must compare the characteristics and costs of each type (Table 1-5). Note also that the cable type you need depends on its implementation, such as network interface cards, hubs, and other devices. For example, a **hub** is a multiport repeater containing one port that connects to the backbone and multiple ports that connect to a group of workstations. The cabling for a hub would require the use of UTP installed in a star topology.

You would also need to compare cable media before installing a cable that spans many kilometers. For example, although fiber is more costly than copper cable on a per-foot basis, using copper for long distances would require **repeaters** to be installed at many points along the cable, to amplify and regenerate the analog or digital signal. The cost of the repeaters could easily exceed the cost of the fiber for the same distance.

Table 1-5 Cable comparisons

Cable Type	Cost	Installation	Capacity	Range	EMI/RFI
Coaxial ThinNet	Less than STP	Easy and relatively inexpensive	10 Mbps typical	185 m	Less sensitive than UTP
Coaxial ThickNet	More than STP, less than fiber	Easy	10 Mbps typical	500 m	Less sensitive than UTP
STP	More than UTP, less than ThickNet	Fairly easy	16 Mbps typical, up to 500 Mbps	100 m	Less sensitive than UTP
UTP	Lowest	Easy and relatively inexpensive	10 Mbps typical, up to 4.8 Gbps	100 m	Most sensitive
Fiber-optic	Among the highest; differs by application	Expensive and difficult	100 Mbps to 200 Gbps	2000 to 3000 km	Insensitive

CABLING DOCUMENTATION

In the field of network cabling, documentation is like a road map. It provides the locations and routes for every cable in your network. Documentation also functions like an inventory, providing a reference for each network element and each item used to create the network. Good documentation saves you time and can make your job easier in the long run.

Although network administrators and telecommunications professionals are happy to acknowledge the importance of documentation, they often are unable to provide any of their own. Most professionals want to provide documentation, but it takes extra time that they never seem to have. Besides, documentation is rarely recognized as an accomplishment, and its absence doesn't keep others from doing their work.

This book elaborates on the importance of documentation in each subsequent chapter. You'll learn how to create a documentation project, what to include in it, the best formats to use for it, and how documentation will make your job easier and more secure.

CHAPTER SUMMARY

▫ The worldwide deregulation of the telecommunications industry began with the divestiture of AT&T in 1984. Divestiture resulted in the breakup of the Bell systems, and eventually to the establishment of standardization.

▫ Several organizations have evolved within the telecommunications industry to set and oversee standards, including the ISO, ANSI, EIA, TIA, ITU, and IEEE.

❑ The protocols defined by IEEE 802 are primarily directed at the Physical and Data Link layers of the OSI model, because hardware and software work together at these layers to specify how data is handled by Ethernet and Token Ring networks. These layers also dictate how electrical signals are amplified and transmitted over the wire.

❑ The original Ethernet was developed in the 1970s by Xerox Corporation as an experimental coaxial cable network. Today, two types of coaxial cable are used in Ethernet networks: ThinNet and ThickNet.

❑ Twisted-pair cable is classified into five grades, from Category 1 through Category 5. Only Category 3 and Category 5 are acceptable for use on an Ethernet LAN. UTP Category 5e, Category 6, and Category 7 are the newest standards for copper cable. They can support bandwidths of 1000 Mbps or more. Their cable segment length is limited to 100 m, but their range can be extended with the use of repeaters.

❑ Fiber-optic cable is immune to EMI and RFI, has a faster data rate than other cable types, and can be run over greater distances than copper cable. It is still more costly than any other cable, but it continues to gain industry acceptance for all uses.

❑ In the field of network cabling, documentation is like a road map. It provides the locations and routes for every cable in your network. Documentation also functions like an inventory, providing a reference for each network element and each item used to create the network.

KEY TERMS

American Wire Gauge (AWG) — The standard for measurement of wire.

baseband — A coaxial cable that uses all of its bandwidth for each transmission.

Building Industry Consulting Service (BICS) — An organization of telephone company engineers created by AT&T and Bell Canada. BICS works with architects, building contractors, and engineers to design and implement cabling plans for pathways and spaces in commercial buildings.

Building Industry Consulting Services International (BICSI) — A not-for-profit telecommunications organization founded to serve BICS.

cable — An assembly of one or more insulated conductors within a sheath, constructed to permit use of the conductors singly or in a group.

Carrier Sense Multiple Access/Collision Detection (CSMA/CD) — An Ethernet protocol that allows nodes to listen for traffic on the network before sending data.

code — A law designed to protect people and property from hazards, and to ensure the quality of construction.

conduit — A pipe that carries cable through a ceiling, wall, or floor.

1

cross-connect — A group of connections used to mechanically terminate and administer building wiring.

demarcation point (d-mark) — The point where the service provider's cabling ends and the customer's cabling begins.

electromagnetic interference (EMI) — Noise generated when stray electromagnetic fields induce currents in electrical conductors.

equipment room — An enclosed space for housing equipment, cable terminations, and cross-connects.

error-checking algorithm — The process used in a frame to check for errors in data transmission.

Ethernet — A networking technology originally developed by Xerox and improved by Digital Equipment Corporation, Intel, and Xerox. Used on most LANs.

hub — A multiport repeater containing one port that connects to the backbone and multiple ports that connect to a group of workstations. Hubs regenerate digital signals.

interbuilding — Refers to connections between one building and other outlying buildings.

intrabuilding — Refers to connections within the same building, usually on different floors.

local area network (LAN) — A network of computers and other devices confined to a single building, or even one office.

megabits per second (Mbps) — A measurement of a network's data rate based on the network's physical characteristics.

National Electrical Code (NEC) — The most comprehensive book on electrical codes in the United States.

network interface card (NIC) — A device that enables a workstation to communicate with a network and other computers.

Open Systems Interconnection (OSI) model — A model for understanding and developing computer-to-computer communication. It divides network architecture into seven layers.

patch cable — A relatively short section of cable (3 to 50 feet) with connectors at both ends that connect network devices to data jacks, or horizontal cables to the horizontal cross-connect.

power-limited applications — Applications with a circuit that limit power (generally to 50 volts and under) to the external wiring in the event of an overload condition.

private branch exchange (PBX) — A large telephone system that switches calls among users on local lines while allowing all users to share a certain amount of external lines.

protocols — The rules that a network uses to transfer data.

radio frequency interference (RFI) — A type of interference that may be generated by motors, power lines, televisions, copiers, fluorescent lights, or broadcast signals from radio or TV towers.

regulation — A local authority's ability to enforce codes and standards to regulate the building and construction industry.

repeater — A connectivity device that regenerates and amplifies an analog or digital signal.

service provider (SP) — A company that provides telecommunications service to a building.

standard — A document of specifications that guarantee a minimum level of performance.

star topology — A physical topology in which every node is connected through a central device.

structured cabling — A method for uniform, enterprise-wide, multivendor cabling specified by ANSI/EIA/TIA-568.

telecommunications service — The cabling and services available from a local service provider.

Token Ring — A networking technology developed by IBM. It employs a ring topology using a token to allow data transmission.

topology — The physical layout of a computer network.

twisted-pair cable — The most common form of cabling used on LANs. Each pair has a different number of twists per inch, depending on the grade, to help eliminate interference.

workstation — A computer intended for individual use.

REVIEW QUESTIONS

1. According to industry specifications, what is the maximum allowable length of a horizontal cable?

   a. 15 meters (50 feet)

   b. 30 meters (100 feet)

   c. 100 meters (328 feet)

   d. 333 meters (1000 feet)

2. What is the ANSI/EIA/TIA-568 standard responsible for?

   a. structured cabling

   b. shielded cable

   c. Project 802

   d. manufacturing and quality-control procedures

1

3. The protocols defined by IEEE 802 are primarily directed at which layers of the OSI model?

   a. Session and Data Link

   b. Data Link and Network

   c. Physical and Data Link

   d. Network and Transport

4. What type of cable is used in the Ethernet 10Base2 specification?

   a. coaxial cable

   b. unshielded twisted-pair cable

   c. shielded twisted-pair cable

   d. fiber-optic cable

5. What type of cable is used in the Ethernet 100BaseT specification?

   a. RG-58 AU coaxial cable

   b. Category 3 cable

   c. Category 4 cable

   d. Category 5 cable

6. What type of cable is used in the Ethernet 10BaseT specification?

   a. RG-58 AU coaxial cable

   b. Category 3 cable

   c. Category 4 cable

   d. Category 3, Category 4, and Category 5 cable

7. Fiber-optic cable offers the possibility of very high bandwidth and immunity to noise. True or False?

8. What is the maximum effective segment length for twisted-pair cable?

   a. 800 meters

   b. 2000 meters

   c. 50 meters

   d. 100 meters

9. The Physical layer provides the foundation for a reliable, high-performance LAN. True or False?

10. The telecommunications room is always in the same location as the main or intermediate cross-connect. True or False?

11. The cabling found in older data networks would most likely be
    _____.

    a. fiber-optic

    b. coaxial

    c. twisted-pair

    d. four-pair

12. A standards-based cabling system will support only one application and hardware vendor. True or False?

13. One purpose of a standard is to ensure a minimum level of performance. True or False?

14. The types of media that can transmit information in the telecommunications world are _____.

    a. copper wire, coaxial cable, fiber, and wireless

    b. hybrid fiber/coax and copper wire

    c. wireless and copper wire

    d. copper wire, coaxial cable, fiber, and hybrid fiber/coax

15. The advantages of structured cabling include _____.

    a. support for multivendor equipment and simplified changes

    b. simplified troubleshooting and support for future applications

    c. both of the above

    d. none of the above

16. The backbone cabling provides interconnection among telecommunications rooms, equipment rooms, and entrance facilities. True or False?

17. In Canada and the United States, building codes and standards regulate
    _____.

    a. service providers

    b. how a system functions

    c. quality of manufacturing

    d. the construction industry

18. Ethernet was developed in the late 1960s by AT&T and Bell Canada. True or False?

1

19. Coaxial ThickNet cable has the same 10-Mbps capacity as coaxial ThinNet but has a shorter range. True or False?

20. Fiber-optic cable offers higher bandwidth and can operate at greater distances than _____.

   a. coaxial cable

   b. UTP cable

   c. neither a nor b

   d. both a and b

21. There are two types of fiber-optic cabling: multistrand and single-strand. True or False?

22. Gigabit Ethernet can be implemented _____.

   a. as a backbone interconnect

   b. to the desktop

   c. between switches and servers

   d. all of the above

23. The term "Category" describes the performance characteristics of UTP cabling systems. True or False?

24. In 1984, IBM introduced Token Ring, which was able to transmit data at _____.

   a. 2 Mbps

   b. 4 Mbps

   c. 10 Mbps

   d. 20 Mbps

25. A telecommunications closet is the area within a building that houses telecommunications cabling equipment, including mechanical terminations and/or cross-connect for the horizontal and backbone cabling system. True or False?

HANDS-ON PROJECTS

Project 1-1

Outline the process and standards required to begin installing a telecommunications system in a 10-person, ground-floor business. What are the required components of this system? What components would you require if the business were on the fourth floor?

Project 1-2

To help you decide whether to become BICSI Level 1 certified, go to *www.bicsi.com* and click **RCDD/Installation**. Scroll down the next page to the Telecommunications Cabling Installation Program heading. In the Program Overview section, click **Installer, Level 1**. Read the Course Overview section and then print it. This overview provides an outline of the main objectives for the Level 1 Certification exam.

Optionally, you can go back to the Telecommunications Cabling Installation Program heading on the previous page. In the Exam Requirements section, click **Installer, Level 1**.

Project 1-3

Go to *www.webopedia.com* and search by keyword for definitions of the following terms, which you will use throughout your career in telecommunications and networking.

- Crosstalk
- Patch cord
- Patch panel
- Attenuation
- Local area network
- Wide area network
- CAT5
- Telecommunications
- Ethernet
- Gigabit Ethernet

Project 1-4

Go to the IEEE Web site at *www.standards.ieee.org* and search the 802 standards. Create a report that lists each standard by number and briefly defines each one. Print your report and turn it in to your instructor. Also print a copy for your files; the information will be helpful throughout this course and your telecommunications career.

Project 1-5

Find information about structured cabling systems and the standard that defines them. Go to *www.anixter.com/techlib*, select **Standards Guides**, then select **ANSI/TIA/EIA-569-A, Pathways and Spaces**.

Project 1-6

Check with the appropriate departments for your city and state, such as the registrar of contractors, the building inspector, and the fire marshal, to find out what local regulations and major building codes you should know before installing cable. Write a brief report that summarizes your findings.

CASE PROJECTS

Case Project 1

The XYZ Company is planning to relocate its corporate office. In a planning session, managers and representatives from each department raise several concerns. You have been asked to address these concerns in the next planning session.

1. Managers don't know which types of cable are available. List the different types of cable and the differences among them.

2. Each department has its own cabling requirements. One user from each department is responsible for administering the department's requirements. What could some of these requirements be?

3. What type of system would you recommend to address these requirements?

Case Project 2

ABC Engineering has just landed a large contract and requires six workstations to be installed two floors up from the server. The managers are concerned that the new users will slow down the network by transferring large files to and from the server. You have been asked to create a document that addresses these concerns.

1. Outline each of the issues you need to address.

2. EMI is a major issue and has been emphasized by your managers. Document the various materials you will use to address EMI.

3. Document the type of cabling you recommend, and how it will address each issue.

Case Project 3

You have been hired by the LB Company to evaluate its telecommunications system and make recommendations for a proposed expansion of 20 workstations and telephones. The company currently has 55 workstations. Based on your reading of this chapter, create a report that summarizes what cabling equipment the company might have, and where it might be located (for example, the equipment room or the telecommunications room).

Case Project 4

The LB Company has also asked you to provide information about newer cabling technology. Create a report that includes the most current information on Category 5e, 6, and 7 cabling standards. Use this book, the Internet, and other sources for assistance.

2

GROUNDING AND BONDING

After reading this chapter and completing the exercises, you will be able to:

♦ Discuss how grounding and bonding work

♦ Differentiate between "grounding and bonding systems" and "grounding and bonding equipment"

♦ Understand cable protection and equipment-grounding practices

♦ Identify the three types of telecommunications circuit protectors

♦ Understand how documentation helps you and your network

The grounding and bonding of telecommunications cable and equipment are essential to any installation. This chapter provides basic information and application instructions for all the key aspects of grounding and bonding. The standards and practices used in this chapter are in accordance with the relevant standards organizations.

Every effort has been made to ensure that the recommendations in this chapter are technically accurate and provide necessary site, equipment, environmental, and safety requirements. However, local or regional conditions may require additional investigations or safeguards. You should always consult the applicable international, federal, state, and local requirements.

A Closer Look at Grounding and Bonding

When studying grounding and bonding, you must understand the applicable codes and standards, their origins, and the basic terms used throughout the specifications. Many of the terms are specific to the practices of grounding and bonding.

Codes, Standards, and Organizations

The organizations responsible for the following standards are the four main sources for information about grounding and bonding codes and practices.

- **National Electrical Code (NEC)** — As stated in Article 90-1 of the NEC, the code's purpose is the practical safeguarding of people and property from electrical hazards. Compliance with the NEC and proper maintenance will result in a hazard-free installation. This safety code is written and administered by the **National Fire Protection Association® (NFPA)**.

- **ANSI/EIA/TIA-607: Commercial Building Grounding and Bonding Requirements for Telecommunications** — This standard specifies a uniform infrastructure for telecommunications grounding and bonding within commercial buildings. It also provides specific guidelines for designing the grounding and bonding system.

- **Underwriters Laboratories UL-497: Protectors for Paired Conductor Communication Circuits** — Underwriters Laboratories Inc. is an independent testing lab that defines safety standards for electrical equipment. UL-497 applies to telecommunications.

- **IEEE Standard 142-1991: Grounding of Industrial and Commercial Power Systems** — This international standard, which is very similar to ANSI/EIA/TIA-607, specifies a uniform grounding system for industrial and commercial power systems within commercial buildings.

Grounding, Bonding, and Effective Ground

Grounding and bonding are actually two separate concepts. One way of distinguishing the two is to consider one as the physical medium and the other as the method for creating that medium. A **ground**, the physical medium, is a conducting connection between an electrical circuit or equipment and the earth, or to some other conducting body that serves in place of the earth. Grounding is the backbone of effective protection for all telecommunications systems.

Bonding, the method, is the permanent joining of metallic parts to form a conductive path that ensures electrical continuity and safely conducts current. An **effective ground** is an intentional connection to a low-resistance earth ground that permits current to discharge into the earth without buildup of hazardous voltages on the **cable**, equipment, or people.

Grounding and Bonding Components

The telecommunications grounding system is made up of several components. When designed and installed following the appropriate codes, specifications, and safety practices, these components create a system that effectively safeguards personnel, property, and equipment. Figure 2-1 illustrates a typical grounding and bonding network.

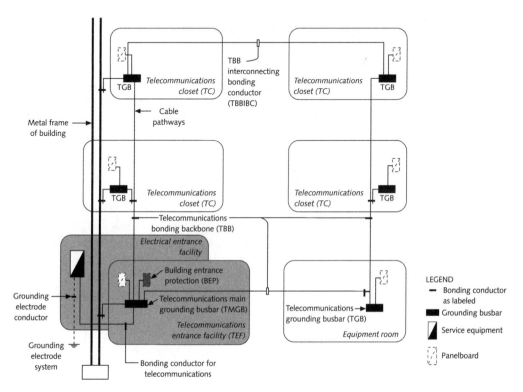

Figure 2-1   Grounding and bonding network

The most common hazard in these networks is electric shock, which occurs from accidental contact with energized devices or circuits. Shock hazards include touching a faulty or improperly grounded electrical component, standing on a damp floor while working on or near electrical equipment, and using or being near conducting material during a lightning storm.

The effects of electrical current on the human body are primarily determined by the magnitude of the current and the duration of the shock. If a person makes contact between an object that has voltage and another object that is grounded, the current will flow through those contact points. The amount of current that can be forced through a body is usually determined by the electrical voltage on the energized circuit. Currents as low as 20 **mA** (20 **milliampere**, or 20/1000 **ampere**) for a fraction of a second are enough to kill a person. Although strong electric shock can kill by damaging vital organs, lower currents can also cause injuries and death from involuntary muscle reflex reactions.

Next you will learn the individual components of a grounding and bonding network. To begin, every building has a **grounding electrode**, a conductor or group of conductors that provides a direct, low-resistance connection to the earth. A **grounding conductor** connects the electrical equipment to the grounding electrode and the building's main grounding **busbar**, a conductor that serves as a common connection point for two or more circuits.

Bonding Conductor for Telecommunications

Any conductor used specifically for bonding is called a **bonding conductor**. For example, the conductor that connects the building's service (power) equipment ground to the telecommunications grounding system is called the **bonding conductor for telecommunications (BCT)**. The BCT is a No. 6 **AWG (American Wire Gauge)** or larger insulated copper conductor that connects the equipment ground to the telecommunications main grounding busbar.

Telecommunications Main Grounding Busbar

The telecommunications main grounding busbar (TMGB) is the foundation of the telecommunications grounding system (Figure 2-2). The TMGB is a solid copper busbar with insulated standoffs. It is ¼" thick, 4" high, has a variable length, and is drilled with rows of holes according to the **National Electrical Manufacturers Association (NEMA)** standards for the attachment of bolted compression fittings.

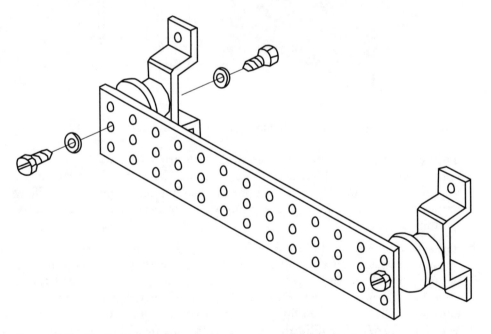

Figure 2-2   Typical telecommunications main grounding busbar

The TMGB serves as an interface between the building's service equipment (power) ground and the telecommunications infrastructure. The TMGB also serves as a central connection point for the telecommunications bonding backbone (TBB) and equipment.

There is usually only one TMGB per building. It is typically located in the **entrance room (facility)**, the entrance to a building for both public and private network service cables, or the **main telecommunications room**. This room is the main equipment room or main cross-connect for the interconnection of entrance cables, first-level backbone cables, and equipment cables. The TMGB should minimize the length of the BCT and TBB.

Telecommunications Grounding Busbar

In each telecommunications room the telecommunications grounding busbar (TGB) provides a common point of connection for systems and equipment bonding to ground (Figure 2-3). The TGB is a solid copper busbar with insulated standoffs and the same dimensions and drill holes as TMGBs. The TGB should be installed as close as possible to the panelboard in the telecommunications room.

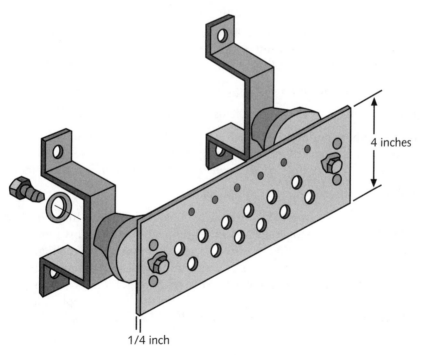

4 inches

1/4 inch

Figure 2-3   Telecommunications grounding busbar

If a **backboard** (a panel for mounting system hardware and equipment) is located in the same room as a TGB, it should be bonded to the TGB.

Telecommunications Bonding Backbone

The TMGB and all TGBs are interconnected by a No. 6 AWG or larger insulated conductor called the telecommunications bonding backbone (TBB). Its primary function is to reduce or equalize differences in the telecommunications systems bonded to it. The TBB is considered a part of the grounding and bonding infrastructure (the telecommunications pathways and spaces in the building structure), but it is independent of all equipment and cable.

The TBB begins at the TMGB and extends throughout the building, using the telecommunications backbone pathways. The TBB is connected to the TGBs in all of the telecommunications rooms. When TBBs and other TGBs are located in the same space, they all must be bonded to one TGB.

When planning the TBB installation, the following design considerations are important:

- Be consistent with the design of the telecommunications backbone cabling system.

- You can use multiple TBBs if the size of the building permits it.

- The bonding conductors used between a TBB and TGB must be continuous and routed in the shortest, most direct path as possible. Plan the route to minimize the length of the TBB.

- Do not use interior water pipe systems of the building as a TBB.

- Do not use metallic cable shields as a TBB in new installations.

- When there are multiple vertical TBBs, they must be bonded together at the top floor, and at a minimum of every third floor in between, using a telecommunications bonding backbone interconnecting bonding conductor.

- Install TBBs without the use of splices.

All of the foregoing items—the grounding electrode, grounding conductor, BCT, TMGB, TGB, and TBB—together form the **ground system**. This system of hardware and wiring provides electrical paths from the telecommunications cabling and equipment to the earth-ground point. The primary responsibility of this system is the safeguarding of personnel, property, and equipment from **foreign electrical voltages** and currents. Foreign voltage is any voltage imposed on a system that is not supplied from the central office, telephone equipment, or the system itself.

GROUNDING AND BONDING—SYSTEM VS. EQUIPMENT

A building has six types of grounding and bonding systems, and each performs a unique function. The combination of the following systems provides the overall protection for the building and its occupants, so their design and installation must be coordinated.

- Lightning protection system

- Grounding electrode system

- Electrical bonding and grounding system

- Electrical power protection system

- Telecommunications bonding and grounding system

- Telecommunications circuit protector system

This chapter focuses on telecommunications bonding and grounding and the telecommunications circuit protector. It is important, however, to understand the purpose of each grounding system.

Each type of telecommunications equipment has its own grounding and bonding specifications. These specifications are separate from grounding systems, and are in addition to the general rules specified in NEC Article 250.

Grounding Systems

The following sections explain each grounding system. These systems are separate from the grounding of equipment, which is described in a later section.

Lightning Protection System

A lightning protection system provides a designated path for lightning current to travel. Lightning protection systems neither attract nor repel lightning strikes; they simply intercept and guide the current to ground, preventing harm to the building and any occupants.

Lightning protection systems are made up of several components, as shown in Figure 2-4. **Air terminals (lightning rods)** are slender rods that are usually installed on a roof at intervals defined by industry standards (not exceeding 20 feet). The **conductors** are copper or aluminum cables that interconnect the air terminals and the other system components. **Ground terminations (ground rods)** are metal rods that are driven at least 10 feet into the earth to guide lightning current harmlessly to ground. To protect computers and other office equipment from rapid rises in current or voltage, called **surges** or **transients**, you should install **surge arresters** at the main electrical panel and **surge suppressors** in each outlet.

The telecommunications ground must be bonded to the lightning protection system within 3.7 meters (12 feet) of the base of the building, and may need additional bonding depending on the spacing, building dimensions, and construction.

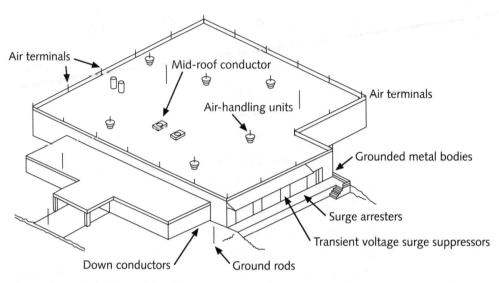

Figure 2-4 Lightning protection system

Grounding Electrode System

The **grounding electrode system** is the end product of bonding together all metal underground water pipes, the metal frame of the building, any electrode that is encased in concrete, any ground ring, and any **made and other electrodes**. These electrodes are not specified in NEC Article 250H, but defined instead in NEC Article 250, section 83, subsections b–d. They include rod and pipe electrodes, plate electrodes, and metal underground systems such as piping systems. The grounding electrode system forms a single, reliable ground for a building. NEC Article 250H, sections 81–86, defines the specifications for this system.

Electrical Bonding and Grounding System and Electrical Power Protection System

Both the electrical bonding and grounding system and the electrical power protection system refer to the general requirements for all electrical installations. They include specific requirements for grounding systems, circuits, and equipment; the circuit conductor ground; the location of grounding connections; the types and sizes of grounding and bonding conductors and electrodes; the methods of grounding and bonding; and conditions in which a substitution for grounding is permitted. All of the specifications are covered in depth in NEC Articles 250A and 250B.

Three scientific principles guide telecommunications bonding conductors:

- **Equalization — Potentials**, the measured voltages between different ground points, are very dependent on the **impedance**, the total opposition to the flow of electrical current between these points. Ground equalization is improved because the additional bonding lowers the impedance between different ground

2

points. Bonding conductors should be routed with minimum bends or changes in direction, with bonding connections made directly to the points being bonded, and without unnecessary connections or splices in the bonding conductors. The shortest, most direct path and the use of large conductors provide for low impedance. Multiple conductors or wide strips provide even lower impedance.

NOTE   When splices are unavoidable, always use approved connectors and make the splice accessible.

- **Diversion** — Because the bonding conductor follows the telecommunications cable and is directly connected to system grounds at each end, electrical transients that are forced down the cable path are diverted by the bonding conductor and are less likely to influence the telecommunications conductors.

- **Coupling** — The closer the bonding conductor is to the telecommunications cable, the greater the mutual electromagnetic coupling. Coupling tends to partially cancel electrical transients when they reach the telecommunications equipment. A tightly coupled bonding conductor or a backbone cable shield is often called a coupled bonding.

The effect of each principle varies from building to building, and depends on a range of factors. It is often difficult to predict or measure specific results, but using any combination or all three principles is usually beneficial to the telecommunications equipment.

The type of bonding conductor (Figure 2-5) used in most commercial buildings depends on the application and the fault-current-carrying capacity needed. Bonding conductors should be copper, must be insulated, and must be at least No. 6 AWG. (The ANSI/EIA/TIA-607 specification also suggests consideration of No. 3/0 AWG copper conductors.) In addition, bonding conductors should not be placed in metal conduits, cable trays, or **raceways**, and must be marked appropriately, using a green label. (A raceway is any enclosed channel designed for holding wires, cables, or busbars.)

NOTE   If you must use metal conduits, cable trays, or raceways, you must bond both of their ends to bonding conductors.

Figure 2-5   Typical grounding and bonding conductors

Equipment Grounding

Each type of grounding equipment has its own set of grounding and bonding specifications, in addition to the general rules specified in NEC Article 250.

Two different methods are used for grounding, and each serves a different purpose. These methods, equipment grounding and earth grounding, must be kept separate except for a connection to prevent differences in potential from a possible flashover during a lightning strike.

The primary purpose of **equipment grounding** (safety grounding) is to remove potentially dangerous voltage from the equipment. It also protects against electrical shock and prevents heat buildup in the equipment due to a **ground fault**, current misdirected from the hot (or neutral) lead to a ground wire, box, or conductor.

Earth grounding is an intentional connection from a circuit conductor, usually the neutral, to a ground electrode placed in the earth. Besides protecting people and equipment, an earth ground provides a safe path for the dissipation of **fault currents**, lightning strikes, static discharges, EMI and RFI signals, and interference.

Earth Grounding and Bonding Specifications

The NEC requires earth grounding and bonding of telecommunications equipment, antennas and lead-in cables, and network-powered broadband communications systems. These specifications and requirements are published in NEC Article 800D-40.

The communications system grounding conductor should be bonded at the nearest accessible location to any of the following earth-ground locations:

- The building or structure grounding electrode system
- The grounded, metallic water-piping system within the building
- Any power service that is external to enclosures, such as exposed metallic service raceways, exposed grounding electrode conductors, or any other approved means for the external connection of a corrosion-resistant conductor to the service raceway or equipment
- The metallic power service raceway
- The service equipment enclosure
- The grounding electrode conductor or the grounding electrode metal enclosure
- The grounding conductor or grounding electrode of a separate building that is grounded to another electrode in a junction box, panelboard, or similar enclosure immediately inside or outside the building

The bonding jumper must be no smaller than AWG 6 copper or equivalent; you must connect it between the communications system grounding electrode and the building's power grounding electrode system.

2

Termination is the connection of a cable or wire to connecting hardware. You must terminate the earth ground to the grounding electrode using one of the following methods:

- **Exothermic welding** — A method of permanently bonding two metals together with a controlled heat reaction that results in a molecular bond. See Figure 2-6 for an example.

- **Listed lugs or listed clamps** — Two types of connectors used for connecting the earth ground to the grounding electrode. These connectors must always be made of the same material as the conductors.

- **Listed pressure connector** — A device that establishes a connection between two or more conductors or between one or more conductors and a terminal. This device uses mechanical pressure to make connections, not soldering.

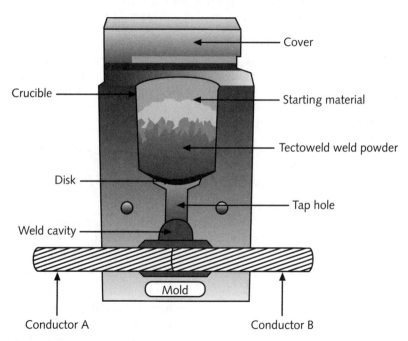

Figure 2-6   Typical exothermic weld

When the earth-ground termination is to a pipe or rod, or is buried, it must be listed for direct burial and clearly labeled.

If you run the earth-ground conductor in a metal raceway, then you must bond both ends of the metal raceway to the earth grounding conductor.

Water Pipes

Underground water pipes historically have been the first choice for a grounding electrode. With the increased use of nonmetallic pipes, however, electrical systems can no longer rely on plumbing systems. Water pipes must be bonded to another electrode type.

Exercise caution when using a water pipe as an intersystem bonding conductor; in such cases, the bonding conductor must be at least AWG No. 6 copper.

Intrinsically Safe Systems

An intrinsically safe system operates by preventing ignition of a flammable or combustible material under normal or abnormal conditions. You can use these systems in **hazardous (classified) locations**, which NEC Article 500 defines as places where fire or explosion hazards may exist due to flammable gases or vapors, flammable liquids, combustible dust, or ignitable fibers.

A primary advantage of intrinsically safe systems is that NEC Article 504-20 allows the use of ordinary wiring. However, the system still must conform to Article 504, which may impose additional requirements that are specific to the hazardous location. Some of these additional requirements are included in Chapters 7 and 8.

Intrinsically safe systems are composed of safe interconnecting cables, cable shields, enclosures, cable trays, and raceways. All of these items must be grounded with an equipment grounding electrode, and bonded using bonding jumpers, bonding fittings, or other approved methods.

Earth Grounding of Communications Systems

The communications systems listed in this section must be earth grounded. When grounding several communications systems, you should bond them all to a common point at the building grounding electrode system. Specifications for each earth-grounded system are summarized in the following list.

- **Low-voltage circuits of less than 50 volts** — Grounding is not required for these systems; however, you must ground them when the primary power supply system exceeds 150 volts to ground, the primary power supply system is ungrounded, or the secondary conductors are installed as overhead conductors outside.

- **Telephone systems** — The protective metallic **sheath** of communications cables and primary protectors must be grounded to the earth grounding electrode as close as possible to the **point of entrance** of the phone cable to the building. Bond the telephone system's ground to an acceptable earth ground, using an AWG No. 14 or larger **insulated** copper conductor. The insulation separates wires and prevents conduction between them. Run the conductor in as straight a line as possible and guard it from any physical damage. If you run the conductor in a metal raceway, bond both ends to the conductor or to the same terminal or electrode to which the grounding conductor is connected.

- **Antennas, satellites, lead-in conductors, and other receiving systems** — You must ground this equipment to the earth grounding electrode. The grounding of the antenna mast and lead-in conductors helps protect the receiving equipment from voltage surges, as well as voltage transients that result from lightning. (A mast is the metal structure that supports receiving antennas; the **lead-in** is the part of the antenna cable that enters the building and continues inside to the final connection.) Each conductor of a lead-in from an outdoor antenna must be connected to a listed **antenna discharge unit**, which can be outside or inside the building as close as possible to the entrance of the conductors to the building. You must ground antenna masts and discharge units to an acceptable earth ground with an AWG No. 10 bare or insulated copper conductor. Run this conductor in as straight a line as possible.

- **CATV systems** — Earth-ground the shield of the coaxial cable as close as possible to the point of entrance to the building. Use an AWG No. 14 or larger insulated conductor that is listed as suitable, has a current-carrying capacity approximately equal to that of the coaxial cable's outer conductor, and is run in as straight a line as possible from the CATV ground to an acceptable earth ground.

- **CCTV and MATV systems** — Closed-circuit television (CCTV) and master antenna television (MATV) circuits within a building do not need to be earth grounded, unless they are connected to coaxial cable that may extend beyond the building structure and be exposed to lightning. The sheath of the coaxial cables that enter the building must be earth grounded as close as possible to the point of entrance to the building. Bond an AWG No. 14 or larger insulated copper conductor from the CCTV or MATV ground to an acceptable earth ground. Run this conductor in as straight a line as possible.

- **Sound (audio) systems** — For metal raceways and enclosures with sound circuits that operate at less than 50 volts, earth grounding is not required unless the cables are exposed to lightning. If the sound circuits operate at 60 volts to ground or more, you must ground their metal enclosures and raceways and provide an equipment grounding conductor.

- **Network-powered broadband communications systems (NPBCS)** — The sheath of an NPBCS cable that enters a building must be grounded to an acceptable earth ground as close as possible to the point of entrance to the building. Use a conductor within the range of AWG No. 14 copper to AWG No. 6 copper for the bonding, depending on the current-carrying capacity of the cable. Run this conductor in as straight a line as possible. If you use metal raceways for the network-powered broadband entrance cable, you must bond them to an acceptable earth ground. Again, the conductor you use should be within the range of AWG No. 14 to AWG No. 6 copper.

CABLE PROTECTION AND EQUIPMENT-GROUNDING PRACTICES

The communications cables, wire, and equipment inside a building are generally considered to be nonexposed. Inside cable and wire is defined by NEC Article 800-52 as any communications cables and wires that run from the equipment to the **protector**, a device used to protect facilities and equipment from abnormally high voltages or currents. These cables and wires have their own special requirements for proper installation, in addition to those for grounding and bonding telecommunications systems in commercial buildings.

All types of communications cables and wires must be rated for resistance to the spread of fire, be suitable for the installation site, and have a voltage rating of at least 300 volts. The conductors in these cables, other than fiber-optic cable, must be copper. For a complete list of cable types, including fire resistance ratings and suitable installation locations, consult NEC Article 800-51.

Specific installation requirements for communications cables and wires include:

- The separation of communications cables and electrical power cabling
- Using approved firestopping methods around the penetrations through firewalls, partitions, floors, or ceilings when cables are installed in hollow spaces, vertical shafts, and ventilation or air-handling ducts. Chapter 7 discusses firestopping in detail.
- The use of a conduit when the installation is in a space used for environmental air
- Using the exterior of any conduit or raceway as a means of support

These specifications are further defined in NEC Article 800-52.

Unshielded Backbone Cable

When you use an unshielded backbone cable, you should use a telecommunications backbone bonding (TBB) conductor with it. The TBB should be a No. 6 AWG insulated copper conductor that is routed along the backbone cable route, with minimal separation between the TBB and the cable along the entire distance. You must bond the TBB to the approved ground using a grounding busbar that is closest to the termination point of the cable.

Shielded Cable

Some indoor cables, such as coaxial, twinaxial, and shielded twisted-pair, rely on their interior shielding as a major factor in their transmission performance. These shields are usually grounded at each end to a connector panel, which you must bond to the closest approved ground with a grounding conductor of the shortest possible length.

Equipment Grounding

All manufacturers, service providers, and customers have their own requirements for grounding telecommunications equipment. The following practices most commonly apply to commercial buildings.

In smaller equipment rooms and entrance facilities, the grounding connections on the installed equipment (e.g., protector panels and PBX cabinets for voice switching) are usually connected directly to the closest approved ground. An electrical contractor generally provides this ground. Usually a coupled bonding conductor is installed directly between the protector's ground terminal and the PBX ground terminal.

In larger buildings that have multiple equipment rooms or separate entrance facilities, multiple TGBs are necessary. Each TGB should be bonded with a minimum No. 6 AWG insulated copper conductor, directly to the nearest approved building ground. This direct bonding results in a connected set of telecommunications grounds that are distributed throughout the building.

When positioning busbars, it helps to place them where the bonding conductors can easily follow the telecommunications cabling, and where the busbars are near their associated equipment. In addition, the TMGB must provide sufficient protection to safely carry lightning and power-fault currents. Typical grounding bars and accessories are shown in Figure 2-7.

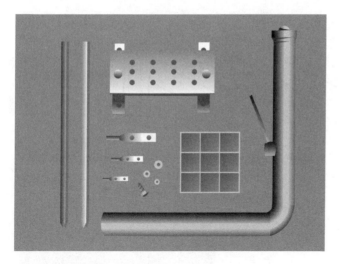

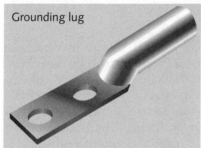

Grounding lug

Figure 2-7   Typical grounding bars and accessories

TELECOMMUNICATIONS CIRCUIT PROTECTORS

A telecommunications circuit protector is a device that protects telecommunications facilities and equipment from abnormally high voltages and currents. High voltage and currents are usually caused by exposure to lightning, accidental contact with electrical light, or power conductors operating at over 300 volts to ground.

Based on Underwriters Laboratories (UL) standards, there are three types of telecommunications circuit protectors:

- **Primary protectors** — Primary protectors are intended for use on exposed circuits, to minimize damage to equipment due to electrical disturbances from lightning, power crosses, power faults, induction, and electrostatic discharge. These protectors must be installed as close as possible to the point where the exposed conductors enter the building. Locating the primary protector so that the grounding conductor is as short as possible will help limit potential differences between communications circuits and other metallic systems (Figure 2-8).

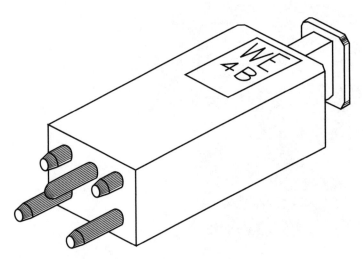

Figure 2-8   Typical primary protector module

- **Secondary protectors** — Although secondary protectors are mentioned by the NEC, they are not required. They are typically used for additional protection behind primary protectors. Besides providing voltage protection, they also protect against **sneak current**, which flows through terminal wiring or equipment at a voltage too low to make the primary protector operate. Secondary protectors can be installed anywhere, including directly behind primary protectors or at telephone set and communications terminal equipment.

- **Data and fire alarm protectors** — These protectors are not required by the NEC, but they must provide primary protection against transients from lightning. They do not protect against power faults and should only be used according to the manufacturer's guidelines.

Because there is some functionality overlap in the available products, always consult the manufacturer concerning specific applications. However, you should always comply with the following general rules for protectors:

- A primary protector is required whenever a circuit may be exposed to electrical power faults and lightning.

- When the circuit may be exposed to lightning surges only, a primary protector or a data and fire alarm protector is required.

- When a circuit may be exposed to sneak currents, a secondary protector or a primary protector with secondary protection is required.

Some manufacturers include secondary and other forms of protection in their primary protectors. These additional functions are known as enhanced protection, and are usually provided for a specific application.

Primary Protectors

Although manufacturers use many types of materials for protection, the following materials are the most typical primary protectors:

- **Carbon blocks** — These are the original protection devices. An air gap between carbon elements is set to arc at about 300 to 1000 volts and conduct surge current to a grounding conductor. When the surge current drops low enough, the arc stops and the protector resumes its normal isolation of the ground. When a surge or fault current overheats the carbon blocks, they short permanently to ground. Carbon blocks are usually installed in pairs and are the least expensive option among primary protectors. However, they tend to wear out quickly under extreme conditions, and can cause leakage and noise on voice circuits.

- **Gas tubes** — These protection devices are an improvement over carbon blocks, although they operate in the same way—by providing an arc over a gap to a grounding conductor. Because they use a special gas, the tubes are set to a higher arc than carbon blocks; as a result, they have a higher rate of reliability. In addition, they have a tighter tolerance on arc breakdown voltage and are usually set to arc at a lower voltage than carbon blocks.

- **Solid state** — This newest type of protection device relies on high-power semiconductor technology. Although it is more expensive than carbon blocks and gas tubes, the cost of solid-state can be recovered over its extended life expectancy. Solid-state protectors are fast acting and well balanced, and do not deteriorate with age below a maximum surge current.

Primary Protector Installation

Before selecting and installing any form of protection, the telecommunications designer should be aware of all customer and manufacturer requirements, as well as the specifications for protectors. In addition, the designer is responsible for ensuring that there are no obstructions around protectors, that protector locations will not be used for storage, and that additional space is allocated in the building entrance facility and the equipment room(s) to accommodate additional protection, even if it is not needed for the existing equipment.

When the protectors are ready to be installed, you should observe the following installation practices:

- Ensure that primary protectors are installed immediately adjacent to the exposed cable's point of entrance, and that the associated grounding conductor is routed as directly as possible to the closest approved ground.

- For long-term reliability, ensure that the installation is in a noncorrosive atmosphere.

- For personnel safety at protector locations, adequate lighting is very important.

- When a protector is installed in a metal box, bond the box with an approved grounding conductor directly to the protector's ground.

- When a new cable and protector are installed in a building beside an existing protector, bond the new protector directly to the old one, and add a separate grounding conductor for the new protector.

- When a protector must be installed outside a building, use cabinets, boxes, and mounting hardware that is listed for that purpose to avoid environmental degradation.

- Never locate primary protectors or their associated grounding near any hazardous or easily ignitable material.

Secondary Protectors

Secondary protectors must coordinate with the lightning transient and power-fault requirements of primary protectors. For this reason, secondary protectors often include one of the previously described protection device materials, and secondary protection is usually available as an option on primary protectors. When secondary protection is provided as an option, the protection device is qualified to both the UL-497 and UL-497A standards.

Because secondary protectors must handle sneak current, they are constructed differently than primary protectors. The materials used to handle sneak current are:

- **Heat coil** — This device has coils that are designed to detect low-level current by heat. The heat melts a spring-loaded shorting contact that permanently shorts the line to ground. If shorted, the heat coil requires manual inspection and replacement.

- **Sneak-current fuse** — This fuse opens the station circuit wiring under a sustained low-level current. When opened, the fuse requires manual inspection and replacement. The fuse is placed on the station side of the protection device.

- **PTC resistors** — Positive Temperature Coefficient (PTC) resistors are used in place of sneak-current fuses. They are designed to limit sustained current as they heat. The advantage of PTC resistors is that they do not need to be replaced after the sneak-current fault is cleared.

2

How Documentation Helps You and Your Network

You know from Chapter 1 that documentation is important and can save you time, but you still don't have a clear picture of why it helps you and your network. The following list summarizes the advantages of keeping accurate documentation:

- It provides a comprehensive reference to help you determine hardware and software requirements for additions to the network.

- It can make additions, moves, and changes to equipment and workstations easier.

- It can be a valuable source of troubleshooting information.

- It can provide the necessary justification for adding staff or equipment.

- It helps determine compliance with standards.

- It provides proof that your installations meet a manufacturer's hardware or software requirements.

- It can help reduce training requirements, which saves time.

- It makes security management more effective.

- It helps you comply with software licensing agreements.

Keeping your documentation current and accurate helps you perform network tasks more quickly and with less chances for error. For example, just moving a workstation from one end of the office to the other can prove difficult and time-consuming unless your network configuration is properly documented. By the same token, proper documentation of the move will make future tasks easier, at least on this area of the network.

CHAPTER SUMMARY

❑ All telecommunications systems require grounding and bonding systems. Several associations provide codes, standards, and minimum requirements for installing these systems. ANSI/EIA/TIA-607, "Commercial Building Grounding and Bonding Requirements for Telecommunications," is the primary source of installation information. The second most important source is the NEC.

❑ A grounding and bonding network is made up of insulated copper conductors. These conductors are run in parallel with the telecommunications cables, and link rooms containing telecommunications equipment to a common ground. The recommended size for these conductors ranges from No. 6 to No. 3/0 AWG insulated copper.

❑ These conductors are bonded to solid copper grounding busbars, which are installed in the entrance facility, the main telecommunications room, and all other telecommunications rooms. In addition to the conductors that run throughout the building, telecommunications equipment, frames, cabinets, raceways, and protectors are grounded to the busbars.

❑ The busbars throughout the building are bonded together with a backbone cable of at least No. 6 AWG insulated copper. This backbone cable is also connected to the main grounding busbar, which is bonded to the electrical service (power) ground and an earth ground.

❑ Telecommunications circuit protectors are used to protect telecommunications facilities and equipment from abnormally high voltages and currents. This protection is in addition to the requirements and recommendations for grounding and bonding telecommunications systems.

❑ Documentation makes your job easier and helps you and your networks work more efficiently.

KEY TERMS

air terminals (lightning rods) — Slender rods installed on a roof at regular intervals to ground lightning current.

American Wire Gauge (AWG) — The system used to specify wire size. The greater the wire diameter, the smaller the value is.

ampere — The basic unit for measuring electrical current.

ANSI/EIA/TIA — The three associations involved in developing telecommunications industry standards. Their full names are the American National Standards Institute, Electronic Industries Alliance, and Telecommunications Industry Association, respectively.

antenna discharge unit — The bonding location for the antenna lead-in cable.

backboard — A panel used for mounting connecting hardware and equipment.

bonding — The permanent joining of metallic parts to form an electrically conductive path that will ensure electrical continuity, the capacity to safely conduct current, and the ability to limit differences in potentials between the joined parts.

bonding conductor — A conductor used specifically for bonding.

bonding conductor for telecommunications (BCT) — The conductor that interconnects the building's service equipment (power) ground to the telecommunications grounding system.

busbar — A conductor that serves as a common connection point for two or more circuits.

cable — An assembly of one or more insulated conductors within a sheath, constructed to permit use of the conductors singly or in a group.

conductors — Copper or aluminum cables that interconnect various system components. Wires through which a current of electricity flows.

earth grounding — An electrical connection to the earth obtained by a grounding electrode system.

effective ground — An electrical connection to a low-resistance ground that permits current to discharge without the buildup of hazardous voltages on the telecommunications cabling.

entrance room (facility) — An entrance to a building for both public and private network service cables.

equipment grounding — An electrical connection of the non-current-carrying metal parts of equipment raceways and other enclosures to the grounding electrode system.

fault current — *See* foreign electrical voltage.

foreign electrical voltage — Any voltage (current) imposed on a system that is not supplied from the central office, telephone equipment, or the system itself. This unwanted voltage is also known as fault current.

ground — A conducting connection, whether accidental or intentional, between an electrical circuit or equipment and the earth, or to some other conducting body that serves in place of the earth. Grounding is the backbone of effective protection for all telecommunications systems.

ground fault — Current misdirected from the hot (or neutral) lead to a ground wire, box, or conductor.

ground system — A system of hardware and wiring that provides an electrical path from a specified location to an earth-ground point.

ground terminations (ground rods) — Metal rods driven into the earth to guide lightning current harmlessly to ground.

grounding conductor — A conductor used to connect electrical equipment to the grounding electrode and a building's main grounding busbar.

grounding electrode — A conductor that provides a low-resistance, direct connection to the earth.

grounding electrode system — One or more grounding electrodes bonded to form a single, reliable ground for a building, tower, or similar structure.

hazardous (classified) locations — A location where fire or explosion hazards may exist due to flammable gases or vapors, flammable liquids, combustible dust, or ignitable fibers.

impedance — Total opposition to the flow of electrical current.

insulated — Coated with dielectric material that physically separates wires and prevents conduction between them.

lead-in — The part of the antenna cable that enters a building and continues inside to the final connection.

lightning rods — Slender rods installed on a roof at regular intervals to ground lightning current.

mA (milliampere) — A measure of a unit of electrical current, equal to 1/1000 of an ampere.

made and other electrodes — Any electrode not specified in NEC Article 250H, but defined in NEC Article 250, section 83, subsections b-d. These electrodes include rod and pipe electrodes, plate electrodes, and metal underground systems such as piping systems.

main telecommunications room — The main equipment room or main cross-connect for the interconnection of entrance cables, first-level backbone cables, and equipment cables.

National Electrical Code (NEC) — An electrical safety code written and administered by the NFPA.

National Electrical Manufacturers Association (NEMA) — A standards association that focuses on electrical power and grounding.

National Fire Protection Association (NFPA) — The association that writes and administers the NEC.

point of entrance — The point at which cabling emerges through an exterior wall, through a floor, or from a conduit. It can also be the point where the local service provider's cabling ends and the customer's cabling begins.

potentials — Measured voltages.

protector — A device used to protect facilities and equipment from abnormally high voltages or currents.

raceway — Any enclosed channel designed for holding wires, cables, or busbars.

sheath — A protective covering over a conductor assembly that may include one or more metallic members, strength members, or jackets.

sneak current — A foreign voltage that is too low to make an overvoltage protector operate.

surge — A rapid rise in current or voltage, usually followed by a fall back to a normal level. Also referred to as a transient.

surge arresters (suppressors) — Devices that are installed in conjunction with a lightning protection system to protect electrical wiring and electronic systems.

termination — The act of connecting a cable or wire to connecting hardware.

2

transient — A rapid rise in current or voltage, usually followed by a fall back to a normal level. Also referred to as a surge.

Underwriters Laboratories — A U.S.-based independent testing laboratory that creates safety tests and standards for electrical equipment.

REVIEW QUESTIONS

1. Which organization produces codes and standards for the grounding and bonding of telecommunications systems in commercial buildings?

   a. IEEE

   b. NEC

   c. ANSI/EIA/TIA

   d. all of the above

2. The most common electric shock occurs from inadvertent contact with energized devices or circuits. Name another common shock hazard to avoid.

   a. touching a faulty or improperly grounded electrical component

   b. standing on a damp floor while working on or near electrical equipment

   c. using or being near conducting material during a lightning storm

   d. all of the above

3. The effects of an electric current on the body are primarily determined by the magnitude of currents and duration of shock. People can die when exposed to currents as low as 20 mA (20/1000 ampere) for a fraction of a second. True or False?

4. Which organization and standard specifies a uniform infrastructure for telecommunications grounding and bonding?

   a. NEC Article 250

   b. ANSI/NFPA 780, Lightning Protection Code

   c. UL-497, Protectors for Paired Conductor Communication Circuits

   d. ANSI/EIA/TIA-607, Commercial Building Grounding and Bonding Requirements for Telecommunications

5. Where must a telecommunications ground be bonded to the lightning protection system ground?

   a. anywhere there is a ground

   b. within 12 meters of the base of the building

   c. within 3.7 meters (12 feet) of the base of the building

   d. within 1 meter of the building

6. At what voltage is safety grounding not required for the metal parts of equipment and electrical raceways of low-voltage systems?

   a. 60 volts or less

   b. less than 50 volts

   c. Safety grounds are not required for low-voltage systems.

   d. less than 100 volts

7. Metal raceways for low-voltage and limited-energy circuits that become energized by higher-voltage systems must be bonded in accordance with which standard?

   a. ANSI/NEMA

   b. IEEE 142-1991

   c. NEC Article 250-92(b)

   d. ANSI/EIA/TIA-607

8. Electrical current can create a fire from excessive heat buildup. What can cause this heat buildup?

   a. If a grounding path has a high resistance, the ground-fault current might not be significant enough to open the circuit protection device to clear the fault. This will result in dangerous voltage in all metal parts, and the buildup of ground-fault current could cause a fire.

   b. a surge of dangerous voltage

   c. an isolated grounding connector that is too long

   d. an overcurrent protection device that has a lower rating than the impedance of the grounding path

9. The NEC requires earth grounding of telecommunications equipment, antennas and lead-in cables, and network-powered broadband communications systems. True or False?

10. To which of the following earth-ground locations must the communications systems be bonded?

    a. building and structure grounding electrode

    b. metal service raceway

    c. building or structure grounding electrode conductor

    d. all of the above

11. Historically, the first choice for a grounding electrode was an underground water pipe connected to a utility distribution system. This is still the best practice today. True or False?

2

12. What are the three scientific principles behind telecommunications bonding conductors?

   a. grounding, diverting, and bonding

   b. equalization, diversion, and coupling

   c. equality, impedance, and resistance

   d. resistance, equalization, and coupling

13. The telecommunications bonding backbone (TBB) is used to interconnect all telecommunications grounding busbars with the telecommunications main grounding busbar (TMGB), and is generally considered part of a grounding and bonding infrastructure, but is independent of equipment or cable. True or False?

14. What is the primary function of the TBB?

   a. to join all of the telecommunications systems

   b. to provide a common ground for all the telecommunications systems bonded to it

   c. to reduce or equalize differences between telecommunications systems bonded to it

   d. to shield the other telecommunications systems that are bonded to it

15. The TMGB serves as _____.

   a. a central point for all the TBBs and equipment to connect

   b. the grounding electrode for the TBBs and equipment

   c. the protection for the telecommunications systems

   d. a dedicated extension of the building grounding electrode system for the telecommunications infrastructure, and as the central connection point for the TBBs and equipment

16. What is the basic function of telecommunications circuit protectors? (Choose all that apply.)

   a. to carry lightning and power-fault currents

   b. to protect against sneak current

   c. to arrest surges or overvoltages that come from exposed circuit pairs

   d. to protect against sustained hazardous currents

17. A busbar where grounding and bonding conductors can be connected is commonly referred to as a _____.

   a. terminal ground

   b. grounding terminal

   c. grounding bus

   d. bus strip

18. Inside cable and wiring is defined by NEC Article 800-52 as any communications cable and wire that runs from _____.

    a. the work area to the TMGB

    b. the telecommunications room to the equipment

    c. the equipment to the protector

    d. the protector to the telecommunications room

19. Why are some indoor cables shielded?

    a. to protect the wires inside the cable

    b. to ensure transmission performance

    c. to prevent EMI

    d. to prevent electric shock

20. What is an overcurrent protective device with a circuit-opening element that is severed (opened) when heated by the passage of an overcurrent?

    a. fuse

    b. coil

    c. bond

    d. ground

21. Which device grounds a conductor when its current time limits are exceeded, and is suitable for sneak current protection?

    a. resistor

    b. circuit

    c. conductor

    d. heat coil

22. What is the total opposition that a circuit offers to the flow of current at a particular frequency?

    a. impedance

    b. resistance

    c. current

    d. inductance

23. What is the name for a network of grounded building components that includes metal underground water piping, a metal building frame, a concrete-encased electrode, a ground ring and rod, and pipe electrodes?

    a. primary protectors

    b. telecommunications grounding busbar

    c. building grounding electrode system

    d. telecommunications bonding backbone

24. The property of a conductor that determines the current produced by a given potential difference, impedes the flow of current, and results in the dissipation of power and heat is called _____ .

    a. impedance

    b. resistance

    c. inductance

    d. current

HANDS-ON PROJECTS

Project 2-1

Each of the following six systems—lightning protection, grounding electrode, electrical bonding and grounding, electrical power protection, telecommunications bonding and grounding, and telecommunications circuit protectors—is recognized as performing a unique function within a building and providing overall protection for the building and its occupants. Proper design and coordination of these systems are important.

1. Using your text, define each system and explain the purpose and importance of each.

2. Visit the following Web sites and read the articles related to the six systems. Summarize any additional or new information you acquire. If you know of any other appropriate Web sites, use them as well.

    ❏ *www.elec-toolbox.com/usefulinfo/lightprot.htm*

    ❏ *www.lightning.org/protect.htm*

    ❏ *www.faqs.org/faqs/electrical-wiring/part1/section-29.html*

    ❏ *www.epanorama.net/documents/groundloop*

    ❏ *www.psihq.com.* Click **Informational Readings** on the home page. Select the articles you want to read from the list.

    ❏ *www.mikeholt.com*

Project 2-2

Three equipment design methods are commonly used to protect large telecommunications equipment from residual circuit surges. List and define each of the design methods, and explain their advantages and disadvantages.

Project 2-3

Article 250 of the NEC covers general rules for telecommunications grounding and bonding. The NEC also covers some specific requirements. What are they, and why are they important?

Project 2-4

Define earth grounding. List and explain the types of protection it provides. Some useful Web sites for this project are *www.sgscorp.com/system.htm* and *www.mikeholt.com*.

Project 2-5

Explain the importance of bonding conductors, then identify and explain the importance of their three design considerations. A useful Web site for this project is *www.uic.edu/depts/accc/telecom/art8.html*.

Project 2-6

1. Define safety grounding and earth grounding, identifying differences between the two.

2. Identify the eight communications systems that must be earth-grounded, and briefly discuss each one.

CASE PROJECTS

Case Project 1

Answer the following questions about the many guidelines for cabling inside a building.

1. Describe what might happen if the electrical power cabling were routed directly next to the communications cable.

2. Explain why the communications cable should be routed as close to the middle of the building as possible.

3. Your company is in an area that is not generally affected by weather. As the communications specialist, however, you have been asked to research lightning protection systems and write a report identifying the pros and cons of installing a system now or later.

4. Explain why it is important to ground or protect the cables leading into the building, and identify possible problems if they are not protected.

Case Project 2

Three types of telecommunications circuit protectors are defined by UL standards. List each type, explain when each one is used, and describe the composition of each type. For more information on UL-497, UL-497A, and UL-497B, go to *http://ulstandardsinfonet.ul.com*. Click **Catalog of Standards**, click **UL Standards & Outlines**, and then scroll to the appropriate standard numbers.

Case Project 3

Discuss the installation practices for choosing a form of primary protection. In your discussion, include actions that the designer should always perform before making the choice. For assistance, go to *www.ch.cutler-hammer.com*. You then have two choices for finding relevant articles: click the **Quick Links** list box and then click **Surge Suppression**, or type **Surge Protection Devices** in the For Documents text box.

Case Project 4

Explain "sneak current" and the components used to handle it. Use the following Web sites for assistance:

❐ *www.its.bldrdoc.gov/fs-1037*. Search the glossary.

❐ *www.itwlinx.com*. Click **Articles** in the Browse box and read any articles you want.

❐ *www.bourns.com/pdf/2400revB1.pdf*

3

CABLES AND THE CABLING INFRASTRUCTURE

After reading this chapter and completing the exercises, you will be able to:

♦ Identify the various types of cable and their characteristics

♦ Compare cable types and characteristics

♦ Identify and differentiate between the various network topologies

♦ Create an effective network design

♦ Identify which network elements you must include in your documentation

Every network needs a solid foundation, regardless of its size. The cables are the framework of that foundation; without the necessary cables in place, no network can exist. Designing the cable layout and selecting the appropriate types of cable for use are crucial to a network's success.

This chapter describes the popular cable types you need to know, as well as their specifications and network topologies. When you are designing a network for an organization, this information helps you to assess the organization's current needs and plans for future growth. Creating a network design that is both sound and flexible provides the solid foundation you need.

CABLE TYPES AND CHARACTERISTICS

When selecting cable for your telecommunications system, you must match your needs with the characteristics of the cable. The three basic types of cable are coaxial, twisted-pair, and fiber-optic. As an alternative to using cable in your system, you might consider **wireless** technologies, which transmit signals through the atmosphere. The five basic characteristics you must consider when choosing cable are its throughput and bandwidth, cost, size and scalability, connectors, and noise immunity. The following sections describe each cable type and its characteristics.

Cable Characteristics

The five characteristics described in this section pertain to all means of **data transmission**, in which signals are generated by voltage and then sent over a designated path. These signals can be either analog or digital. **Analog** signals are variable voltages that create continuous waves of sound, resulting in inexact transmissions. **Digital** signals are precise voltages that create pulses with specific values called bits, resulting in more precise transmissions. You must consider the following characteristics when selecting data transfer **media** for transmitting signals:

- **Throughput and bandwidth** — **Throughput** is the amount of data that a cable can transmit during a given period. This time is usually measured in **megabits** (1,000,000 bits) per second, or Mbps. Throughput potential is determined by the physical nature of the cable. If you try to send more data through a copper wire than it is designed to handle, the result will be lost data and data errors. Noise and other devices connected to transmission media can also limit throughput. **Bandwidth** is the measure of the difference between the highest and lowest frequencies that media can transmit. The range of these frequencies is expressed in **hertz (Hz)**, and is directly related to throughput. The higher the bandwidth, the higher the throughput, because higher frequencies can transmit more data in a given period than lower frequencies.

- **Cost** — Because the cost for different types of cable varies and depends on the available hardware, several factors can influence the final cost of choosing one type of cable over another. You should consider the costs of installation, the transmission rate as it affects productivity, and the obsolescence potential of the media. You should also consider whether a new infrastructure is needed or the existing one is sufficient; the maintenance and support costs for new and existing systems play a part in this decision.

- **Size and scalability** — Three specifications determine a cable's size and **scalability** (growth ability and potential): maximum nodes per segment, maximum length per segment, and maximum network length. Each of these specifications is based on a physical characteristic of the wire. **Attenuation**, the amount of signal loss over a given distance, limits the maximum number of nodes and the maximum length of a segment. Maximum network length is determined by **latency**, the delay between entering commands on your computer and their acceptance by the server.

- **Connectors** — **Connectors** are the hardware that connects the cable to the network device. Each type of cable requires a specific connector. The connectors you choose affect the cost of installation and maintenance.

- **Noise immunity** — Noise can distort data signals. Two types of noise that can affect data transmission are **electromagnetic interference (EMI)** and **radio frequency interference (RFI)**. Both EMI and RFI are waves that emanate from cables carrying electricity or electrical devices, including cabling motors, power lines, televisions, copiers, and fluorescent lights. RFI can also be caused by a strong broadcast signal from a radio or television station.

Cable Types

Now that you understand the characteristics of cables, you need to learn more about each type of popular cable and how it works.

Coaxial Cable

Coaxial cable, also called "coax" for short, was the foundation for Ethernet networks in the 1980s and remained a popular medium for many years. Coaxial cable consists of a central copper core surrounded by an insulator, a braided metal shielding called braiding, and an outer plastic cover called a sheath or jacket. Figure 3-1 depicts a typical coaxial cable. The copper core carries the electromagnetic signal, and the braiding acts as both a shield against noise and a ground for the signal. The insulator layer usually consists of a ceramic or plastic material such as polyvinyl chloride (PVC) or Teflon®. The insulator protects the copper core from the metal shielding to prevent a short circuit in case the two touch. The jacket protects the cable from physical damage and is usually manufactured from a flexible, fire-resistant plastic.

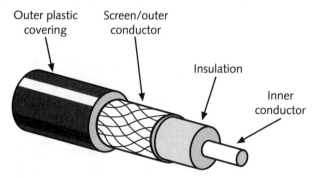

Figure 3-1   Coaxial cable

Coaxial cable has a high resistance to interference from noise due to its insulation and protective braiding. Coax can also carry signals farther than twisted-pair cabling before signal amplification is necessary, although not as far as fiber-optic cabling. Coax is more expensive than twisted-pair cable and generally supports lower throughput. Coax requires each end of its segments to be terminated with a 50-ohm resistor to control **signal bounce** (sometimes called signal reflection), a phenomenon in which data signals travel endlessly between the two ends of the network. Coax also requires each cable to be grounded on one end.

Coaxial cable comes in a variety of types with different specifications; however, only two or three types of coax are used today. In telecommunications, the most important specification for coaxial cable is its **impedance**, the measurement of a conductor's opposition, or resistance, to the flow of alternating current. Each unit of this resistance is expressed as an **ohm**.

To better understand the concept of resistance, visualize an open window. Wind easily blows through it, but if a mesh screen is placed over the window, it creates opposition to the wind. Each time another, more tightly woven mesh screen is placed over the window, resistance to the wind increases. Placing a piece of glass over the window provides total opposition to the wind.

Each type of coaxial cable is defined by its own specifications, as shown in Table 3-1.

Table 3-1 Types of coaxial cable

Designation	Type	Impedance	Description
RG-58 /U	Thinwire	50 ohms	Solid copper core
RG-58 A/U	Thinwire	50 ohms	Stranded copper core
RG-58 C/U	Thinwire	50 ohms	Military version of RG-58 A/U
RG-59	CATV	75 ohms	Broadband cable, used for cable TV
RG-8	Thickwire	50 ohms	Solid core; approximately 0.4-inch diameter
RG-11	Thickwire	50 ohms	Stranded core; approximately 0.4-inch diameter
RG-62	Baseband	90 ohms	Used for ARCnet and IBM 3270 terminals

Twisted-Pair Cable

Twisted-pair cable is the most common form of cabling used on LANs today. It is relatively inexpensive, flexible, and easy to install. It does not span as great a distance as coax, but it can span significant distances before requiring the use of a **repeater** to regenerate and amplify signals. Twisted-pair cable can easily accommodate a variety of network layouts, or **topologies**, and can handle faster networking transmission rates than coaxial cable. Because of its flexibility, twisted-pair is more prone to physical damage than coaxial cable. The benefits of twisted-pair, however, outweigh this drawback.

Twisted-pair cable is the type of cable used to wire telephones. Different applications may call for different grades of twisted-pair cable; however, no matter what the grade or application, all twisted-pair cable consists of insulated copper wires, each with a diameter of 0.4 to 0.8 mm, twisted in pairs around each other and encased in a plastic coating (Figure 3-2). The telephone industry refers to these pairs as the tip and ring. One of the wires in the pair, the **tip**, is connected to the positive side of a battery, which is the telephone industry's equivalent of a ground in a standard electrical circuit. The other wire, the **ring**, is the DC negative wire (–48 volts) that carries the signal.

The twists in the pairs, also referred to as **balanced–pair**, help to reduce the effects of **crosstalk**, the infringement of the signal from one wire pair on another wire pair's signal. Crosstalk is quantified in **decibels (dB)**, a measurement unit of signal strength or of a sound's intensity. Silence measures 0 dB, a sound that is 10 times more powerful measures 10 dB, and a sound that is 100 times more powerful is 20 dB (not 100 dB). **Alien crosstalk**, which occurs when signals from one cable interfere with an adjacent cable's transmission, is another form of crosstalk. It is often caused by bundling too many cables in a conduit that is too small.

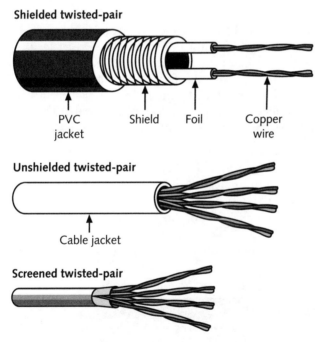

Shielded twisted-pair

PVC jacket   Shield   Foil   Copper wire

Unshielded twisted-pair

Cable jacket

Screened twisted-pair

Figure 3-2   Shielded, unshielded, and screened twisted-pair cable

The number of twists per inch in a pair of wires determines how resistant the pair will be to noise. Better, more expensive twisted-pair cable has more twists per foot, an amount known as the **twist ratio**. One drawback of a high twist ratio is the possibility of greater attenuation.

Twisted-pair cable falls into three categories: shielded twisted-pair, unshielded twisted-pair, and screened twisted-pair.

- **Shielded twisted-pair (STP)** — STP consists of twisted pairs that are individually insulated and surrounded by a shielding made of a metallic substance, such as foil or braided metal, that must be properly grounded. The shielding acts as an antenna by converting the noise into a current that induces an equal, yet opposite, current on the twisted pairs it surrounds. The noise on the shielding mirrors the noise on the twisted pairs, allowing the two to cancel each other out. The effectiveness of the shield depends on the environmental noise to which the STP is subjected; the grounding mechanism; and the material, thickness, symmetry, and consistency of the shielding.

- **Unshielded twisted-pair (UTP)** — UTP consists of one or more insulated pairs of wires encased in a plastic sheath. Because it does not contain additional shielding, it is less expensive and less resistant to noise than STP and screened twisted-pair (ScTP). UTP protects against EMI and RFI by providing an electrical balance between the two conductors in a pair and a uniform twist, also referred to as balanced-pair.

- **Screened twisted-pair (ScTP)** — ScTP consists of one or more insulated pairs of wires contained in a full foil laminate shield, with at least one tinned, copper drain wire encased in a plastic sheath. Because of its construction, ScTP offers superior immunity to radio frequency fields and reduced crosstalk. ScTP protects against EMI and RFI by providing an electrical balance between the two conductors in a pair and a uniform twist. The drain wire and screen must always maintain continuity and a single point of ground.

In 1991 the American National Standards Institute (ANSI), Electronic Industries Alliance (EIA), and Telecommunications Industry Association (TIA) released their joint standard, called the ANSI/EIA/TIA-568 Commercial Building Wiring Standard. Also known as structured cabling, this standard was designed for uniform, enterprise-wide, multivendor cabling systems. The standard accomplishes two objectives: It divides twisted-pair wiring into several categories, as shown in Table 3-2, and suggests how networking media can be best installed to maximize performance and minimize maintenance.

Table 3-2   Twisted-pair categories, data rates, and applications

Category	Maximum Data Rate	Usual Application and Information
CAT1	20 Kbps	Voice communications, doorbell wiring
CAT2	4 Mbps	Not usually found on modern networks, but still used on IBM cabling systems and Token Ring networks
CAT3	Usually 10 Mbps, but 16 Mbps is possible	Voice and data on 10-Mbps Ethernet networks and 4-Mbps Token Ring networks
CAT4	16 Mbps to 20 Mbps	16-Mbps Token Ring (not used much); guaranteed up to 20-MHz (megahertz) signal
CAT5	100 Mbps	100-Mbps Ethernet and ATM (Asynchronous Transfer Mode); guaranteed up to 100-MHz signal

Table 3-2   Twisted-pair categories, data rates, and applications (continued)

Category	Maximum Data Rate	Usual Application and Information
Enhanced CAT5	1000 Mbps or 1 Gbps (gigabits per second)	Fast Ethernet and other fast technologies; signal rates as high as 200 MHz, with advanced methods for reducing crosstalk
CAT6	1000 Mbps	Fast Ethernet and other fast technologies. Same as Enhanced CAT5, but better performance. Guaranteed signal rates of 250 MHz.
CAT7	Unknown at this time	Same as CAT6, with signal rates of 600 MHz. The CAT7 standard was still in testing at press time.

Fiber-Optic Cable

Fiber-optic cable, also called fiber, contains one or more glass fibers in its core. Data is transmitted by converting electrical signals at the sending end into optical signals, which are then transmitted through the central fibers via a pulsing light sent from a laser or light-emitting diode (LED), and reconverted into electrical signals at the receiving end. Around the fibers is a layer of glass, called **cladding**; it has a lower refractive index than the core. The **refractive index**, which measures the ability to bend light, enables the cladding to act like a mirror, reflecting light back to the core in patterns that vary depending on the transmission mode. This behavior is known as total internal reflection; it allows the fiber to bend around corners without diminishing the integrity of the signal. Over the cladding is a layer of plastic and a braiding of Kevlar® (an advanced polymeric fiber), also known as the buffer, that protect the inner core. A plastic jacket covers the braiding. Figure 3-3 shows the different layers of a typical fiber-optic cable.

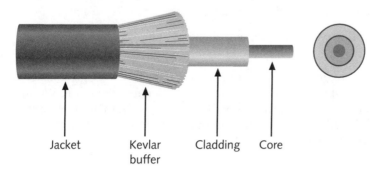

Jacket   Kevlar buffer   Cladding   Core

Figure 3-3   Basic optical fiber

Fiber comes in a number of different types, but all of its variations fall into two categories: single-mode and multimode. **Single-mode fiber** carries a single mode of light to transmit data from one end of the cable to another. Data can travel faster and farther on single-mode fiber, but the cost is extremely high. **Multimode fiber** carries up to hundreds of thousands of modes of light simultaneously, and is the type of fiber-optic system used by most data networks.

COMPARING CABLES AND THEIR CHARACTERISTICS

Now that you are familiar with the various cable types and the characteristics that pertain to all media, you can compare these cables. This comparison helps you make the best decisions when selecting cable for your applications. The terms that define the types of media used by a network include 10Base5, 10Base2, 10BaseT, and 100 (or 1000)BaseT. The "10" (or "100," or "1000") refers to the data speed or throughput in Mbps. The "Base" refers to baseband, which means that the cable uses all of its bandwidth for each transmission. The "5" is short for 500 m and the "2" is short for 185 m, both of which refer to the maximum cable segment lengths. Finally, the "T" refers to twisted-pair. Understanding these terms helps you identify cable immediately.

ThickNet (10Base5)

ThickNet (10Base5) cabling is also known as ThickWire Ethernet, Yellow Ethernet, and Yellow garden hose, due to its yellow sheath. The following list describes ThickNet's characteristics:

- ThickNet has a maximum transmission rate of 10 Mbps and uses **baseband** transmission, in which digital signals are sent through direct-current pulses applied to the wire. The signal requires exclusive use of the wire's capacity, which means that only one signal can be transmitted at a time.

- Although ThickNet is less expensive than fiber-optic cable, it is significantly more expensive than ThinNet or twisted-pair cable.

- ThickNet requires the use of a **vampire tap** (a connector that pierces a hole in the wire) to connect to a transceiver, and a drop cable to connect the telecommunications devices. A vampire tap is shown in Figure 3-4.

- Because of its wide diameter and shielding, ThickNet has the highest resistance to noise of any commonly used cabling option.

- ThickNet's high noise resistance allows data to travel for greater distances than most other types of cabling. The maximum segment length is 500 m. ThickNet can accommodate a maximum of 100 nodes per segment. Its total maximum network length is 1500 m. To minimize interference between stations, devices must be separated by at least 2.5 m.

ThinNet (10Base2)

ThinNet cabling (10Base2) is also known as thin Ethernet or black Ethernet for its black sheath. It was the most popular medium for Ethernet LANs in the 1980s. The following list describes ThinNet's characteristics:

- ThinNet can transmit data at a maximum rate of 10 Mbps, and uses baseband transmission.

- ThinNet is less expensive than ThickNet and fiber-optic cable, but more expensive than twisted-pair cable. Prefabricated cables are available for the low cost of approximately $1 per foot, which is why ThinNet is sometimes referred to as "cheapnet."

- ThinNet uses **BNC (British Naval Connector)** and **BNC/T** connectors to connect the wires to devices (Figure 3-5). The BNC is the connector that goes on the cable, and the BNC/T is a T-shaped adapter that connects on one end to the station's network interface card. The bus connects to the other two ends.

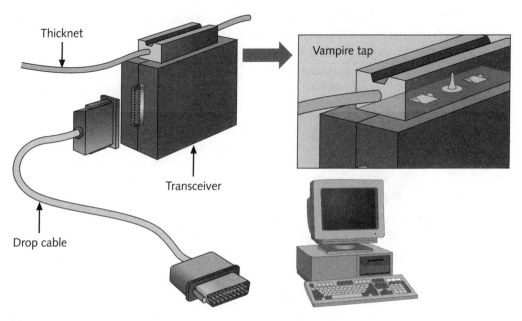

Figure 3-4   Vampire tap

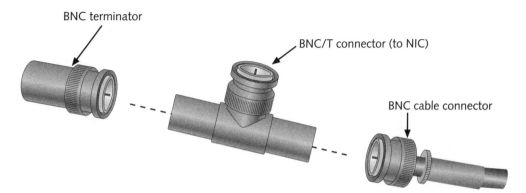

Figure 3-5   BNC and BNC/T connectors

- Because of its insulation and shielding, ThinNet is more resistant to noise than twisted-pair cable, but not as resistant as ThickNet.

- ThinNet has a maximum segment length of 185 m and can accommodate 30 nodes per segment. The total maximum network length for ThinNet is slightly more than 550 m. To minimize interference between stations, devices must be separated by at least 0.5 m.

Twisted-Pair: Shielded, Unshielded, and Screened (10BaseT)

Whether shielded, screened, or unshielded, all twisted-pair cables share many of the same characteristics. The following list describes the characteristics of STP, ScTP, and UTP cable, and highlights their similarities and differences:

- Both STP and UTP can transmit data at 10 Mbps. CAT5 UTP can transmit data at 100 Mbps, and enhanced CAT5 and CAT6 can transmit data at 1000 Mbps (1 Gbps).

- The costs of STP, ScTP, and UTP vary and depend on the grade of copper used, the category rating, and any enhancements. However, STP and ScTP are usually more expensive than UTP, enhanced CAT5 usually costs about 20 percent more than regular CAT5, and CAT6 is even more expensive than enhanced CAT5.

- All twisted-pair cables use 8-pin **RJ-45 connectors** and jacks, which look very much like standard telephone connectors and jacks, as shown in Figure 3-6.

- Because of their shielding or screening, STP and ScTP are more resistant to noise than UTP. UTP is the least noise-resistant of the major cable types. UTP may use filtering and balancing techniques to offset the effects of noise.

- The maximum segment length for STP and UTP is 100 m; for ScTP, it is 98 m. These are shorter spans than those for coaxial cable, because twisted-pair is more susceptible to noise. Twisted-pair can accommodate a maximum of 1024 nodes per segment. The maximum overall network length depends on the transmission method used.

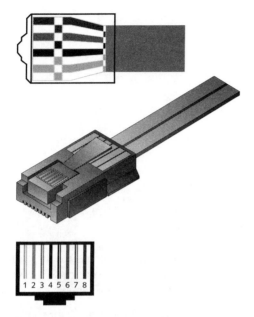

Figure 3-6   RJ-45 connector

Fiber-Optic Cable

Fiber-optic cable is also known as fiber. Until recently, fiber was used primarily as a **backbone cable**. This is the cabling that connects one telecommunications room (TR) to another, as well as connecting TRs to equipment rooms and one building's equipment room to another's. The following list describes the characteristics of fiber-optic cable:

- Fiber has always been able to reliably transmit data at rates as high as 1 Gbps. With the use of **dense wave division multiplexing (DWDM)**, which combines and transmits multiple signals simultaneously at different wavelengths on the same fiber, data has been transmitted at guaranteed rates in excess of 40 Gbps. Such high throughput is partly due to the physics of light traveling over glass. Light encounters virtually no resistance, so it can travel at a faster rate.

- Fiber is one of the most expensive types of cable. The cost of running it to a desktop was once prohibitive, and is only now becoming affordable. Not only is the cable more expensive, but network communication devices used with fiber, such as **network interface cards (NICs)** and **hubs**, can cost up to five times more than similar devices designed for twisted-pair networks.

- Fiber is more difficult to install and modify than most other cabling. Installing and splicing fiber is extremely difficult and precise work, and requires hiring a certified fiber cable installer, which costs more than hiring a twisted-pair cable installer. Many manufacturers of fiber-optic cable and accessories have begun to develop products that make fiber-optic installations easier.

- Fiber cabling uses several different types of connectors. The industry standards are the **ST** and **SC connectors**, as shown in Figure 3-7, and the MT-RJ small form factor connectors.

ST connector

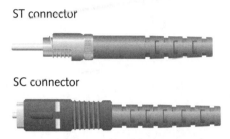

SC connector

Figure 3-7   ST and SC fiber-optic connectors

- Fiber is immune to both EMI and RFI, and therefore has the best noise immunity of any cabling. This high noise resistance is one reason that fiber can span such long distances before requiring repeaters to regenerate the signal.

- Fiber can transmit signals over much greater distances and carry information at significantly greater speeds than coax or twisted-pair cable. The maximum network segment length for fiber is 100 m. The maximum overall network length varies depending on the type of fiber-optic cable used. With multimode fiber, the maximum network length is 2 km; with single-mode fiber the limit is 3 km. However, single-mode fiber is used primarily in long-distance network infrastructure and almost never for local networking, except as a trunk.

Wireless Technologies

Wireless networking refers to computers that communicate using standard network rules or protocols, but without the use of cabling to connect the computers. Instead, the computers send and receive information by means of wireless signals produced by infrared or radio waves. Infrared waves require the sending and receiving equipment to be in a direct line of sight, but radio waves do not.

A wireless network can be installed as the sole network in an organization, or it can extend a wired network to areas where wiring would be too difficult or expensive to implement. Wireless networks can be configured to provide the same network functionality as any wired network.

Wireless networks require NICs to be installed in the network device, just like any wired network, but the wireless NIC contains a built-in antenna. Wireless networks use **access points**, which work like the hubs used in a wired network. The access point broadcasts and receives signals to and from surrounding computers via the NIC. Access points also provide the interconnection point between a wireless and wired network.

Wireless networks currently transmit data at a rate of approximately 11 Mbps. This rate depends primarily on the number of network users and the size of the files being transferred. The rate also depends on the computer's distance from the access point, and on the material of any structures that may be in the line of sight. In addition, because the network's range may extend beyond the walls of a building, additional security measures may be necessary to ensure that data is protected.

Network Topologies

There are two types of network topologies. The first type, **physical topology**, is the physical layout of the network, including the configuration of the cables and devices. The second type, **logical topology**, refers to the method used to communicate between devices. You must understand physical topologies before you design a network, because they can affect the logical topology you choose (for example, Ethernet or Token Ring), how your building is cabled, and what kind of media you use. Understanding a network's physical topology is also necessary for troubleshooting its problems or making changes in its infrastructure.

Physical topologies are classified according to three geometric shapes: bus, ring, and star. These shapes can also be mixed to create hybrid topologies. A fourth type of topology, referred to as fault-tolerant mesh, is often required for high-availability networks.

Bus Topology

A **bus topology** consists of a single cable that connects all the nodes on a network without intervening connectivity devices. A bus topology requires the use of a 50-ohm resistor, called a **terminator**, at each end. Most bus topologies use Ethernet as their communication method. Figure 3-8 shows a typical bus topology.

Figure 3-8   Bus topology

The single cable is called the bus, and it can support only one channel. As a result, every node shares the total capacity of the bus. A bus topology can be considered a **peer-to-peer** topology, because every device on the network shares the responsibility for getting data from one point to another. Also, every node is alerted about every transmission, and every transmission passes through each node, although only the intended recipient of the transmission reads and processes it.

A bus topology offers the following advantages:

- It is easy to install and add devices.
- It requires less cable than other topologies.
- It is less expensive to install than other topologies.

Unfortunately, a bus topology also has its disadvantages:

- The bus requires 50-ohm resistors, called terminators, at each end.
- The entire network shuts down if the cable breaks.
- It is difficult to troubleshoot problems if the network shuts down.
- A bus topology is not designed for large applications. The limit is about 10 connections.

Ring Topology

In a **ring topology**, each node is connected to the two nearest nodes so that the entire network forms a circle (Figure 3-9). Data is transmitted in one direction around the ring. Each node receives every transmission; when passing on a transmission, the node acts as a repeater, a device that regenerates signals. A ring network has no ends, and data stops at its prescribed destination, so it does not require terminators. The ring topology generally uses token passing as its communication method, which prevents network collisions.

The token-passing method controls a node's ability to transmit data. Before a node can transmit data, it must first possess the token. While a node has the token, no other node can transmit data until the active node is finished. The data packet is attached to the token and passed around the ring until it reaches the target node. The target node receives the data and sends the token back around the ring until the original transmitting station picks it up, checks the token to determine that the data has been received, and then releases the token back to the ring for another node to use.

The ring topology is used primarily by Token Ring and FDDI networks. A **Fiber Distributed Data Interface (FDDI)** contains two rings: a primary ring and a secondary ring. The secondary ring provides fault tolerance (redundancy) and backup if the primary ring fails (Figure 3-9). This redundancy is crucial to modern implementations and avoids the point-of-failure problem of single-ring topologies.

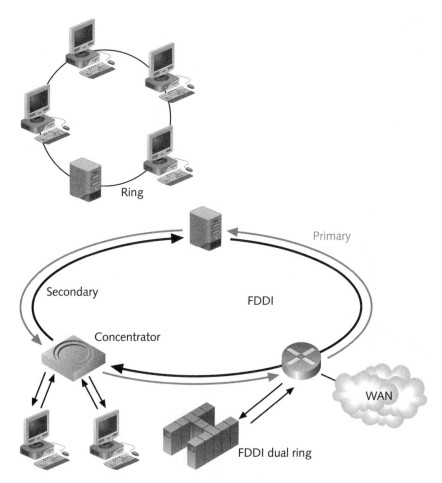

Figure 3-9 Ring topology and FDDI dual ring

A ring topology includes the following advantages:

- No network collisions occur, due to the data transmission method it uses.
- Each node functions as a repeater, so the need for additional network hardware is limited.
- Less cable is required than with other topologies.

The ring topology also has the following disadvantages:

- A single malfunctioning workstation can disable the entire network.
- It is not very flexible or scalable, because response time slows with each additional node.
- Before making additions or changes or performing maintenance, you must shut down the network, because all nodes are wired together.

Star Topology

In a **star topology**, every node is connected through a central device, such as a hub. Figure 3-10 shows a typical star topology. Any physical cable in a star topology connects to only two devices, so a cabling problem will affect only two nodes at most. All nodes transmit data to the hub, which then retransmits the data to the segment that contains the destination node.

Star topologies require more cable and configuration than other topologies, but a single malfunctioning cable or workstation will not disable the entire network. A hub failure can disable an entire segment, but usually will not shut down the entire network.

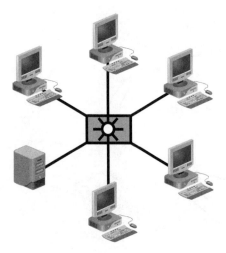

Figure 3-10   Star topology

Because of the way star topologies are wired, they are easy to move, isolate, or interconnect with other networks. Adding nodes, performing maintenance, or making other changes will not affect or disable the network. Because star topologies offer more flexibility and scalability than other topologies, most modern Ethernet networks use them.

Star topologies offer the following advantages:

- A break in one cable does not affect all other stations, because there is only one station per segment.

- The star topology is more reliable because there is only one station per segment.

- Troubleshooting a star topology is easier because symptoms usually point to one station or segment.

- No terminators are necessary because media are terminated at the station and the hub.

- The star topology is more flexible and scalable than other topologies.

Although a star topology offers many advantages, it has a few disadvantages as well:

- Star topologies use more cable than most other topologies.

- Hubs are usually more expensive than terminators.

- A hub failure can take down an entire LAN segment.

3

Mesh Topology

In a **mesh topology**, all devices share many redundant interconnections with each node, as shown in Figure 3-11. There are two types of mesh topologies: full mesh and partial mesh.

In a full-mesh topology, every node is interconnected with every other node in the network, providing multiple routes for data to travel from origin to destination with the greatest amount of redundancy. If one route has a problem or fails, data can be directed to any one of the other routes. Full mesh is generally reserved for use in network backbones.

In a partial-mesh topology, some nodes are connected using the full-mesh scheme, while others are connected to only one or two other nodes. This approach still provides redundancy, but to a lesser degree than the full mesh. Partial-mesh topologies are commonly found in LANs that are connected to a full-mesh backbone.

Mesh topologies offer the following advantages:

- If one connection fails, data can be redirected to multiple alternate paths.

- Mesh topology provides a high level of security, because each device has its own connection to every other device.

- There are few problems with troubleshooting a mesh topology.

- The mesh offers greater stability and reliability.

Even though mesh topology offers many advantages, it still has a few disadvantages:

- It uses much more cable than any other topology.

- It is more expensive to install than other topologies.

- It can be difficult to install and configure on very large networks.

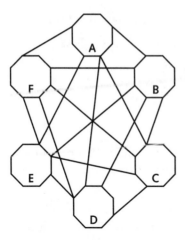

Figure 3-11   Mesh topology

CREATING AN EFFECTIVE NETWORK DESIGN

Before you begin designing a network, you must know its relative scale and what your customer expects the network to accomplish. The prerequisites of network design include assessing functional requirements, sizing the network, and defining connectivity needs. Once you complete the preliminary assessment, you can begin your design work.

This section discusses the steps for ensuring that your design is flexible and solid, and that it meets your customer's expectations. The following list helps you make these determinations:

- **Assessing functional requirements** — Make a list of the tasks that should be automated or made more efficient. Determine which business applications need support, and determine whether the network will simply provide shared access to word-processing files or support multiuser databases. Also, identify other needs such as electronic mail, Web servers, point-of-sale operations, and Internet access.

- **Sizing the network** — Determine the network's expected size by establishing the number of users and their intensity of use. Plan for future growth by building in extra capacity from the beginning. Calculate the possible network capacity in two or three years by estimating the number of potential new users; also, account for possibly dramatic increases in the average user's data storage needs, based on your customer's business strategy. Plan your design to accommodate easy growth with incremental additions of existing technology.

- **Connectivity** — Define which types of external connections you need. Determine the need for Internet access and whether the network requires a dial-up connection or a full-time, dedicated link. Also, determine the amount of required bandwidth and the need to connect with any private (external) networks.

Once you complete the prerequisites, you can begin the design work. Network design involves several layers, and you need to make decisions about each of them:

- **Network type** — The options include Ethernet, ATM, and Token Ring. The relative bandwidth that the network must support is a significant factor in choosing a network type.

- **Physical network** — This includes the cabling, faceplates, and other components of the basic infrastructure. The kind of cabling you install depends on the network type your customer selects.

- **Network communications equipment** — The network requires devices such as hubs and routers before it can operate.

- **Network operating system** — Microsoft Windows NT Server, Windows 2000 Advanced Server, Windows XP, and Novell NetWare are currently the dominant systems. However, they are not the only available systems. Be aware that your customer may already have made this decision.

- **Client workstations** — Consider which hardware the customer needs. These decisions depend on which network operating system and workstation operating system the customer selects.

- **Network server hardware**

- **Data backup hardware and software**

NETWORK ELEMENTS YOU NEED TO DOCUMENT

Before you begin your documentation project or define your documentation policies, you must first decide what you need to document. Every network is unique and has its own documentation needs. In this section, you will learn which network elements you most likely need to document.

The first section of your documentation manual should describe the network. This description should give any reader a basic understanding of how the network works and what it includes. This section should include information about the network topology, the network architectures used, the installed operating systems, and the number of devices and users served. This section should also provide contact information for people who are responsible for various aspects of the network, and for key vendors. Use this section as an overview of your network; you can describe the finer details in later sections.

The next section, which documents your cable plant, is among the most critical documentation tasks. This is the most frequently used section; it defines the physical layout of your network cabling, the terminations used, and the conventions for labeling your cable and connectivity equipment. You must also include the results of any tests completed on the cable plant. Every time the network requires additions, moves, or changes, this documentation will probably be consulted and modified. Therefore, the documentation must be kept current—incorrect or outdated information can be worse than no documentation at all. For example, outdated documentation can result in a critical piece of equipment being disconnected, instead of the workstation that was just removed from service.

Proper documentation of the items in each equipment room, including their location, is crucial to a customer's ability to troubleshoot problems quickly and effectively. The equipment rooms house internetworking devices, servers, and telephone equipment, and are the junction points for horizontal and backbone cabling.

Your efficiency in modifying and troubleshooting networks is greatly enhanced when you document the internetworking devices. When describing these devices, you must first list the devices themselves, then document which devices are connected to other devices, and list each device's capabilities and limitations. Also, list the available network management features on each device, as well as the device's port usage, physical and logical addresses, model numbers, serial numbers, and hardware and software revision numbers.

Any computers that provide shared resources or network services are referred to as servers, and require detailed documentation. Include the hardware configuration, operating system and application version numbers, NIC information, and the system model and serial numbers in your server documentation.

Documentation of workstations is often the most difficult to maintain, for several reasons. For example, workstations and their users usually create most support and troubleshooting tasks. By documenting each workstation's hardware and software configurations, along with its physical and logical addresses, you can save considerable time and effort when resolving a problem. In addition, your network policies should limit the changes that users can make to their workstations. If you enforce these policies, maintaining current records will be much easier.

CHAPTER SUMMARY

- Cabling is the basic framework of a solid network foundation. To successfully design a network cable layout, you need a thorough knowledge of cable types, their specifications, and network topologies. This information helps you to assess the organization's current needs and plans for future growth.

- All cabling media have five basic characteristics you must consider when selecting cable for your telecommunications systems: throughput and bandwidth, cost, size and scalability, connectors, and noise immunity.

- The three basic types of cable are coaxial, twisted-pair, and fiber-optic. Coaxial cable has a high resistance to interference, can carry signals for a greater distance than twisted-pair cable before requiring repeaters, and must be terminated with a 50-ohm resistor at each end of a segment. Twisted-pair cable is the same as the cable used to wire telephones, and is the most common form of cabling used on LANs today. Twisted-pair is relatively inexpensive, flexible, and easy to install. It can be shielded, unshielded, or screened. Fiber is among the most expensive media, but has the highest throughput and bandwidth. It transmits optical signals in the form of light over glass fibers.

❑ There are two categories of fiber: multimode and single-mode. Single-mode fiber transmits in a single mode of light, which allows data to travel more rapidly and for greater distances. Multimode fiber transmits up to hundreds of thousands of modes of light simultaneously, which allows more data to be transmitted at one time. However, data cannot travel as fast or as far on multimode fiber.

❑ The coaxial cables used for networks are ThickNet (10Base5) and ThinNet (10Base2). Both were used extensively in the early years of Ethernet.

❑ Wireless networking refers to computers that communicate using standard network rules or protocols, but without the use of cabling to connect the computers. A wireless network can be installed as the sole network in an organization, or it can extend a wired network to areas where wiring would be too difficult or expensive to implement. Wireless networks can be configured to provide the same network functionality as any wired network.

❑ Network topologies come in three basic geometric shapes: bus, ring, and star. A fourth type of topology, referred to as fault-tolerant mesh, is often required for high-availability networks. The bus topology is the least expensive and the most difficult to troubleshoot. The ring topology is difficult to troubleshoot for the same reasons, but is not subject to network collisions because of its communication method. The star topology is the most commonly used, and offers the most advantages. It is more expensive because it uses more cable than other topologies, but it is more reliable because of its wiring. If one station goes down in a star topology, the rest of the network is not affected.

❑ Before you begin designing a network, you must know its relative scale and what your customer expects the network to accomplish. The prerequisites of network design include assessing functional requirements, sizing the network, and defining connectivity needs. Once you complete the preliminary assessment, you can begin your design work.

❑ Before you begin your documentation project or define your documentation policies, you must first decide what you need to document. Every network has its own documentation needs.

KEY TERMS

access points — The wireless equivalent of the hubs used in a wired network. Access points broadcast and receive wireless signals to and from surrounding computers via a NIC. Access points also provide the interconnection point between a wireless and wired network.

alien crosstalk — The interference of signals from one cable with an adjacent cable's transmission.

analog — Analog signals are variable voltages that create continuous waves of sound, resulting in inexact transmissions.

attenuation — The amount of signal loss over a given distance.

backbone cable — The cabling that connects one telecommunications room (TR) to another, TRs to equipment rooms, or one building's equipment room to another's.

balanced-pair — The twists in cable pairs that help to reduce the effects of crosstalk.

bandwidth — The measure of the difference between the highest and lowest frequencies that media can transmit.

baseband — The transmission of digital signals through direct-current pulses applied to the wire. Baseband requires exclusive use of the wire's capacity, which means that only one signal can be transmitted at a time.

BNC (British Naval Connector) and **BNC/T** — The type of connector used on ThinNet (10Base2) cable. The BNC is the connector that goes on the cable. The BNC/T is a T-shaped adapter that connects on one end to the station's network interface card. The bus connects to the other two ends.

bus topology — A single cable that connects all the nodes on a network without intervening connectivity devices.

cladding — In fiber-optic cable, a layer of glass around the fibers that acts like a mirror and reflects light back to the core.

coaxial cable — Cable that consists of a central copper core surrounded by an insulator, a braided metal shielding called braiding, and an outer cover called a sheath or jacket.

connector — A piece of hardware that connects the cable to the network device.

crosstalk — The infringement of the signal from one wire pair on another wire pair's signal.

data transmission — The sending of signals generated by voltage over a designated path.

decibel (dB) — A measurement unit of signal strength or of a sound's intensity.

dense wave division multiplexing (DWDM) — The combination and transmission of multiple signals simultaneously at different wavelengths on the same fiber.

digital — Digital signals are precise voltages that create pulses with specific values called bits, resulting in more precise transmissions.

electromagnetic interference (EMI) — Waves that emanate from electrical devices or cables carrying electricity.

Fiber Distributed Data Interface (FDDI) — In a ring topology, this interface contains two rings: a primary ring and a secondary ring. The secondary ring provides fault tolerance (redundancy) and backup if the primary ring fails.

fiber-optic cable — Cable that contains one or more glass fibers in its core. Data is transmitted by converting electrical signals at the sending end into optical signals, which are then transmitted through the central fibers via a pulsing light sent from a laser or light-emitting diode (LED), and reconverted into electrical signals at the receiving end.

hertz (Hz) — The unit for measuring a range of frequencies.

hub — A multiport repeater containing one port that connects to a network's backbone and multiple ports that connect to a group of workstations. Hubs regenerate digital signals.

impedance — The measurement of a conductor's opposition, or resistance, to the flow of alternating current.

latency — The delay between entering commands on your computer and their acceptance by the server.

logical topology — The method used to communicate between devices.

medium — A means of transmitting signals, usually via cable. The plural form of the word is *media*.

megabit — One million bits of data.

mesh topology — A system in which all nodes and devices share many redundant interconnections.

multimode fiber — Fiber that carries up to hundreds of thousands of modes of light simultaneously.

network interface card (NIC) — The device that enables a workstation to connect to the network and communicate with other computers.

ohm — A measurement of resistance.

peer-to-peer — A means of networking computers using a single cable.

physical topology — The physical layout of the network, including the configuration of the cables and devices.

radio frequency interference (RFI) — Waves that emanate from electrical devices or cables carrying electricity. RFI can also be caused by a strong broadcast signal from a radio or television station.

refractive index — The measure of a material's ability to bend light.

repeater — A connectivity device that regenerates and amplifies an analog or digital signal.

ring — One of the wires in a pair, in twisted-pair cabling. The ring is connected to the DC negative wire (–48 volts) that carries the signal.

ring topology — In this system, each node is connected to the two nearest nodes so that the entire network forms a circle. Data is transmitted in one direction around the ring. Each node receives every transmission; when passing on a transmission, the node acts as a repeater, a device that regenerates signals.

RJ-45 connectors — The 8-pin connectors used with twisted-pair cable.

SC connector — One of the most popular connectors made for fiber-optic cable.

scalability — Growth ability and potential.

signal bounce — A phenomenon in which data signals travel endlessly between the two ends of the network.

single-mode fiber — Fiber that carries a single mode of light to transmit data from one end of a cable to another.

ST connector — One of the most popular connectors made for fiber-optic cable.

star topology — In this system, every node is connected through a central device, such as a hub. Any physical cable on a star topology connects to only two devices, so a cabling problem will affect only two nodes at most. All nodes transmit data to the hub, which then retransmits the data to the segment that contains the destination node.

terminator — A resistor at the end of a bus network that stops signals after they reach their destination.

throughput — The amount of data that a cable can transmit during a given period of time.

tip — One of the wires in a pair, in twisted-pair cabling. The tip is connected to the positive side of a battery, which is the telephone industry's equivalent of a ground in a standard electrical circuit.

topology — The physical layout of network components.

twist ratio — The number of twists per meter or foot in twisted-pair cable.

twisted-pair cable — Cable that consists of insulated copper wires, each with a diameter of 0.4 to 0.8 mm, twisted around each other and encased in a plastic coating.

vampire tap — A connector that pierces a hole in a ThickNet cable.

wireless — Technology that transmits signals through the atmosphere.

REVIEW QUESTIONS

1. What type of network design helps provide a solid foundation?
   a. one that has the right workstations
   b. one that is sound and flexible
   c. one that has the right network operating system
   d. one that has the proper cable installed

2. What is the physical layout of the networking components called?
   a. cabling
   b. floor plan
   c. physical components and cable plan
   d. topology (physical)

3. What are the three most common topologies?
   a. bus, circle, and star
   b. bus, ring, and star
   c. circle, star, and torus
   d. ring, arc, and star

3

4. What is one advantage of a bus topology?

   a. All workstations run to a central device.

   b. It is the easiest topology for troubleshooting problems.

   c. It is inexpensive.

   d. It is difficult to design and implement.

5. What is one advantage of a ring topology?

   a. It prevents network collisions due to the media access method or architecture required.

   b. All workstations are wired to one another with termination points.

   c. Each station functions as a repeater, but the topology still requires additional network hardware, such as hubs.

   d. Because all stations work together, it is easy to add a station.

6. What are two of the primary differences between a star topology and the other topologies?

   a. A data signal from one station is transmitted to all other stations on the network.

   b. All computers are wired directly to a central location.

   c. A data signal from any station goes to a central device, which transmits the signal according to the established access method for the type of network.

   d. The star topology uses the least amount of cable.

7. What are two of the biggest advantages of a star topology?

   a. Problems are easier to locate because symptoms often point to one station.

   b. A break in one cable does not affect all other stations, because there is only one station per segment.

   c. It is the least expensive topology to install.

   d. It is the best topology to use when you have very few users.

8. Which type of cable is most often used on the backbone of a network?

   a. twisted-pair

   b. hybrid

   c. thick coaxial

   d. fiber-optic

9. Coaxial cable has a very large bandwidth, which means it can handle large volumes of data at high speed and is better protected from electromagnetic interference than other types of cable, so it can carry signals over much greater distances before the signal degrades. True or False?

10. Coaxial cable requires a termination at each end of each segment with a
    _____.

    a. vampire tap

    b. 55-ohm resistor

    c. 50-Mhz connector

    d. 50-ohm resistor

11. Why is twisted-pair cable the most common form of cabling used in LANs today?

    a. It is less expensive to install than other forms of cabling.

    b. It is flexible.

    c. It is easy to install.

    d. all of the above

12. What is throughput?

    a. the amount of time it takes to transmit data

    b. the amount of data a cable can transmit during a given time period

    c. the frequency at which data is transmitted

    d. the range of frequencies that data uses for transmission

13. In fiber optics, signals are converted from electrical into modulated optical signals, transmitted through a thin glass fiber, then reconverted into electrical signals. True or False?

14. What is bandwidth?

    a. a range of frequencies

    b. the amount of data that can be transmitted at one time

    c. the amplification of a data signal

    d. the measure of the difference between the highest and lowest frequencies that media can transmit

15. What are the two categories of optical fiber?

    a. multistrand and single-strand

    b. multicore and single-core

    c. multiple and single

    d. multimode and single-mode

16. Multimode fiber is more expensive than single-mode because it can carry multiple paths as it travels from the transmitter to the receiver. True or False?

17. What is latency?

    a. the time it takes data to travel from one network to another network

    b. the transmission speed of your data

    c. the transmission distance of your data

    d. the delay between entering commands on your computer and their acceptance by the server

18. EMI is electronic magnetic interruption. True or False?

19. Crosstalk occurs when a signal traveling on a nearby wire pair infringes on another wire pair's signal. True or False?

20. Fiber-optic cable offers very high bandwidth and can operate at distances in excess of _____.

    a. 1000 meters

    b. 500 meters

    c. 100 meters

    d. 2000 meters

21. Baseband transmission is _____.

    a. several signals transmitting at the same time

    b. only one signal transmitting at a time

    c. several signals transmitting over the same cable, but taking turns

    d. There is no such thing as baseband transmission.

22. Which type of cable has the best noise immunity and thus has the longest maximum network lengths?

    a. fiber-optic

    b. twisted-pair

    c. coaxial

    d. none of the above

23. What is attenuation?

    a. the loss of signal power between points

    b. information-carrying capacity

    c. total opposition of a circuit to the flow of current

    d. the bending of a signal

24. What is cladding?

    a. the radius of curvature that a cable can bend without hurting performance

    b. the layer of glass (or other transparent material) surrounding the light-carrying core of an optical fiber

    c. a device that cuts an optical fiber in a flat, smooth, and perpendicular manner

    d. a device mounted on the end of an optical fiber and used for joining it to another fiber end, light source, or detector

25. Coaxial cable consists of a central copper core surrounded by an insulator, a braided metal shielding called braiding, and an outer plastic cover called a sheath. True or False?

HANDS-ON PROJECTS

Project 3-1

When choosing transmission media for your network, you need to consider the five basic characteristics of cable. For this project, you will create a chart of the three major cable types and then list the various subtypes under each major cable type. Complete the chart by identifying each of the five basic characteristics for each type.

NOTE Most of the information you need is in the first three chapters of your text. You can also search the Internet. If you use information from any Web sites, note them as references on your chart before turning it in.

Project 3-2

Survey organizations and businesses in your area to determine which cabling types, transmission speeds, and transport models are used on their LANs. From this information, you should be able to determine the most popular networking design approaches, which approaches may grow in popularity, and which ones may become obsolete.

1. Identify at least five businesses, civic organizations, or schools in your area that use networking technology. For example, you can identify insurance agencies, school districts or particular local schools, retail store chains, utility companies, and architectural firms.

2. For each of your choices, find the contact information for the Information Technology (IT) department manager.

3. Call the IT department manager and ask the following questions:

    ❏ What is the transmission speed of your network?

    ❏ What type of cabling is used for your network backbone?

❏ What type of wiring does your network use? Do you use the same type of wiring for the backbone as you use for connecting workstations?

❏ Which topology does your network use?

❏ How many nodes are on your network?

❏ Are all your network devices in one building? If not, where are the others, and how are they connected?

❏ If you had an unlimited budget, what types of upgrades would you make to your network?

❏ If you only had enough money in your budget for one upgrade, which one would you make?

4. Compile the answers from all the managers. Which network transmission speed is most popular? Which type of backbone? Which topology? Which type of interbuilding connection? Which network upgrade?

5. From the list you compiled, which items should grow in popularity, and why? Which items may become obsolete, and why?

Project 3-3

Knowing what type(s) of cable to use, and when, is only part of your training as a telecommunications professional. Understanding network design is another important tool. In this exercise, you will go to an Internet site and read four good articles about designing networks.

1. Using a workstation in your class that has Internet access, go to the following Web site:

    www.networkcomputing.com/netdesign/soho1.html

2. Read the first article. You can then keep clicking the Next Page button to read the remaining articles, or you can change the address in your browser. The address should remain the same except for the */soho1.html*. For each additional article, change *soho1* to *soho2*, *soho3*, and *soho4*.

3. After reading all four articles, write a summary of each. Include the most important points to remember for your future work in this field.

4. At the end of each summary, list what you learned from each article.

Project 3-4

Answer the following questions about fiber-optic cable and write a summary of your findings.

1. What is fiber-optic cable?

2. Define each physical component of fiber-optic cable.

3. What is the most ideal use for "basic" optical fiber?

4. For which other applications is fiber available?

In addition to using your text, you can find information at *www.commspecial.com/fiberguide.htm*.

NOTE

Project 3-5

HANDS-ON PROJECTS

List the procedures to follow when designing an effective network, and explain why each step is important. Use your text and any appropriate source material, and identify the source(s) in your report.

Project 3-6

HANDS-ON PROJECTS

Define the following networking and telecommunications terms:

◻ Host (to a dumb terminal)

◻ Carrier Sense Multiple Access with Collision Detection (CSMA/CD)

◻ Hub (active and passive)

◻ Cable terminator (coaxial)

◻ Token Ring

◻ Ethernet

◻ Network collision

◻ Repeater

◻ Network access method

◻ Transceiver

◻ Broadband

◻ Baseband

◻ Network interface card (NIC)

◻ Vampire tap

The following Web sites will help you find these definitions:

◻ *www.whatis.com*

◻ *www.about.com.* Type **glossary** in the **Search** box, then click the links that appear.

◻ *www.techfest.com/networking/cabling/cableglos.htm*

CASE PROJECTS

Case Project 1

Create a proposal for prewiring a new building. The building has one floor with 15 private offices, one work area with 15 employees, and one telecommunications closet. The equipment room is the entrance facility for the building, and is next to the telecommunications closet. The distance from the telecommunications closet to the most distant workstation is 70 meters. Good speed and bandwidth are desirable in your proposal, but size and scalability are more important. Cost is not a major factor, but it is a consideration. Your proposal should include the type(s) of cable you would use (workstation, horizontal, backbone), the approximate cost of the cable, and explanations for your selection(s).

NOTE

Use the Internet to obtain cable pricing. Some useful Web sites for cable and equipment pricing are:

- *www.sfcable.com*
- *www.cablemaster.com*
- *www.directron.com*

Case Project 2

Describe an optical fiber system. Identify and explain its three basic components. Include the various types of each component and their characteristics.

Case Project 3

Identify and thoroughly explain each of the factors that most commonly affect the performance of an optical fiber system.

Case Project 4

Research information about the construction of fiber-optic cable, and then report your findings. In your report, discuss the two types of buffering in use today; the three basic, tight-buffered fiber cable types; when and how each one is used; and the three categories of optical fiber cable designated for building use. For this project, use sources from the library and the Internet.

4

INSTALLING CABLES AND SUPPORTING STRUCTURES

After reading this chapter and completing the exercises, you will be able to:

♦ Identify the different pathways and why they are necessary

♦ Understand the layouts of equipment rooms and telecommunications rooms

♦ Discuss proper cable installation procedures

♦ Identify good cable management practices and understand their importance

♦ Document your network

In the previous chapter you learned about the various cable types and network topologies. This information helps you make informed and intelligent decisions about the equipment you will use for cabling applications.

In this chapter you will learn how to install the cables. Proper installation requires knowledge of different pathways, the layout and composition of equipment rooms, pulling tension, bend radius, and practices for good cable management.

PATHWAYS

Cabling **pathways** provide the means for placing cables between the equipment room, the telecommunications rooms, and the work areas. This chapter explains two types of pathways: horizontal and vertical.

Choosing proper pathway components at the design stage makes it easier to perform cable-related work and maintenance later. Choosing the proper horizontal cabling components allows the use of a variety of technologies.

Generally, your cabling choices should not dictate your pathway choices. The pathways must accommodate all standards-compliant cabling and allow for necessary changes later. Compromising the pathway system to accommodate specific cabling components may lead to increased costs of long-term maintenance and operations. During new construction, you should focus on the pathway component, largely ignoring the cabling component until later in the design process. This strategy helps ensure robust pathways that respond well to cable work over the facility's life cycle.

Cable-related maintenance such as additions, moves, and changes are common in a horizontal distribution system. Therefore, do everything you can at the design stage to reduce the time and cost of subsequent replacement materials, labor, and disruptions.

Horizontal Pathway Systems

Horizontal pathway systems are used to distribute, support, and provide access to the **horizontal cabling**. This cabling links the **distribution field** (connecting hardware) of the cross-connect system in the telecommunications room to the **telecommunications outlet/connector** in each work area. This connector is terminated with a jack for plugging in telecommunications equipment. All of these components make up the content of the horizontal pathways and spaces, and together are called the horizontal distribution system. The system includes the pathway itself (e.g., cable trays, conduit, and J-hooks), as well as related spaces such as pull boxes, splice boxes, and **consolidation points** that provide access to the cable and connecting hardware.

The following sections discuss a number of methods for routing horizontal cables to the work area. One of the most common methods is **zone cabling**, in which cable bundles are run to a particular area from the telecommunications room along J-shaped hooks (**J-hooks**) suspended in a plenum or above a ceiling. Upon reaching the zone, cables are fanned out and dropped through interior walls, support columns, or raceways, and then terminated at the telecommunications outlet/connector (also called the **work area outlet**).

NOTE

When selecting a distribution method, you must consider the fire rating of the ceiling or floor space of your building, the proximity to sources of electromagnetic interference (EMI), and cable security. Because fire rating requirements vary among regions and countries, contact your local fire inspector to confirm acceptable requirements.

Underfloor Duct

An underfloor duct system is a network of metal raceways, usually single-level or dual-level rectangular ducts, that are embedded in concrete. The system includes the main **feeder ducts** (also called header ducts), which carry the cables from the telecommunications room to **distribution ducts** (Figure 4-1), which in turn carry the cables to a specific floor area. The system also includes **junction boxes**, openings in the ductwork that provide access to the duct system for pulling cables and routing them to the workstations. All parts of the underfloor duct system are available in different sizes to suit a variety of purposes.

4

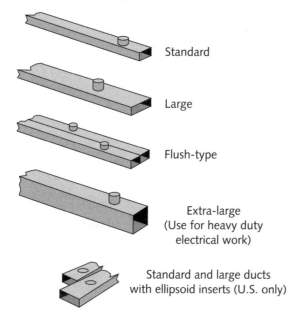

Standard

Large

Flush-type

Extra-large
(Use for heavy duty
electrical work)

Standard and large ducts
with ellipsoid inserts (U.S. only)

Figure 4-1   Distribution ducts

In feeder ducts, different types of services such as power and telecommunications must be separated, either by providing a dedicated duct for each service or by using a flat, metal **trench duct**, which is divided into separate compartments for each service (Figure 4-2). Feeder ducts also distribute cables to specific floor areas with the help of distribution ducts; these ducts are installed with preset inserts to provide cable access during and after installation.

Junction boxes are installed in planned locations in the duct system to permit changes in the direction of a cable run and provide access to the duct for pulling cables. The maximum allowable distance between junction boxes is 18 meters (60 feet). A typical junction box is shown in Figure 4-3.

A final component of underfloor duct systems is a **splice box**. This opening in the system provides access for making connections in the cable.

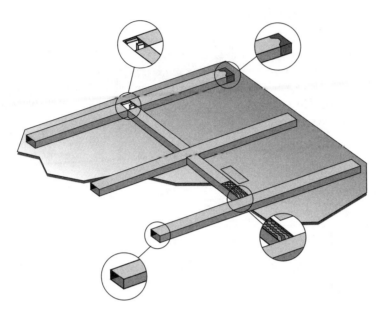

Figure 4-2 Trench duct

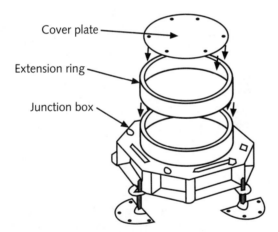

Figure 4-3 Junction box

Conduits

Conduits are rigid or flexible, metallic or nonmetallic pipes that cable is placed in and pulled through. They are installed from the telecommunications room to the work area outlets in the floor, walls, or columns of a building. The following types of conduit are rated as suitable for use in buildings:

- Rigid metal conduit made of high-strength steel

- Intermediate metal conduit that is as strong as rigid conduit, but lighter and more economical

- Electrical metal tubing (EMT) made from high-grade mild strip steel

- Rigid conduit made of a nonmetallic material, usually PVC (polyvinyl chloride)

- Any other material permitted by the appropriate electrical codes

"Flex conduit," or **flexible conduit**, is not recommended for use in buildings. This conduit is made by wrapping a strip of metallic material around itself and slightly overlapping it to form a pipe. When cable is pulled through flexible conduit, the conduit tends to creep or shift, and can damage the cable's sheath or jacket.

NOTE Use flexible conduit when it is the only practical solution. For example, use it to connect rigid pathways to other pathways that may not join in exact alignment. If you must use flexible conduit, increase the conduit size by one trade size.

When using conduits for your pathways, observe the following design and installation guidelines:

- Run cable in the most direct route possible.

- A continuous section must not be longer than 30 meters (100 feet).

- A continuous section should have no more than two 90° angles.

- If one section will exceed the maximum length of 30 meters, a junction box must be installed.

- Each conduit must be bonded to ground on one or both ends, in accordance with national or local requirements.

- Ensure that the conduit can withstand the environment in which it is installed.

Cable Trays

Cable tray systems are commonly used as distribution systems for cabling within a building. They are often preferred to conduit and raceway systems because of their greater accessibility and ability to accommodate change.

Cable trays are rigid, prefabricated structures that route and support telecommunications or power cables (Figure 4-4). Typically, cable trays are open and equipped with sides that allow cable to be laid within the tray's entire length. When installed, the trays must meet the codes defined in NEC Article 318.

NOTE You should not use the same cable trays to distribute both telecommunications and power cables. If cable trays must be shared, the power and telecommunications cables must be separated by a grounded metallic barrier.

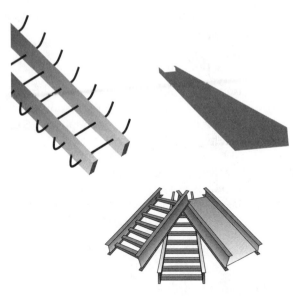

Figure 4-4   Cable trays

When cable trays are used in the ceiling area, conduit should be provided from the end of the tray to the telecommunications outlets, except where **loose cables** are permitted by the code. These cables are run in the ceiling without the use of conduits.

The five basic types of cable trays are described in Table 4-1.

Table 4-1   Cable tray structures

Type of Cable Tray	Structural Description
Ladder	Two side rails connected by individual transverse members; the tray looks very much like a stepladder
Ventilated trough	A ventilated bottom with side rails
Ventilated channel	A channel section with a one-piece bottom that is no more than 150 mm (6 inches) wide
Solid bottom	A tray with a solid bottom and longitudinal side rails
Spine	An open tray with a central rigid spine and cable support ribs along the length at 90° angles

Access (Raised) Floors

An **access floor**, also called a raised floor, sits above the existing subfloor and provides access to the space under the floor panels (Figure 4-5). Access floors are most often found in computer and equipment rooms. The floor panels are available in combustible, non-combustible, and composite material. They can also be designed to meet seismic conditions and many other special conditions.

The two basic types of access flooring are standard-height floors and low-profile floors. Standard-height floors are generally 150 mm (6 inches) high, or higher, and are the most common type of access floor. Low-profile floors have heights of less than 150 mm, and are often used on sites with structural limitations, such as insufficient slab-to-slab height. The measurements in Figure 4-5 refer to a typical floor panel size, and may vary depending on the manufacturer.

4

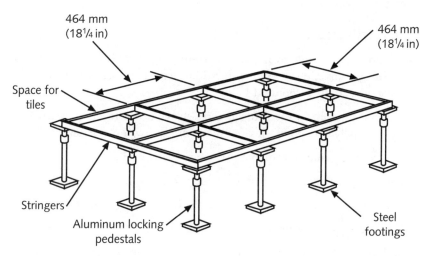

Figure 4-5   Access floor

Access floors typically consist of the following components:

- Steel footings rest on the subfloor to provide distributed support for floor loads.

- Pedestals support and interlock with lateral bracing (also called stringers) and panels. These pedestals are evenly spaced on the steel footings and are adjustable to compensate for any unevenness of the subfloor.

- Modular floor panels rest on the stringers and pedestals. Floor panel sizes typically range from 450 to 600 mm (18 to 24 inches) square. The panels are available in plain or carpeted surfaces to accommodate the functional and aesthetic needs of their area.

The minimum finished height of access floors depends on use and location. When used in general office areas, the finished floor should be at least 200 mm (8 inches) high. In a computer or control room environment where a plenum is used, the finished floor must be at least 300 mm (12 inches) high. A **plenum** is a chamber to which air ducts are connected to form part of a heating, ventilating, and air conditioning (HVAC) system.

Regardless of the height of the finished floor, there should always be at least 50 mm (2 inches) of free space between the top of the cable tray side rails and the underside of the stringers. When using cable trays with covers or raceways, ensure that the free space above the tray allows for easy removal of the cover.

Although ANSI/EIA/TIA-569-A specifies 150 mm (6 inches) as the minimum finished height for standard-height access floors, a height of at least 200 mm (8 inches) is necessary to provide sufficient space for cable trays and other means of cable management.

NOTE

Ceiling Distribution

To distribute horizontal cable from the telecommunications room to the work area, ceiling distribution systems use the open, interstitial space between the structural ceiling and an accessible grid ceiling suspended below it.

There are several guidelines for using ceiling distribution to service work areas. These methods are generally acceptable if they meet the following criteria:

- The ceiling space is available for cabling pathways.

- The ceiling space is used only for horizontal cables serving the floor below.

- The ceiling access is controlled by the building owner.

- All code requirements for design, pathways, and installation are met.

- Building owners are aware of their responsibility for any damage, injury, or inconvenience to occupants that may result from technicians working in the ceiling.

- The areas used for cabling pathways are fully accessible from the floor below (e.g., not obstructed by fixed ceiling tiles, drywall, or plaster).

- The ceiling tiles are removable and no more than 3.4 meters (11 feet) above the finished floor.

The **ceiling zone** method is commonly used in ceiling distribution (Figure 4-6). In this method the overall usable floor area is divided into zones of approximately 46 square meters (about 500 square feet). For every 500 square feet of usable office area, you must provide a pathway of one conduit, raceway, or cable tray within the ceiling from the telecommunications room to an appropriate point of the zone (generally the midpoint). Where convenient, the zones should be divided by building columns. From that point, the pathway should extend to the top of the wall conduit or to **utility columns**, which extend from the ceiling to the floor to guide wiring or cable.

Plenum-rated cable trays or raceways may be required. Refer to the NEC for local restrictions on the use of cable trays.

NOTE

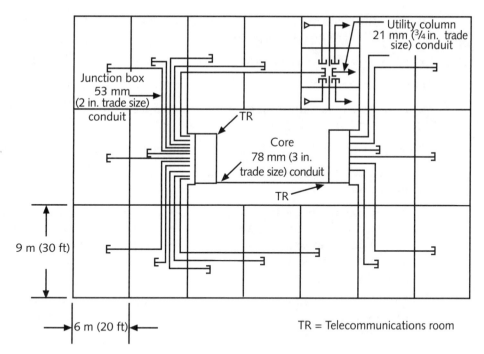

Note: Only one zone is completed.

Figure 4-6 Typical zoned ceiling distribution

Vertical Pathways

Vertical pathways are spaces that provide distribution access of backbone cabling between communications rooms in multistory buildings. Vertical pathways also provide distribution of station cabling between office locations and telecommunications rooms.

When installing vertical pathways, you must follow some important design requirements. First, the pathways should be stacked above each other on each floor of the building, and be accessible from each floor. They must also contain at least three 4-inch conduits, or **sleeves** (Figure 4-7), that line an opening through which cables pass between the floors. Finally, the pathways should have a 100-watt fixture with a bulb and a 20-amp, 100-volt electrical outlet, and the pathway entrances should be secured with a mortised combination lock.

When you install high-pair-count cables in the vertical pathways between floors, you can either lower the cables from the top level or pull them up from the bottom level. Each method has specific guidelines that will be explained later in this section; however, some installation guidelines are common to both methods:

- Ensure that all installation personnel have adequate training and experience with the installation equipment and methods.

- Establish adequate spacing between cables and any other facilities that use the same or adjacent vertical pathway.

- Know the local code requirements for installing cables in vertical pathways.

- Consult the manufacturer's guidelines for installation and use.

- Remove any hazards from each floor, including anything that a person could trip over or slip on.

- Secure any loose cables to keep them out of the way and avoid tangles.

- Complete all necessary preparations (e.g., drilling, installing straps) before the installation.

- Choose the raising or lowering method and then set up all necessary associated hardware, including shoes, sheaves, and winches. A **shoe** (Figure 4-7) is a curved plastic apparatus that guides cables and protects them from corner abrasions during cable pulling. A **sheave** is a curved apparatus used to guide vertical cable into a sleeve (Figure 4-8).

- Set up safety measures such as perimeters, cones, and **reel and sheave blocks**. These blocks apply a break at the reel or sheave when you raise or lower cable through vertical pathways.

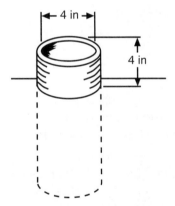

Conduit sleeve through floor

Figure 4-7   Sleeve and cable shoe

Lowering vertical cable requires less equipment than raising cable, but it does require the ability to bring large cable reels to the building's top level. There must also be adequate space for reels and equipment.

Follow these guidelines when lowering cable:

- Position the cable reel away from the opening.
- Use a shoe or sheave to direct the cable into the opening.
- Ensure that adequate braking measures are set up, because the cable reel may not be designed to hold the cable's vertical weight.
- Unreel the cable slowly from the top, guiding the cable through each floor.
- Secure the cable as soon as it is in position, starting at the bottom level.
- Allow for adequate slack where it is needed.

Raising cable generally requires more equipment than lowering cable, and has several important guidelines of its own:

- Secure an opening sheave and **power winch**, which provides pulling force for raising vertical cables (Figure 4-8).
- Lower the pulling line from the top floor.
- Ensure that adequate braking measures are set up, because the cable reel may not be designed to hold the cable's vertical weight.
- Use the manufacturer's pulling eye or a **core hitch** (Figure 4-9) to attach the vertical cable to the winch.
- Slowly pull the cable up through the floors.
- Secure the cable as soon as it is in position, starting at the bottom.
- Allow for adequate slack where it is needed.

Choosing the Right Cable and Documenting It Before Installation

Before you begin installing cable, you must know where it needs to start and end, its intended route, how to identify it after installation, and how to ensure that the cable is appropriate for the purpose. By following the steps in this section, you can take care of all these concerns.

1. Create a detailed floor plan that identifies the locations of every relevant piece of equipment, including cable trays, conduits, ducts, and junction boxes. The floor plan must also show all equipment rooms and telecommunications rooms, all pathways, offices, work areas, and telecommunications outlets, as well as the complete grounding and bonding system, the entrance facility, and all termination hardware and cross-connects. A sample floor plan is shown in

Figure 4-10; note that it comes complete with **administrative labeling**, which identifies every element in the floor plan with a unique ID.

Figure 4-8   Sheave and power winch

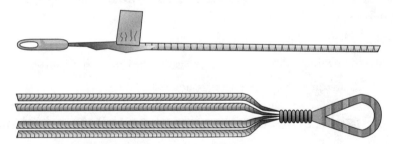

Figure 4-9   Typical core hitches

2. Follow the example of Figure 4-10 by identifying every element in your floor plan with a unique ID number. Use a consistent standard for applying these ID numbers.

3. Before you begin running the cable, consult the floor plan for the cable ID number. Apply this ID to the end of the cable you are pulling and to the box or reel from which the cable is fed. When the cable is in place, cut the other end from the cable box or reel, and apply the same ID to the newly cut cable. Using this approach ensures that both ends of the cable will have the same ID.

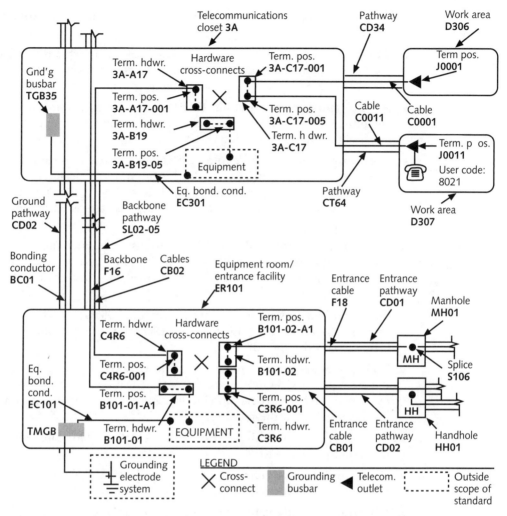

Figure 4-10   Floor plan with administrative labeling

4. To ensure that the cable you are using is appropriate for the intended purpose, you must understand the information on the cable jacket. This information appears on all cable, and is repeated every two feet along its entire length. The information includes the cable manufacturer, its listing status and type (either UL or NEC), the number of pairs and their AWG size, the cable's category and verification, the date of manufacture, the manufacturer's traceability code, and the cable length, which appears in descending footage. The markings also include the cable type; usage and installation guidelines for each cable type are defined in NEC Article 800, Section E, paragraphs 49–51 and 53, and

Tables 800-50 and 800-53. This information is summarized for your convenience in the following list:

- **Communications plenum cable (CMP)** — This cable is suitable for use in ducts, plenums, and other spaces used for environmental air. It has adequate fire resistance and produces minimal smoke.

- **Multipurpose plenum cable (MPP)** — You can also use MPP in ducts, plenums, and other spaces used for environmental air, as long as the cable meets all the requirements of CMP.

- **Communications riser cable (CMR)** — This cable is suitable for use in a vertical run in a shaft, or from floor to floor. Its fire-resistant characteristics prevent it from carrying fire from floor to floor. Floor penetrations that require CMR must contain only cables that are listed as suitable for riser or plenum use.

- **Multipurpose riser cable (MPR)** — This cable must meet the same primary requirements as MPP. It can be installed in a vertical run that penetrates more than one floor, or in vertical runs in a shaft, as long as it meets all the requirements of CMR.

- **Communications general-purpose cable (CMG)** — This cable is suitable for general-purpose use, with the exception of risers and plenums. It is resistant to the spread of fire.

- **Multipurpose general-purpose cable (MPG)** — This cable must meet the same primary requirements as CMG. It can be installed in locations other than plenums, risers, distributing frames, and cross-connect arrays, as long as it meets all the requirements of CMG.

- **Multipurpose general-purpose cable (MP)** — This cable must meet all the requirements of MPG.

- **Communications general-purpose cable (CM)** — This cable must meet all the requirements of CMG.

- **Communications cable, limited use (CMX)** — This cable is suitable for use in dwellings and raceways. It is listed as flame-retardant.

- **Undercarpet communications wire and cable (CMUC)** — This cable is suitable for use under carpeting. It is listed as flame-retardant.

5. Record the length of each cable run. First, note the length marking on the jacket closest to the pulling end at the beginning of the run. Then, note the length marking at the end of the run, closest to where you cut the cable from the box or reel. The difference between the two markings is the length of the run; you must include this measurement in your system documentation.

EQUIPMENT ROOMS AND TELECOMMUNICATIONS ROOMS

The equipment rooms and telecommunications rooms in a building act as junctions between the backbone and horizontal pathways. Both may house such items as the main distribution frame, small telephone systems called **private branch exchanges (PBXs)**, secondary voltage protection, active voice and data telecommunications equipment, termination fields, and **cross-connect** wiring. This wiring connects a circuit from one facility to another in a network.

The ANSI/EIA/TIA-569-A standard provides a guide for designing dedicated rooms for telecommunications equipment. This standard is intended to ease future changes by helping you plan the rooms beforehand; it is discussed in detail in the next two sections.

Equipment Room

The equipment room is essentially a large telecommunications closet that usually houses the **main distribution frame**, a steel-bar framework that typically holds the phone company's central office protective devices, serves as the major cross-connect point for the central office lines and the customer's wiring, and interconnects loop cable pairs and line-equipment terminals on a switching system. The equipment room also houses the main telephone switching equipment and secondary voltage protection. This room is often appended to the entrance facility or a computer room, to allow sharing of air conditioning, security, fire control, lighting, and restrictions on access. The amount of space needed for an equipment room can vary, depending on the number of user locations within the building. According to the standard, a good rule of thumb is to provide 0.75 square feet of equipment room floor space for every 100 square feet of workstation area. A second means of determining the floor space needed for equipment rooms is shown in Table 4-2.

Table 4-2   Equipment room floor space recommendations

Number of Workstations	Equipment Room Floor Space (square feet)
1–100	150
101–400	400
401–800	800
801–1200	1200

Besides floor space, you need to consider several other design guidelines for the equipment room:

- **Location** — Rooms should be located away from sources of electromagnetic interference (transformers, motors, radios, radar), and sources of flooding should be avoided.

- **Perimeters** — There should be no false ceilings, all surfaces should be treated to reduce dust, and walls and ceilings should be painted white or pastel to improve visibility.

- **Limited access** — The room should be equipped with single or double 36-inch × 80-inch lockable doors. No piping, ductwork, mechanical equipment, or power cabling should be allowed to pass through the equipment room, and it should not be used for any unrelated storage.

- **HVAC** — Keep the equipment room at a constant temperature of 64° to 75° F, with humidity at 30 percent to 50 percent. Maintain a positive pressure at all times.

- **Lighting** — The lights must be adequate and uniform. They should typically be 8.5 feet high and provide 50 foot candles of intensity at 3 feet above the floor.

- **Electrical** — Rooms require at least two dedicated 15A, 110VAC duplex outlets on separate circuits. Other convenience outlets can be placed at 6-foot intervals around the perimeter, and emergency power should be supplied if available.

- **Dust** — The environment must be relatively dust-free; a room's air should measure less than 100 micrograms/cubic meter of dust per day.

Telecommunications Room

The telecommunications closet on each floor provides the junction point between the backbone and horizontal pathways. These rooms contain active voice and data telecommunications equipment, termination fields, and cross-connect wiring.

More than one telecommunications closet per floor is required if the distance to a work area exceeds 100 meters (300 feet), or if the floor area being served exceeds 10,000 square feet. The recommended size of the telecommunications closet is 10 feet by 11 feet for each 10,000-square-foot area served. A typical telecommunications room is shown in Figure 4-11.

Requirements for power, lighting, air conditioning, and limited access are the same as for the equipment room. In addition, at least three 4-inch firestopped conduits or sleeves should be placed in the floor at the left side of a plywood termination field near the door. (**Firestopping**, the installation of specialty materials into penetrations of fire-rated barriers, is discussed in detail in Chapter 7.) You should also connect a smoke detector to the building fire alarm panel and provide an approved fire extinguisher.

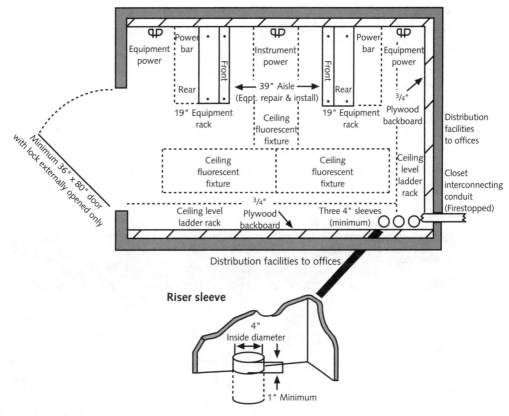

Figure 4-11   Typical telecommunications room

CABLE INSTALLATION GUIDELINES

Typically, cabling installations begin with the placement of all the large backbone and intra-building cables, followed by the smaller horizontal cabling and then the interconnect cables.

The ANSI/EIA/TIA-569-A standard provides important instructions for ensuring successful installations, including information on conduit capacity, cable pulling tensions, pathway and cable support, cable bend radius, cable stress, termination practices, and cable jackets. The following sections provide detailed guidelines and instructions from this standard.

Conduit Capacity

A conduit's capacity, the number of cables it can hold, depends on the size of the cables and the conduit. Typically, the conduit size for outlets of data and voice cables is 21 mm (¾-inch trade size).

In general, high- and low-signal level cables should not be run in the same conduit. In addition, the NEC forbids the installation of telecommunications cables in the same conduit as power cables.

Table 4-3 is based on the maximum number of cables permitted in a conduit by the NEC, the diameters are calculated on the area of the cables with 40 percent of the conduit filled. For conduit runs of 50 to 100 feet, the installed number of cables should be reduced by 15 percent, or the next larger conduit size should be used. Each 90° conduit bend may be estimated as equal to the friction of 30 feet of straight level conduit. If there are more than two 90° bends or the conduit run is more than 100 feet, you should insert a **pull box**, an opening in the duct system that provides access for pulling cables. Using cable lubricants when pulling cable is recommended, and can increase the fill ratio.

Table 4-3   Conduit capacity chart

Conduit Inside Diameter (mm) and Trade Size (inches)		Cable Outside Diameter mm (inches)									
		3.3 (0.13)	4.6 (0.18)	5.6 (0.22)	6.1 (0.24)	7.4 (0.29)	7.9 (0.31)	9.4 (0.37)	13.5 (0.53)	15.8 (0.62)	17.8 (0.70)
16	0.5	1	1	0	0	0	0	0	0	0	0
21	0.75	6	5	4	3	2	2	1	0	0	0
27	1	8	8	7	6	3	3	2	1	0	0
35	1.25	16	14	12	10	6	4	3	1	1	1
41	1.5	20	18	16	15	7	6	4	2	1	1
53	2	30	26	22	20	14	12	7	4	3	2
63	2.5	45	40	36	30	17	14	12	6	3	3
78	3	70	60	50	40	20	20	17	7	6	6
91	3.5							22	12	7	3
103	4							30	14	12	7

The preceding table provides guidelines on cable capacity for horizontal conduits that have no more than two 90° bends (180° total) and are no longer than 30 meters (100 feet). Additional information on telecommunications conduit fill is provided in ANSI/EIA/TIA-569-A.

NOTE   Table 4-3 shows the conduit fill ratio guidelines for horizontal cables; however, the number of cables that can be installed is actually limited by the maximum pulling tensions of the cables. This fill requirement does not apply to sleeves, header ducts, underfloor systems, access floors, or conduit runs that have no bends or are less than 15 meters long (50 feet). Fill ratios can be increased further by use of lubricants.

Pulling Tension

Copper will begin to permanently stretch under a stress of approximately 15,000 pounds per square inch. Table 4-4 lists the maximum recommended pulling tensions for specific conductor sizes. For multiconductor cables, multiply the appropriate value by the total number of conductors. During installation, the total pulling tension must be equally distributed among all conductors.

Table 4-4   Maximum pulling tensions

Conductor Size	Maximum Pulling Tension per Conductor
24 AWG	4 lbs.
22 AWG	7 lbs.
20 AWG	12 lbs.
18 AWG	19 lbs.
16 AWG	30 lbs.
14 AWG	48 lbs.
12 AWG	77 lbs.

Pull force should be monitored closely during installation to ensure that the manufacturer's pull-force requirements are never exceeded. The following factors determine pull force:

- Cable type, number of pairs, and quantity of cable
- Conduit type, size, and length
- Number and configuration of conduit bends
- Use of cable lubricants

During installation, pulling the cable may damage the first portion of it, so you should cut off this portion before the cable is terminated. Existing cable can be damaged as well; therefore, you should avoid pulling new cable through a partially filled conduit.

To avoid stretching the conductors of 4-pair horizontal distribution cable, limit the pulling tension to 25 pounds per foot. When pulling several cables together over fixed edges or guides, take special care because the cable adjacent to the guide is bearing the total weight of the bundle being installed. The friction on the cable jacket is much higher for bundled cables than for individually installed cables.

Pathway and Cable Support

Every ceiling distribution system must properly support cables from the telecommunications room to the work area it serves. Ceiling conduits, raceways, cable trays, and cabling must be suspended from or attached to the structural ceiling or walls, using hardware or other installation aids specifically designed to support their weight. Ceiling panels, support channels (T-bars), and vertical supports are not proper supports for horizontal pathways or cables.

All devices must have adequate support to withstand pulling the cables, and must be installed with at least 75 mm (3 inches) of clear vertical space above the ceiling tiles and support channels to ensure accessibility. Also, you should try to provide up to 150 mm (6 inches) between the suspended ceiling and the telecommunications pathways and cables, so you can install the cables, maneuver them, and store ceiling tiles during service.

Where building codes permit telecommunications cables to be placed in suspended ceiling spaces without conduit, ceiling zone distribution pathways may consist of cable trays and J-hooks (Figure 4-12). J-hooks are one of the most cost-effective methods for supporting horizontal cabling. When cables are in confined areas that do not accommodate cable trays and raceways, J-hooks provide flexible, efficient, and economic options for support. J-hooks maintain the correct cable bend radius, making them less likely to pinch. This helps ensure the integrity of the cabling system.

Figure 4-12   J-hook

NOTE   When using J-hooks, locate them on centers of 1.2 to 1.5 meters (4 to 5 feet) to adequately support and distribute the cable's weight. These types of supports may typically hold up to fifty 6.4-mm (0.25-inch) diameter cables.

There is evidence that support devices can hurt the transmission performance of higher-quality cabling systems if the device's surface area is too small to support horizontally placed cable. When you have a choice, select a device with a wider surface area to avoid potential problems. As an added precaution, you should reduce the distance between the support devices.

Cable Bend Radius

The **bend radius** is the amount that a cable can bend before it is damaged or its performance is impaired (Figure 4-13). Once the bend radius has been exceeded, cable performance can no longer be ensured. Maintaining the correct bend radius is critical when terminating wire pairs and creating **service loops**. This extra wire is stored in a wall, ceiling, or floor, and is used to repair damaged wire, repair installation errors, and assist in the moving, changing, or addition of devices.

Typically, the minimum bend radius for cables with six or fewer pairs is four times the outside diameter of the cable. For cables with more than six pairs, the minimum bend radius is 10 times the cable's diameter.

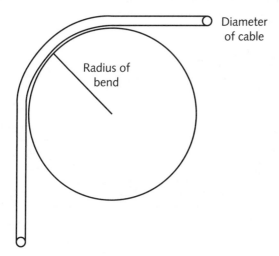

Figure 4-13   Cable bend radius

Cable Stress

Cable stress can occur in many ways, but it can usually be avoided by observing the following good installation practices:

- Support suspended cables every four to five feet to minimize stress.
- Fasten cable ties so they rotate easily around the cables.
- During installation, ensure that the cable is not crushed and that pulling tensions are not exceeded.
- Make sure that cables do not snag during installation; snags can cause excessive stress.

If cables are to be run freely in a ceiling space, they should be loosely **dressed**, or tie-wrapped in bundles, then secured to the underslab or metal structure at intervals of no greater than 6 feet. Dressing ensures that cables are neat, symmetrical, and properly aligned for termination. Cable ties should be hand-tightened, but not so tightly that the sheath becomes deformed.

Termination Practices

Proper cable termination can be the difference between a sound telecommunications system that requires little or no servicing and one that is plagued by service problems. Horizontal and backbone cables must be terminated on connecting hardware that meets applicable requirements for the type of cabling used. Because horizontal and backbone cables are always terminated on separate connectors, use patch cords or jumpers to connect these cables. **Patch cords** (Figure 4-14) are cables with connectors on one or both ends that join telecommunications circuits at the cross-connect. **Jumpers** are like patch cords, but are terminated using a punch-down tool.

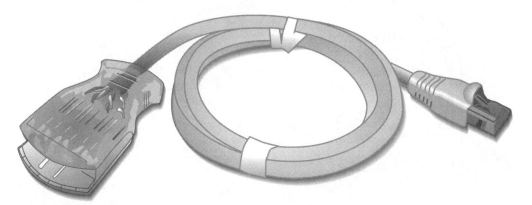

Figure 4-14   Patch cord

While most cabling is sensitive to transmission discontinuities caused by poor terminations, the performance of twisted-pair systems is particularly sensitive to near-end crosstalk, which can be caused by conductor untwisting and other installation practices that disturb pair balance and cause impedance variations. In addition to signal degradation, improper termination practices can create loop antenna effects, resulting in signal radiation levels that can exceed regulatory emission requirements.

To prevent these problems, always observe the following guidelines:

- Remove only as much cable jacket as needed for termination and trimming.
- Follow the manufacturer's instructions for mounting, termination, and cable management.
- Minimize the amount of untwisting in a pair as a result of termination to connecting hardware.

When untwisting cable pairs, maintain the pair twists as close as possible to the termination point. The amount of untwisting must not exceed 25 mm (1 inch) for Category 3 cables and 13 mm (0.5 inch) for Category 5 and higher cables.

NOTE This requirement is intended to minimize untwisting of wire pairs and the separation of conductors within a pair. It is not intended as a twist specification for cable or jumper construction.

For termination fields that require frequent access (for example, cross-connects used for configuring a network), one way to control termination consistency is to use factory-assembled patch cords and patch panels that meet appropriate performance requirements. Jumpers can provide comparable performance, but typically require a more highly skilled technician to implement changes.

When terminating twisted-pair cables at the patch panel or telecommunications outlet, keep jacket removal to a minimum and do not exceed 14 inches (35.6 cm).

CABLE MANAGEMENT PRACTICES

Connector and cable components that meet transmission performance requirements are crucial to your installed cabling system, but they do not ensure success. Performance may be degraded by poor or improper cabling practices as they relate to:

- Connector terminations
- Cable installation and management
- Use of cross-connect jumpers and patch cords
- Multiple connections in close proximity

The cable and connecting hardware may degrade if initial installation and cable management recommendations are not followed. Installation and maintenance practices for the more permanent horizontal and backbone cabling differ greatly from those for the cross-connects.

Cross-connects are designed for flexibility to allow for moves, additions, and changes. The structured cabling system user is typically responsible for altering cross-connects to implement network changes. Skill levels among users vary, and should be considered when designing the cross-connect facility, providing training for it, and managing it.

Follow the guidelines in the next few sections to manage horizontal and backbone cables, cross-connects, vertical and horizontal pathways, and ceiling zone distribution.

Horizontal and Backbone Cable Management

The recommended minimum bend radius for a cable during installation is typically greater than the same radius after the cable is installed. The increased bend radius minimizes tension and deformation as the cables pass around corners during installation. The maximum pull-force guideline for 4-pair, horizontal twisted-pair cables is 25 pounds per foot. Meeting this guideline helps to avoid stretching conductors during installation and prevents the transmission degradation that can be associated with excessive stretching. The maximum pull-force guideline for 2- or 4-fiber cables is 50 pounds per foot. The minimum bend radius for 2- or 4-fiber cables is 25 mm (1 inch) under no-load conditions and 50 mm (2 inches) under pulling tension.

In both the cable pathways and the telecommunications room, use appropriate cable routing and dressing fixtures to organize and manage the different cable types. This type of management can eliminate cable stress caused by:

- Tension in suspended cable runs; limit the **spans** (lengths) between support points to 1.5 meters (5 feet) or less
- Tightly clinched cable bundles, which cause jacket deformation
- Twisting the cable jacket during installation

 Never use staples to fasten telecommunications cabling.

NOTE

Cross-Connect Management

Cross-connect systems were introduced for terminating and cross-connecting voice cabling. Today there is a broad range of products for voice, data, and control installations. The two most common products are the BIX cross-connect system and the 110 cross-connect system. See Figure 4-15 for an example of a typical 110 cross-connect system.

Keep voice and data fields separate for the sake of administration and maintenance. Also, use the color field concept to identify the various termination areas in a cross-connect system. The ANSI/EIA/TIA-569-A standard defines color-coding requirements. The uniform color-coding scheme used today was devised by AT&T in the 1960s as a way to identify wire pairs. Color coding is discussed in detail in Chapter 5.

Patch cord or jumper slack is a major contributor to poor management, cable stress, and loose connections at the cross-connect. To manage this slack, use appropriate dressing fixtures, horizontal and vertical cross-connection managers, or patch-cord adjusters after the cross-connect is installed. Provide easy access to patch cords and jumpers to facilitate changes and rapid identification.

4

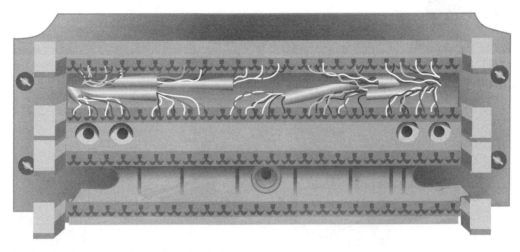

Figure 4-15   110 cross-connect kit, 100-pr

If the cross-connect system has to be wall-mounted, make sure there is adequate wall space. You should use fire-rated, ¾-inch (19-mm) plywood. To assist in cable management, the plywood should be furred out 4 inches (101 mm) so that the cables can be run in behind the plywood and brought out through the hole in a cross-connect panel.

When they are unmanaged, cross-connect cable and jumpers can have uncontrolled bend radii at connector interfaces, as well as throughout the cable and jumper length within the management field. Observe the following precautions to manage cross-connects:

- Eliminate or minimize patch cord and jumper slack in the management field after each cross-connection is completed.

- In cross-connections that use twisted-pair or fiber patch cords, bend radius can become uncontrolled. To manage the connections and ensure channel performance for twisted-pair, maximize the patch cord bend radius. For fiber patch cords, control the bend radius.

Vertical and Horizontal Pathway Management

Vertical cable management channels made of copper provide cable and patch cord protection and routing space. Vertical cable management channels made of fiber contain 10 uniquely designed wire guides to maintain the recommended bend radius for fiber cable and patch cords.

All vertical cable management channels can be easily fastened on either side of the racks. They can also be equipped with a removable swing-out door with magnetic strips for positive closure (Figure 4-16).

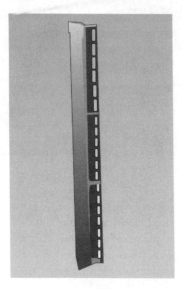

Figure 4-16 Vertical cable management channel

Horizontal cable management channels also provide patch cord protection and routing space. They are usually equipped with a front-cover panel fastened with plastic rivets. These channels provide cable protection at the top and bottom of the rack, and feature a large channel for easy cable routing (Figure 4-17).

Figure 4-17 Horizontal cable management channel

Ceiling Zone Distribution Management

To effectively manage the cabling of a suspended ceiling zone distribution system, per-form the steps in the following procedure.

1. Pull or place cables into the zone pathway.

2. Leave sufficient slack in the ceiling cables to reach any work area outlet within the zone.

3. Where zone pathways are not provided, divide the floor area into direct-run telecommunications zones.

4. Run all the cables to the center point of their zones.

5. From the center point of each zone, distribute the cables to work areas within that zone.

6. At the center point of each zone, support all cables with a cable tie made of Velcro® rather than the standard nylon cable ties. You can easily cinch a nylon tie too tightly, which could impede cable transmission. Velcro ties offer much more control for cinching.

7. Coil any cable that is not in service back to the end of the zone pathway. When required, cable-tie these coiled cables.

8. Label the cables and pathways for easy recognition, and establish a working database for their identification and maintenance. This process is described in ANSI/EIA/TIA-606.

Cable Management and ANSI/EIA/TIA-606

ANSI/EIA/TIA-606, the Administration Standard for the Telecommunications Infrastructure of Commercial Buildings, defines administration as a necessary foundation for effective cable management and reliable infrastructure. Administration includes basic system documentation and timely updating of all related drawings, labels, and records. In addition to coordinating voice, data, and video communications, administration should encompass all other building signal systems, including security, audio, alarms, and energy management. You can use either paper records or computer-generated records for administration.

Commercial buildings have a long life expectancy. As tenants move or companies expand, system additions, moves, and changes are inevitable. Administrative recordkeeping plays a crucial role in managing these frequent changes.

DOCUMENTING YOUR NETWORK

Anyone who works on a network, including cable pullers, new network technicians, and specialized consultants, must know how the network works in order to be effective. Good network documentation accounts for the following elements:

- A diagram of the network
- The topologies and network architecture in use
- Protocols and logical addressing schemes
- Operating systems in use
- Directory services
- Cabling standards

- Conventional practices

- A list of manufacturers of all the equipment in use

- Contact information for your company and vendors

These elements are discussed in more detail throughout this section. When reviewing these elements, keep in mind that every network is different. Not all networks require all these elements; some networks will include all of the elements listed here, and more.

Diagram of the Physical Network

The diagram of the physical network should specify the types and locations of all major internetworking devices, major servers, and workstations. The diagram should also describe the network architecture, topologies, network addressing, and media types used in the network.

There are no set rules for creating a network diagram, but many applications are available to help. A favorite application among professionals is Microsoft Visio, which comes in two versions—Standard and Professional. The Professional version can help you create basic network designs. An add-on, Visio Enterprise Network Tools, allows you to create extremely detailed network drawings. It can also perform network discovery, provide reports, and provide access to an extensive library of network equipment shapes.

Other diagramming tools include netViz, which is specifically designed for creating network diagrams, and ConfigMaker by Cisco, which lets you create diagrams that involve Cisco equipment. For more information on these products, go to *www.netviz.com* and *www.cisco.com*, respectively. At the time of this writing, you could download ConfigMaker for free.

Topologies, Architectures, and Protocols

Your network diagram should include a written explanation of the topologies and architectures the network uses. Identify each area of the network, the architecture used in it (such as Ethernet, Token Ring, or FDDI), the reason you selected the architecture, and the speed that the architecture uses. If you use WAN architectures such as frame relay or ISDN, include them in the diagram as well.

You must clearly specify which protocols are used on the network, the network address for each protocol, and the different resources available with each one. If the list of protocols is extensive, you can create a table to summarize the information.

Operating Systems and Directory Services

As part of your network description, you must detail which operating systems you use and explain their purposes in the network. Beginning with your servers, explain how each operating system is used and document how many users are obtaining services. After the server section is complete, identify all desktop operating systems and describe where they are used. You can document this information in written form or as a computer-generated report.

Always explain the rationale for choosing a particular operating system. This rationale helps explain a network's configuration, demonstrates to readers that thought and planning went into the configuration, and provides a reference for the logic behind previous network and configuration decisions.

The term **directory services** refers to the database and network services that store and provide access to network resources and security information. The two best-known examples are Novell Directory Service (NDS) and Active Directory from Microsoft. Whether you use a single directory service such as NDS to manage all the resources, or multiple directory services to manage specific portions of the resources, you must clearly define these directory services in your documentation. You should also include an explanation of how the various resources are organized within the directory. You may even include a diagram that shows the most critical resources. If multiple servers participate in directory service management, describe these servers, and identify who has administrative control over the various branches of the directory tree.

Cabling Standards and Network Conventions

In this section of your documentation, detail which types of cabling you are using and which areas of the network use each type. Document how the cable is terminated and the predominant standards in use. A simple description includes the cable manufacturer, the category verification, and the type of cable used from the horizontal cross-connect to the jack. For all terminating hardware, such as jacks or patch panels, include the manufacturer, category rating, and type of termination in your documentation. Also include the length, cable type, and termination type of all workstation and cross-connect cables.

Including this information in your documentation not only helps the people who work on the network, it encourages you to adhere to chosen standards. If these standards change, note your reasons for the changes in the documentation, as well as which network areas use the new standard.

Conventions are common practices or methods that help make procedures easier to follow and remember. For example, you might decide to always use red patch cables when connecting horizontal cabling to the horizontal cross-connect. This convention makes it easy to walk into a telecommunications room and immediately identify all horizontal cabling.

You can also use conventions for naming and labeling components. In your documentation, provide a brief explanation of your naming conventions for servers and internetworking devices. These conventions can minimize errors during configuration and troubleshooting, reduce the learning curve for new employees or consultants, and enhance understanding of how the network is configured.

Documenting Manufacturers and Vendors

Document the names of all the manufacturers that have products in your network, as well as which network devices they provided. Include contact information and names for representatives in each manufacturer's Sales, Customer Service, and Support departments. Also include any special procedures and information you use when contacting a manufacturer, including sales and support account numbers, passwords, and Web site logins. Remember to keep this documentation up to date; incorrect information can be worse than none at all.

Many items you use on a regular basis, such as cabling, patch panels, and jacks, are probably purchased from a vendor. Vendors are the companies you use when you do not buy directly from a manufacturer. The documentation you need for vendors is similar to that for manufacturers. If you can buy the same product from multiple vendors, you may want to include comparative notes about each vendor's price, shipping policies, and timeliness in product delivery. These comparisons can help you select the best vendor for each product.

Every person who works on the network in your organization, including consultants, contract workers, and service technicians, should be listed in the documentation. Along with names and contact information, you may want to describe each person's expertise and network responsibilities. You can even include short biographies.

CHAPTER SUMMARY

- Cabling pathways provide the means for placing cables between the equipment room, the telecommunications rooms, and the work areas. These pathways can be horizontal or vertical.

- A common method of horizontal cabling is zone cabling, in which cable bundles are run to a particular area from the telecommunications room along J-hooks suspended above a plenum ceiling. Upon reaching the zone, cables are fanned out and dropped through interior walls, support columns, or raceways, and terminated at the work area outlet.

- The equipment rooms and telecommunications rooms in a building act as junctions between the backbone and horizontal pathways. Both rooms may house such items as the main distribution frame, PBXs, secondary voltage protection, active voice and data telecommunications equipment, termination fields, and cross-connect wiring.

- Typically, cabling installations begin with the placement of all the large backbone and intrabuilding cables, followed by the smaller horizontal cabling, and then the interconnect cables. The ANSI/EIA/TIA-569-A standard provides important instructions for ensuring successful installations, including information on conduit capacity, cable pulling tensions, pathway and cable support, cable bend radius, cable stress, termination practices, and cable jackets.

❏ Connector and cable components that meet transmission performance requirements are crucial to your installed cabling system, but they do not ensure success. Performance may be degraded by poor or improper cabling practices relating to connector terminations, cable installation and management, use of cross-connect jumpers and patch cords, and multiple connections in close proximity.

❏ Make your network documentation more effective by including a complete network diagram, along with specific information about hardware, software, topologies, conventions, cabling standards, and configurations. The more you document the network, the better equipped everyone will be to work on it. Remember to keep this documentation up to date; incorrect information can be worse than none at all.

4

KEY TERMS

access floor — A system of removable and interchangeable floor panels that are supported on pedestals, stringers, or both to allow access to the area beneath.

administrative labeling — The process of identifying every element in a floor plan with a unique name and/or number.

bend radius — The maximum radius that a cable can bend without causing physical or electrical damage or adverse transmission performance.

cable tray — A device used to route and support telecommunications cable or power cable. It is typically equipped with sides so that cables can be placed within the tray's entire length.

ceiling zone — A means of distributing horizontal cable from the telecommunications room to the work area.

conduit — A rigid or flexible, metallic or nonmetallic pipe through which cables can be pulled.

consolidation point — An interconnection point or transition point for horizontal cabling.

conventions — Common practices or methods that help make procedures easier to follow and remember.

core hitch — Hardware that connects vertical cable to a winch.

cross-connect — A point in a network where a circuit is connected from one facility to another by cabling between the equipment.

directory services — The database and network services that store and provide access to network resources and security information.

distribution duct — The duct that carries the cable from the feeder duct to a specific floor area in an underfloor duct system.

distribution field — The connecting hardware that provides the link between the cross-connect and the telecommunications outlet.

dressing — Placing cables into a neat and symmetrical pattern for proper alignment and positioning for termination.

feeder duct — In cellular and underfloor duct systems, the main duct used to bring cable from telecommunications rooms to distribution ducts or cells.

firestopping — The installation of specialty materials into penetrations of fire-rated barriers.

flexible conduit — A type of conduit, usually made of flexible metal that allows it to be bent in different directions without distorting it. Flexible conduit is normally used to connect rigid pathways to other pathways that may not join in exact alignment.

horizontal cabling — The cabling between the work area telecommunications outlet/connector and the horizontal cross-connect (floor distributor) in the telecommunications room. It may be installed in either a horizontal or vertical plane.

J-hook — A J-shaped supporting device for horizontal cables that is attached to building structures. Horizontal cables are laid in the niche formed by the J for support.

jumpers — Devices that are similar to patch cords but terminated using a punchdown tool.

junction boxes — Openings in the ductwork that provide access to the duct system for installing and servicing cable.

ladder cable tray — A tray with two side rails connected by individual transverse members. The tray looks very much like a ladder.

loose cables — Cables that are run in the ceiling without the use of conduits.

main distribution frame — A steel-bar framework that usually holds the phone company's central office protective devices and serves as the major cross-connect point for the central office lines and the customer's wiring. It is also used to interconnect loop cable pairs and line-equipment terminals on a switching system.

patch cord — A length of cable with connectors on one or both ends that join telecommunications circuits and links at the cross-connect.

pathway — A sequence of connections for network devices or networks on an internetwork. Also, a pathway is the vertical and horizontal route of the telecommunications cable.

plenum — A chamber to which one or more air ducts are connected to form part of an air distribution system. Cables installed in an air distribution system require a higher fire rating.

power winch — A piece of equipment that provides pulling force for raising vertical cables.

private branch exchange (PBX) — A small, local telephone office, either manually or automatically operated, that serves extensions in a business complex and provides access to the public domain.

pull boxes — Openings in the duct system that provide access for pulling cables.

reel and sheave block — Equipment that provides a means of applying a break at the reel or sheave when raising or lowering cable through vertical pathways.

4

service loops — Extra wire that is stored in a wall, ceiling, or floor, and used to repair damaged cable, repair installation errors, or assist in the moving, changing, or addition of devices.

sheave — A curved apparatus used to guide vertical cable into the sleeve.

shoe — A curved plastic apparatus that guides cables and protects them from corner abrasions during cable pulling.

sleeve — A short section of conduit, either metallic or nonmetallic, that lines an opening in the wall or floor for cables to pass through.

solid bottom cable tray — A tray with a solid bottom and longitudinal side rails.

span — The length between two cabling support points. In an aerial plant, the span is the space between two poles or building connection points.

spine cable tray — An open tray with a central rigid spine and cable support ribs along the tray's length at 90° angles.

splice boxes — Openings in the underfloor duct system that provide access for making connections in the cable.

telecommunications outlet/connector — The location in the work area that is terminated with a jack for plugging in telecommunications equipment.

trench duct — A flat, metal duct that is divided into sections to provide separate compartments for different services.

utility column — An enclosed pathway that extends from the ceiling to furniture or to the floor, and guides electrical wiring, telecommunications cable, or both.

ventilated channel cable tray — A channel section with a one-piece bottom that is no more than 150 mm wide.

ventilated trough cable tray — A tray with a ventilated bottom and side rails.

work area outlet — *See* telecommunications outlet/connector.

zone cabling — Cabling that runs from the telecommunications room to the open office area, using a consolidation point or multiuser telecommunications outlet.

REVIEW QUESTIONS

1. The horizontal cable links the telecommunications outlet in the work area to the cross-connect distribution field. True or False?

2. Which of the following methods can be used to route horizontal cables to the work area?

   a. conduits

   b. ceilings

   c. cable trays

   d. all of the above

3. Which of the following considerations is important when choosing a distribution method?

   a. fire rating

   b. proximity of EMI sources

   c. security

   d. all of the above

4. Underfloor ducts are plastic raceways used to access the cross-connect distribution field. True or False?

5. Why do you need to use distribution ducts?

   a. to provide access to the telecommunications room

   b. to separate cables that provide different types of service

   c. to distribute cables from a feeder duct to specific floor areas

   d. to distribute cables from a cable tray to specific floor areas

6. Why are junction boxes placed at planned locations in a duct system?

   a. to provide access to the telecommunications room

   b. to provide access to the system for pulling cable

   c. to provide access to cable for work area termination

   d. to allow a cable run to be longer

7. What is the maximum cable length allowed between junction boxes and other access points?

   a. 100 feet

   b. 20 feet

   c. 80 feet

   d. 60 feet

8. What is the main disadvantage of using flexible conduit in a building?

   a. creep

   b. bend

   c. EMI

   d. separation

9. In the United States, which code defines the requirements for cable tray use?

   a. NEC Article 300

   b. ANSI/EIA/TIA-607

   c. NEC Article 318

   d. NEC/ANSI-318

10. Stringered systems have lateral bracing between the pedestal supports. Why?

    a. difficulty in frequent removal and replacement of floor panels

    b. improved lateral stability

    c. less support for the panels

    d. none of the above

11. Which of the following criteria must be met when using ceiling distribution systems?

    a. code requirements for design, installation, and pathways

    b. Ceiling tiles are removable and no more than 3.4 meters (11 feet) above the finished floor.

    c. Ceiling space is available for cabling pathways.

    d. all of the above

12. Cabling installation typically starts with the placement of smaller horizontal cabling. True or False?

13. In which of the following ways are high-pair-count cables installed between floors?

    a. by pulling the cable up to the top level through any appropriate shaft

    b. by pulling the cable up through vertical shafts

    c. by lowering cable from the top level through sleeves

    d. by lowering cable from the top level through vertical shafts

14. Which standard provides cable capacity guidelines for conduits ranging from 16 mm (½-inch trade size) to 103 mm (4-inch trade size)?

    a. ANSI/EIA/TIA-607

    b. NEC/ANSI-607

    c. NEC/ANSI-569-A

    d. ANSI/EIA/TIA-569-A

15. Which of the following factors determines pull force?

    a. conduit size

    b. number and configuration of conduit bends

    c. cable type and quantity

    d. all of the above

16. Which of the following problems may occur when the recommended bend radius is exceeded?

    a. No serious problems will occur; Category 5 cable performance will remain the same.

    b. The cable jacket may transmit RFI.

    c. The cable pairs may separate.

    d. Category 5 cable performance can no longer be ensured.

17. What is one of the easiest ways to avoid cable stress?

    a. Suspended cable should be supported every 4 to 5 feet.

    b. Cable ties should be as tight as possible.

    c. Run cables freely.

    d. Secure cables to metal structures every 6 feet or more.

18. To minimize the amount of jumpers or patch cords needed, you should always terminate horizontal and backbone cabling on the same connectors. True or False?

19. Which of the following guidelines should you observe when managing horizontal and backbone cable?

    a. Pay strict attention to the bend radii and maximum pulling tension during installation.

    b. In cable pathways and telecommunications rooms, use appropriate cable routing and dressing fixtures to organize and manage the different cable types.

    c. Eliminate cable stress caused by suspended cable runs.

    d. all of the above

20. In cross-connection management, which two items are important to remember?

    a. Appropriate dressing fixtures, managers for horizontal and vertical cross-connection, or patch cord adjusters can be used to manage patch cord and jumper slack.

    b. Voice and data fields should be separated for the sake of administration and maintenance, and color fields should be used to identify various termination areas in a cross-connect system.

    c. Do not wall-mount the system.

    d. Make access to patch cords and jumpers difficult to provide additional security.

21. Which of the following can provide cable and patch cord protection and routing space?

    a. patch cord management system

    b. tie wraps on the cable every two feet

    c. vertical cable management channels of copper and fiber

    d. cable racks

22. Before cables can be run freely in a ceiling space, they must be tightly dressed and secured. True or False?

23. Which of the following is an option for installing cables in a ceiling where zone pathways are not provided?

    a. Run the cables from the telecommunications room to the most distant work area outlet, and then branch them out to the various locations from there.

    b. Run the cables in any manner that is easiest for the installer.

    c. Do not run any cable that is not in a zone.

    d. Divide the floor area into direct-run telecommunications zones.

24. ANSI/EIA/TIA-606 defines the process of labeling cables and pathways for easy recognition, and for establishing a working database for identification and maintenance. True or False?

25. Which of the following will reduce the time and cost of unit changes, and have a great impact on the long-term maintenance and operating costs of the horizontal distribution system?

    a. careful consideration during the design stage in selecting pathway and cabling components

    b. careful consideration to the planning of cabling zones

    c. careful consideration during the design stage to the technologies being accommodated

    d. focusing on cabling early in the design stage, and on the pathways later

HANDS-ON PROJECTS

Project 4-1

Knowing the fire rating requirements for your building is important. For this project, contact your local fire inspector and obtain all the information you can about fire rating requirements for all cabling projects in commercial buildings. Next, write a report that lists and explains the requirements. If any requirements are not covered in this text, research them and then explain them in your report. Include references to any sources you use other than this text.

Project 4-2

1. Outline or summarize the components of cable management and cabling practices.

2. Define the components and practices.

3. Explain why these components and practices are important.

In addition to your text, the following Web sites contain information and articles you may want to read:

❑ Cable management shake-up — *www.networkmagazine.com/article/NMG20000508S0020*

❑ Wire and cable management — *www.archrecord.construction.com/CONTEDUC/ARTICLES/09_02_4.asp*

❑ Cabling practices for commercial buildings — *www.kraycabling.com/technical_info/tech_index4.html*. Click **Communications Cabling Practices: Commercial Buildings** on the page that appears. The best sections are 3.1 to 3.1.3.2, but the other sections are also recommended.

Project 4-3

You will often need to install cross-connects or jumpers, either in your new installation or as a result of additions, moves, or changes. In this exercise, you will practice terminating wires on a 110 cross-connect system to connect a workstation to the network.

For this project, you need a 110 punch-down tool, a patch panel with 110 block connections on the back and RJ-45 receptacles on the front, a wire cutter, a wire stripper, a length of cable, one workstation outlet (jack), one patch cord, and a simple client/server network system that is set up on the patch panel and verified as working. (Your instructor will provide the 110 punch-down tool, patch panel, patch cord, and the simple network.)

1. Use the wire cutters to make a clean cut at both ends of the UTP cable.

2. Use the wire strippers to remove approximately 1 inch of the jacket from one end of the UTP cable, being careful not to damage the insulation on the twisted pairs inside.

3. Separate the four wire pairs slightly, while keeping the individual pairs twisted.

4. Next, carefully separate each pair by untwisting its wires, but do not untwist them more than ½ inch from each other.

5. Using the 110 punch-down tool, connect the wires to the 110 punch-down block side of the patch panel at port 3. The 110 connector with color markings is shown in Figure 4-18.

Figure 4-18   110 connector with color markings

6. For the other end of the UTP, follow the directions in Steps 1 through 5, but instead of punching the cable down on the panel, punch it down on the workstation outlet (jack). The color code is the same as in Step 5.

7. Plug one end of the patch cord into the workstation and the other end into the RJ-45 connector on the patch panel at port 3.

8. Test your workstation. Can you log in to the network? Can you open a file?

9. If you cannot communicate with the network, repeat all steps and continue testing until you can log in to the server from the workstation you created.

Project 4-4

You have been hired to install the entire telecommunications system in a new office for a small accounting firm. The building has 12 offices, one area for a receptionist, and a small work area for four employees. Every desk will have a phone and computer. Three offices will have Internet access through dial-up modems. The copier and fax are in the storage area behind the receptionist's desk. You need to prepare a floor plan for this project that includes all cables, jacks, and connecting hardware. After you complete the floor plan, prepare the documentation for this project, as described in the documentation sections in Chapters 1 through 4.

Project 4-5

You need good information to successfully manage cable. In this exercise, you will research the ANSI/EIA/TIA-606 standard, called the Administration Standard for the Telecommunications Infrastructure of Commercial Buildings.

1. Using a workstation with Internet access, go to *www.anixter.com/techlib/ standard/cabling/d0502p25.htm*.
2. Select ANSI/EIA/TIA-606 from the main page and read all sections of this document.
3. Write a summary of the standard, and emphasize the main points you learned. List the steps you think are most necessary for successfully managing cable.

Project 4-6

As you work in this field, you will often need to create the design for your cabling project. In this exercise, you will draw a simple ceiling zone distribution, either by hand or in Visio. Some basic information about the building is provided in the following list. When no information is provided, you can create it yourself, but include that information with your drawing.

◻ The building's usable floor space is 11,250 square feet (75 feet by 150 feet).

◻ There are building columns every 25 feet.

◻ The ceiling is plenum rated.

◻ A total of 162 workstation cables must be evenly distributed throughout the building.

◻ The telecommunications room is in the center of the building.

1. First, draw the basic building, including the information you have.
2. Divide the overall usable floor space into zones and place them in your drawing. How many zones did you create? What size? Why?
3. Draw the pathways to each zone. What are you using for your pathways? Where do they start and stop?

4. What type(s) of cable are you using for your ceiling zone distribution? Why?

5. Draw all of your cable runs and work area outlets. Show where each cable starts and stops, as well as its route.

6. Be sure to label all cables and pathways according to the guidelines in ANSI/EIA/TIA-606.

CASE PROJECTS

CASE PROJECTS

Case Project 1

A large corporation in your area has asked your company to design the cabling system for its new main building and warehouse. These buildings must share the same telephone system and be on the same network.

The three-story main building and two-story warehouse will sit side by side on one city block. The main building will house the corporate offices as well as the Sales, Marketing, and Accounting departments. The main building will have telephones and computers with high-speed Internet access in each office and in the three conference rooms (one on each floor). Each floor will have its own telecommunications room, and the entrance facility will be on the first floor.

The warehouse next door will house only a few departments and require only a few offices with telephones and computers, but they must be on the same systems as the main building. High-speed Internet capabilities are not as important in the warehouse, but department managers need access to the corporate offices more often than other warehouse employees, and thus need higher speeds. All warehouse offices must have voice communication, and all departments in the warehouse need at least one networked computer.

What type of transmission media would you use for these buildings? Why? How would you run the cables in the two buildings? How would you interconnect the two buildings?

CASE PROJECTS

Case Project 2

Numerous products are available for voice, data, and control installations. The most common are the BIX cross-connect system and the 110 cross-connect system. Research both systems, then write a report defining each one, including its most common uses, advantages, and disadvantages. Explain which system you think would be best for most installations. Next, explain which system would be best for the buildings in Case Project 1.

Case Project 3

From your work in Case Project 1, take one floor of one building and draw a cabling diagram using an access floor. Label all parts of the diagram. When your drawing is complete, write a brief report that explains what you used and why.

Case Project 4

This chapter discussed five different types of pathways. Write a report that defines each type and its primary uses, and describes a situation in which each pathway would be the best solution. Include references to any sources you use other than this text.

4

5

BACKBONE AND HORIZONTAL DISTRIBUTION SYSTEMS

After reading this chapter and completing the exercises, you will be able to:

♦ Understand backbone distribution systems

♦ Discuss the types of cross-connection in a backbone system

♦ Differentiate between interbuilding and intrabuilding backbone systems

♦ Understand horizontal distribution systems

♦ Discuss design guidelines and work areas in horizontal distribution systems

♦ Document the cable plant

♦ Document equipment rooms

The process of connecting telecommunications rooms, equipment rooms, entrance facilities, and work areas is called distribution. The two types of distribution systems, backbone and horizontal, are responsible for connecting different portions of the telecommunications cabling system.

In this chapter you will examine the elements, functions, and design guidelines of backbone and horizontal distribution systems. You will also learn which media and hardware are best suited for each system.

BACKBONE DISTRIBUTION SYSTEMS

Both the backbone and horizontal cabling systems are part of the **premises distribution system**, a generic term that includes all the components of the telecommunications distribution system. A **backbone distribution system** connects the equipment rooms, telecommunications rooms (TRs), and entrance facilities.

A backbone distribution system normally provides two types of connections. Intrabuilding connections are made between the floors of multistory buildings, and interbuilding connections link a **campus environment** of multiple, related buildings. The **intrabuilding backbone** links all of the building's **cross-connects**; these wall- or rack-mounted connection points mechanically terminate and administer building wiring. The **interbuilding backbone** links the intermediate cross-connects in other buildings to the main cross-connect.

The design requirements for backbones vary because they depend on different factors. For example, data backbones have more stringent, complex design requirements than those for voice backbones. The following sections address design requirements and topologies for cabling backbones.

Backbones and Cross-Connects

All backbone cabling in the distribution system links three types of cross-connects: **horizontal cross-connects (HCs)**, which connect horizontal cabling using jumpers, patch cords, and other hardware; **main cross-connects (MCs)**, the primary connection and flexibility point within a network; and **intermediate cross-connects (ICs)** between first- and second-level backbone. Each type of cross-connect depends on the others for connectivity throughout the system. This section describes how each type of cross-connect works and interconnects with the others.

Building cabling begins in the entrance facility, where the service provider's lines end and the building wiring begins. This cabling is often part of the equipment room or adjacent to it. The equipment room also houses large telecommunications and data equipment. The main cross-connect should be near or even within the main equipment room. Ideally, the main cross-connect should be at the center of the buildings being served, have adequate space for cross-connect hardware and equipment, and have suitable pathways that link it to other buildings. The main cross-connect is typically a wall of punch-down blocks where the service provider's systems connect to the building wiring (Figure 5-1).

Backbone cabling connects the equipment and runs from the equipment room to the various TRs. Depending on the size of the building(s) involved, these TRs house either the intermediate cross-connects or the horizontal cross-connects. Figure 5-2 shows a large campus environment in which the backbone cabling links the main cross-connect to an intermediate cross-connect, and then to the horizontal cross-connect. In smaller environments, an intermediate cross-connect may not be necessary; instead, the backbone cabling links the main cross-connect directly to the horizontal cross-connect (Figure 5-3).

Figure 5-1   Main cross-connect

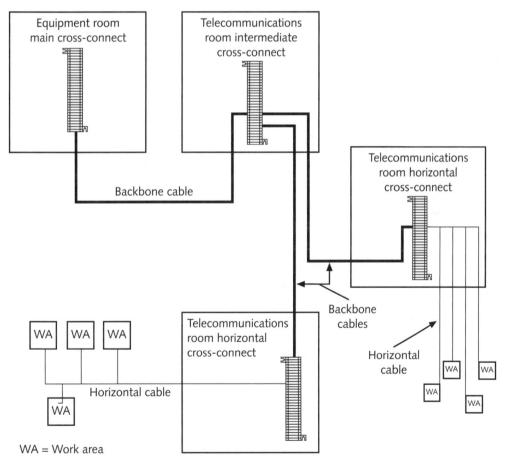

Figure 5-2   Intermediate cross-connect

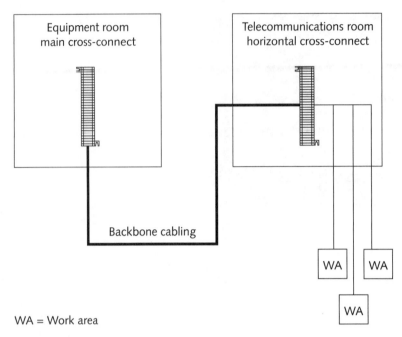

WA = Work area

Figure 5-3   Horizontal cross-connect

Intrabuilding Backbones

The intrabuilding backbone cabling consists of multipair copper or optical-fiber cables and their supporting hardware. Intrabuilding backbones connect all the horizontal cross-connects or intermediate cross-connects in a building to the main cross-connect. The design of an intrabuilding backbone is straightforward, but you still have various options for planning it.

Intrabuilding Topology

The ANSI/EIA/TIA-568-A standard requires the topology for all backbone cabling to be a star or hierarchical star. Backbone topology differs from the network topology discussed in Chapter 3. As you recall, network topology refers to the physical configuration or layout of network devices, and defines how they will connect and communicate. Backbone topology differs from network topology in the following ways:

- Backbones connect multiple network segments or LANs.
- Backbones can connect and support different topologies.
- Backbones provide support for all modes of communication.
- Backbones provide the necessary interconnection that enables communication between segments.

The two topology options for an intrabuilding backbone are the star and the hierarchical star. In the **star topology**, individual nodes are linked to the horizontal cross-connect, which is connected directly to the building's main cross-connect. In the hierarchical star, some or all of the horizontal cross-connects are linked to an intermediate cross-connect, which in turn is linked to the building's main cross-connect. These topology options are shown in Figures 5-4 and 5-5.

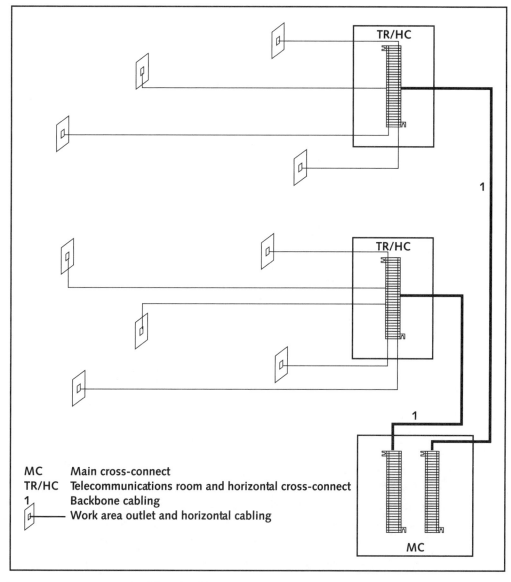

MC   Main cross-connect
TR/HC   Telecommunications room and horizontal cross-connect
1   Backbone cabling
     Work area outlet and horizontal cabling

Figure 5-4   Star intrabuilding backbone

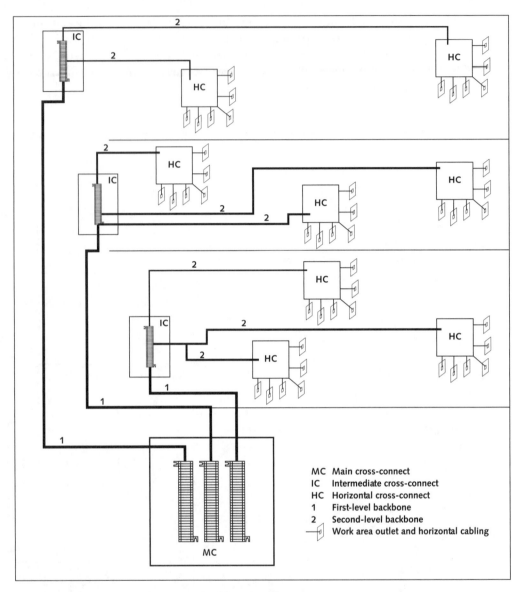

Figure 5-5   Hierarchical star intrabuilding backbone

In general, the star topology is the better design choice. In large buildings such as high-rises, however, it may be more prudent to use the hierarchical star. Use the following criteria to help you select the most cost-effective topology for your purposes:

- The types and sizes of cable available for use with each topology

- The hardware necessary with each topology

- The size of the site and number of end users

- The labor required for the installation of each topology

- The application(s) to be used

- The range of services to be accommodated

Interbuilding Backbones

Interbuilding backbones link the horizontal cross-connect or intermediate cross-connect in various buildings to the main cross-connect. Interbuilding backbone cabling is the network segment that gives distribution designers and users the most options, especially in major networks such as those in universities, industrial parks, and military bases. It is also the network segment most affected by physical considerations, such as duct availability, right of way, and physical barriers.

Interbuilding Topology

You must use the hierarchical star topology for interbuilding backbones, as specified by the ANSI/EIA/TIA-568-A standard. Depending on the size of the network, you will use either a single-level or multilevel hierarchical star. The configurations of these two design options are shown in Figures 5-6 and 5-7.

The better design choice for a small network, based on the number of buildings and the geographical area involved, is a single-level hierarchical star. This design links all the TRs and their horizontal cross-connects in one building to an intermediate cross-connect in the same building. The intermediate cross-connect is then linked to the main cross-connect. This method creates essentially the same effect as directly connecting all the TRs in each building to the main cross-connect.

The single-level hierarchical star has the following advantages:

- It provides a single point of control for system administration.

- It allows testing and reconfiguration of the system's topology and applications from the main cross-connect.

- It allows for easy maintenance and security against unauthorized access.

- It provides increased flexibility.

- It allows for the easy addition of future interbuilding backbones.

Larger networks that connect numerous buildings and wide geographical areas may require more hierarchical levels. Such designs provide an interbuilding backbone that uses selected intermediate cross-connects to serve a number of buildings, and then links these intermediate cross-connects to the main cross-connect. This approach works better than linking all the buildings directly to the main cross-connect.

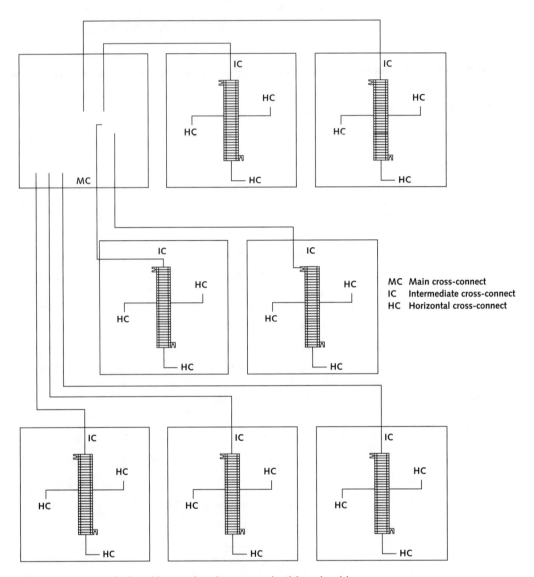

Figure 5-6 Single-level hierarchical star interbuilding backbone

You should consider using the network design in Figure 5-7 when the available pathways do not allow all cables to route directly to a main cross-connect, or when geographical or user groupings require segmenting the network.

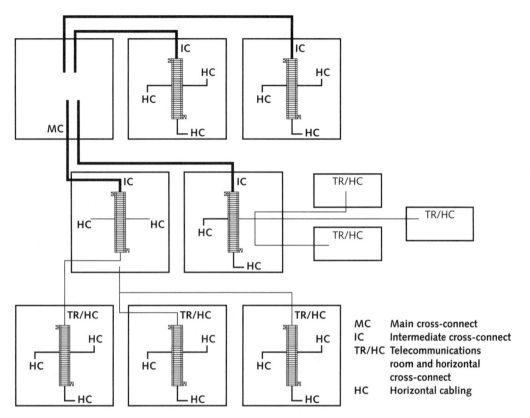

Figure 5-7   Multilevel hierarchical star interbuilding backbone

Considerations for Selecting Backbone Distribution Media

As a backbone system designer, you must choose cable based on a variety of requirements and trade-offs to match the wide range of services and site sizes that the system accommodates. The recognized cable types for backbone systems are:

- 62.5/125-μm or 50/125-μm optical fiber (multimode)
- Single-mode optical fiber
- 100-ohm twisted-pair cable

Each of these cable types has useful characteristics for many situations, but often a single cable type will not satisfy all user requirements. If you need to use more than one medium in the backbone wiring, make sure the different media all use the same facility architecture, including the same locations for cross-connects, mechanical terminations, interbuilding entrance facilities, and other facilities.

Although your choice of transmission media depends on their specific applications, you should consider the following factors when making selections:

- The flexibility of the medium with respect to the services to be supported
- The required useful life of the backbone wiring
- The size of the site and the number of end users

The telecommunications service needs of a commercial building will vary as time passes and the occupants change, so the future uses of the backbone wiring may change as well. Whenever possible, you should first determine the different service requirements, then group similar services into categories such as voice, display terminal, local area network (LAN), and other digital connections. Next you should identify the individual media types and project the quantities required within each group you created.

When the service requirements are uncertain, use worst-case estimates to help you evaluate the wiring alternatives. The more uncertain these requirements are, the more flexible the backbone wiring system must be.

Remember also that separate backbone cables are recommended for voice and data implementations. Design requirements are different between voice and data backbones, and keeping the cables separate helps you perform administrative and maintenance tasks.

When deciding on your backbone cable size, you first need to know the number of workstations being served by each telecommunications room and the number of pairs provided in the horizontal cabling. To determine the size of voice backbone cable, you typically use half the number of backbone pairs as the number of horizontal pairs that are terminated, then add 25 percent for growth. For example, a telecommunications room might serve 100 **work areas**, places where users operate workstations or PCs. If each of these work areas has two voice lines, and each workstation has four terminated pairs per line, then the recommended voice backbone cable for that telecommunications room would be 1000 pairs (100 work areas $\times$ 2 lines $\times$ 4 pairs/line = 800 + 25% = 1000). If you want full flexibility, use the same number of pairs in the backbone cabling and the horizontal cabling.

When selecting your backbone cable, you need to know the maximum backbone distances for each medium. Figure 5-8 shows a typical backbone cabling layout and the maximum distances for various media from different points.

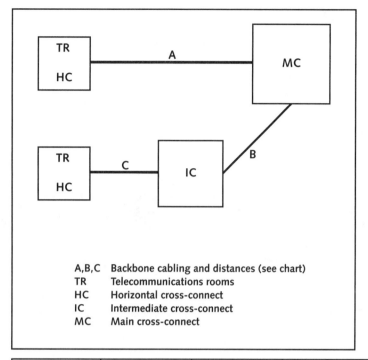

TR	
HC	A → **MC**

A, B, C Backbone cabling and distances (see chart)
TR   Telecommunications rooms
HC   Horizontal cross-connect
IC   Intermediate cross-connect
MC   Main cross-connect

Media Type	A (MC to HC)	B (MC to IC)	C (IC to HC)
UTP/STP (Voice)	800 m (2624 ft)	300 m (984 ft)	500 m (1640 ft)
UTP/STP (Data)	90 m (295 ft)	N/A*	N/A*
Multimode fiber 62.5/125 μm	2000 m (6560 ft)	1500 m (4920 ft)	500 m (1640 ft)
Single-mode fiber	3000 m** (9840 ft)	2500 m (8200 ft)	500 m (1640 ft)

* For high-speed data applications, the use of Category 3, 4 or 5 100-ohm UTP or 150-ohm STP-A backbone cable shall be limited to a total distance of 90 m (295'); this assumes 5 m (16') at each end for connection to equipment.

** The capability of single-mode optical may allow for distance up to 60 km (37 miles). However, this is outside the scope of the standard for backbone cabling.

Figure 5-8   Typical backbone cabling and maximum distance chart

NOTE

In a data backbone, the maximum distance depends on the system to be installed. However, when the total channel length exceeds 100 meters, optical fiber is recommended for the data backbone.

Fiber-Optic Cable

Fiber-optic cables are available with different sheaths for indoor (in-building) and outdoor (interbuilding) applications. Backbone **fiber-optic cable** consists of optical fibers with individually colored buffer jackets of flame-retardant polymer. The cable is stranded around a central strength member, which helps provide a rugged and flexible cable that is easy to pull through conduit.

Table 5-1 provides guidelines for cable distances and data rates when using fiber-optic cable for backbone cabling in premises applications.

Table 5-1   Fiber-optic cable distances and data rates

Application	Multimode Distance/Data Rate (62.5/125 µm or 50/125 µm)	Single-Mode Distance/Data Rate
Backbone	2 km (1.2 miles)/155 Mbps	3 km (1.9 miles)/10 Gbps
Horizontal	90 m (295 ft)/2.5 Gbps	N/A

NOTE

Recently developed applications now support 10-Gbps transmission over 50/125-µm multimode fiber for lengths of more than 300 meters (984 feet).

When using fiber-optic cable for the backbone, you should plan to use at least a six-fiber cable for each TR, if feasible. However, a 24-fiber cable is highly recommended. Typically, six optical fibers are reserved for LANs, six optical fibers are reserved for redundancy, and 12 optical fibers are reserved for growth. To satisfy your present and future needs, your backbone should consist of both multimode and single-mode fiber.

Plastic Insulated Conductor (PIC) Cable

Plastic Insulated Conductor (PIC) cable is twisted-pair cable designed to ease cable-pair identification. Each pair in the cable is color-coded in groups of 25 pairs, as shown in Figure 5-9. These pairs are placed together in a **binder group**, which is identified by a color-coded binder wrapping. PIC cables are usually available in sizes ranging from 6 to 4200 pairs (for large cables, many manufacturers use "supergroups"). The cables are manufactured in various designs for aerial, buried, underground, and in-building applications.

25-Pair Cable

Pair Number	Color Code	
	Tip	Ring
1	White-Bl	Blue-Wh
2	White-Or	Orange-Wh
3	White-Gn	Green-Wh
4	White-Br	Brown-Wh
5	White-Sl	Slate-Wh
6	Red-Bl	Blue-Rd
7	Red-Or	Orange-Rd
8	Red-Gn	Green-Rd
9	Red-Br	Brown-Rd
10	Red-Sl	Slate-Rd
11	Black-Bl	Blue-Bk
12	Black-Or	Orange-Bk
13	Black-Gn	Green-Bk
14	Black-Br	Brown-Bk
15	Black-Sl	Slate-Bk
16	Yellow-Bl	Blue-Ye
17	Yellow-Or	Orange-Ye
18	Yellow-Gn	Green-Ye
19	Yellow-Br	Brown-Ye
20	Yellow-Sl	Slate-Ye
21	Violet-Bl	Blue-Vi
22	Violet-Or	Orange-Vi
23	Violet-Gn	Green-Vi
24	Violet-Br	Brown-Vi
25	Violet-Sl	Slate-Vi

100-Pair Cable

Ring→ Tip↓	Blue (Binder 1)		Orange (Binder 2)		Green (Binder 3)		Brown (Binder 4)		Slate	
White	1	26	2	27	3	28	4	29	5	30
	51	76	52	77	53	78	54	79	55	80
Red	6	31	7	32	8	33	9	34	10	35
	56	81	57	82	58	83	59	84	60	85
Black	11	36	12	37	13	38	14	39	15	40
	61	86	62	87	63	88	64	89	65	90
Yellow	16	41	17	42	18	43	19	44	20	45
	66	91	67	92	68	93	69	94	70	95
Violet	21	46	22	47	23	48	24	49	25	50
	71	96	72	97	73	98	74	99	75	100

Binder 1 - Blue (1-25)
Binder 2 - Orange (26-50)
Binder 3 - Green (51-75)
Binder 4 - Brown (76-100)

Figure 5-9   Color code (tip and ring) for 25-pair and 100-pair PIC cable

Selecting the Main Cross-Connect and Hardware

The main cross-connect is the primary connection and flexibility point within a network. It provides the means of terminating and cross-connecting intrabuilding and interbuilding backbone cables, backbone cables from the entrance facilities, and equipment cables at one common administration point.

Depending on the number of copper pairs you need to terminate at the main cross-connect, the cross-connection hardware can be wall-mounted or rack-mounted. For wall-mounted installations, you generally should terminate no more than 14,400 pairs. If this maximum is exceeded, then use a rack system such as a customer premises distribution frame for cable installation. You can also install a BIX or 110 frame system, especially for terminating all **riser cable** pairs, which run between the floors or sections of a building. **BIX** is the trade name of a NORDX/CDT in-building termination and cross-connect system for unshielded twisted-pair (UTP) cables.

You must segregate voice, data, and control fields to facilitate administration, operation, and maintenance.

When using a fiber cross-connect, you should design it to terminate at least six fiber cables for every telecommunications closet in the building, although 12-fiber cables are highly recommended. Between two buildings, use 24-fiber cables.

The main cross-connect is generally located in the equipment room or adjacent to it. When selecting the location for the equipment room, consider the following criteria:

- The room should be accessible for the delivery of large equipment.

- Expansion of the equipment room should not be restricted by building components, such as elevators, outside walls, or other fixed walls.

- The equipment room should not be below the water level. If it is, take preventive measures against water infiltration.

- Do not locate the equipment room near sources of electromagnetic interference, such as transformers, motors, generators, x-ray equipment, and radio or radar transmitters.

HORIZONTAL DISTRIBUTION SYSTEMS

As you learned in Chapter 4, the horizontal distribution is the part of the cabling system used to distribute, support, and provide access to the **horizontal cabling**. This cabling system provides the physical means for transporting signals between the telecommunications outlet/connector in the work area and the horizontal cross-connect in the TR. The cabling and its associated connecting hardware make up the content of horizontal pathways. These pathways include the cable pathway itself (e.g., cable trays and conduits), as well as the related spaces, such as pull boxes, splice boxes, and intermediate **consolidation points**, which provide access to the cable and the connecting hardware. A typical horizontal cabling system is shown in Figure 5-10.

At least two cable runs are required to each work area, but the pathway design should allow for at least three cable runs per work area, to facilitate additions and changes as users' needs evolve. If these minimum requirements are met, additional cables and outlets may be provided to support other applications such as cable television (CATV).

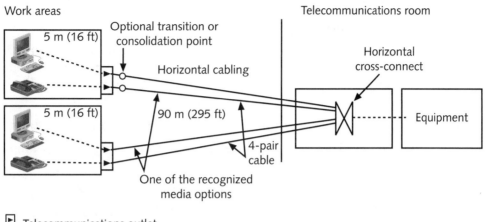

Figure 5-10   Typical horizontal cabling system

General Design Guidelines for Horizontal Distribution

The installation of the horizontal distribution system must satisfy all current requirements and should also accommodate future maintenance and equipment changes. The
horizontal cabling is usually less accessible than other cabling, and is subject to the greatest amount of activity in the building, so a good design is crucial. You must also consider the proximity of cables to possible sources of electromagnetic interference.

You must use a star topology in a horizontal distribution system. Each telecommunications outlet/connector in the work area must be directly connected to a horizontal
cross-connect in a TR on the same floor. No matter which media type you use, the maximum cable distance for this connection is 90 meters (295 feet). Remember that you
cannot connect wires by **splicing** two or more segments together to create one continuous wire.

For each horizontal cable, a maximum distance of 10 meters (30 feet) is permitted for
work area cords, patch cords and jumpers, and any equipment cords. **Patch cords** are
cables with connectors on one or both ends that join telecommunications circuits at the
cross-connect, and **jumpers** are unjacketed groupings of twisted pairs. At the horizontal cross-connect, the length of these patch cords and jumpers must not exceed 6 meters
(20 feet). The length of the work area cord should not exceed 3 meters (10 feet).

Several types of distribution media are recommended for horizontal distribution systems:

- Four-pair, 100-ohm UTP cable
- Two-pair, 150-ohm shielded twisted-pair (STP-A) cable
- Two-fiber, 62.5/125-μm fiber-optic cable

Note that 50-ohm coaxial cable is still an approved medium, but is no longer recommended for new installations.

Hybrid cables contain multiple types of media under a single sheath. You can use hybrid cables for horizontal distribution if each recognized cable type meets transmission requirements and color-code specifications. A hybrid cable that contains both fiber-optic cable and copper conductors may be called **composite cable**.

When considering the use of hybrid cables, keep the following points in mind:

- 100-ohm UTP cables of mixed categories should not reside within the same sheath.

- The cables of a hybrid cable must meet crosstalk specifications.

- You must be able to distinguish hybrid UTP cables from multipair UTP backbone cables.

Each work area must be equipped with at least two telecommunications outlets/connectors. Associate one outlet with voice and the other with data. The first outlet must be a 4-pair, 100-ohm UTP cable, Category 3 or higher. The second outlet may be supported by any of the following media:

- Four-pair, 100-ohm UTP Category 5 cable

- Two-fiber, 50/125-μm fiber-optic cable

- Two-fiber, 62.5/125-μm fiber-optic cable

Work Area Components for Horizontal Distribution

Work area cables are the modular cords that connect the telecommunications outlet to the work area equipment. This equipment includes telephones, fax machines, data terminals, and computers. Work areas often require many changes, so you should design them to allow such changes.

The modular cord in the work area should have a maximum length of 3 meters (10 feet), and all four-pair UTP cables must be terminated in eight-position modular jacks (RJ-45) in the work area, following the T-568 standard. The telecommunications outlet/connector (Figure 5-11) must meet standard interface and minimum reliability requirements. The connector must be mounted on the outlet faceplate to make it accessible for work area connections, and must terminate directly to the horizontal cable with **insulation displacement connections (IDCs)**. IDCs connect copper wire in a manner that makes it unnecessary to strip the insulation away from the wire, because the connecting hardware has receptacles that house a small piece of metal capable of piercing the insulation.

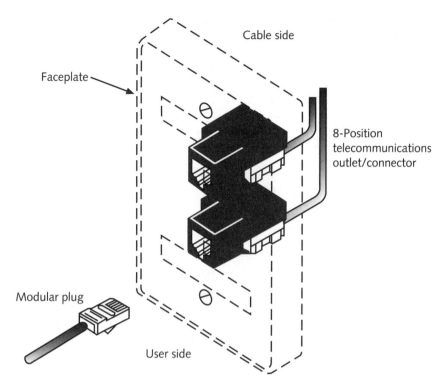

Cable side

Faceplate

8-Position
telecommunications
outlet/connector

Modular plug

User side

Figure 5-11   Typical telecommunications outlet (RJ-45)

The pin/pair assignment for 100-ohm UTP cable should follow the two widely accepted wiring schemes in the T-568 standard: T-568-A and T-568-B. They use the same colors of the cable color code, but they switch the positions of the white/green pair and the white/orange pair. When adding work areas to an existing system, be sure to identify which configuration is in use, and make certain that you follow it on all additions. Figure 5-12 shows the telecommunications outlet pin/pair designation, along with both configurations of the T-568 standard.

Pin Number	T-568-A	T-568-B
1	White-green	White-orange
2	Green-white	Orange-white
3	White-orange	White-green
4	Blue-white	Blue-white
5	White-blue	White-blue
6	Orange-white	Green-white
7	White-brown	White-brown
8	Brown-white	Brown-white

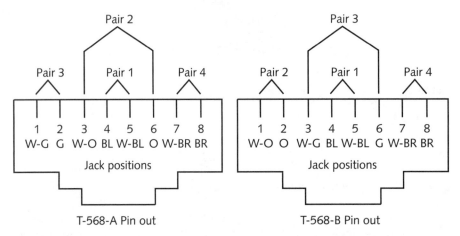

Figure 5-12   Telecommunications outlet pin/pair designation for T-568-A and T-568-B

Horizontal Cables and Their Cross-Connects

Link each telecommunications outlet to the horizontal cross-connect with a dedicated 4-pair, 24-AWG, Category 5 (or 5e) UTP cable. The length of this horizontal cable should not exceed 90 meters. If you must exceed this limit, make provisions for additional telecommunications rooms on the same floor.

The horizontal cross-connect consists of cable terminations and cabling hardware to help link the horizontal cables to the telecommunications and control equipment. Use the BIX or 110 IDC cross-connect system with modular RJ-45 patch panels to connect either voice or data cabling. Note that the horizontal cables for voice, data, video, and control services should be terminated on different fields.

The horizontal cross-connect is located in the TR. Each floor should have at least one TR; provide additional TRs when the total floor area to be served exceeds 1000 square meters (10,000 square feet) or the maximum horizontal cable run exceeds 90 meters (295 feet).

DOCUMENTING THE CABLE PLANT

The **cable plant** includes all the cables and termination points in an installation, such as work area outlets, patch panels, and punch-down blocks. The cable plant information is probably the most useful and important component of your documentation—once cables are run through ceilings or floors and terminated, finding a particular cable that is causing problems can be almost impossible if you didn't label it. Also, the cable plant documentation tells you which cables can and cannot be disconnected when you move equipment or make other changes.

Unfortunately, the cable plant documentation is also the most disliked by professionals. It is tedious and difficult. Installing cable is a physical job; it's hard to think about labeling cables, jacks, and patch panels while standing at the top of a ladder with your head inside a hot ceiling. However, no matter how much you just want to finish the job and move on, taking the extra time to label components during installation can save you time and headaches later.

The following sections discuss how to document your cable plant. You will learn how to document cable terminations, create cut sheets, and describe cable runs, patch panels, and jacks. These sections also explain how to document cable test results and known problems with a cable plant.

Documenting Cable Types and Terminations

Begin your cable plant documentation by describing the types of cables you use in your network, their purposes, and the types of terminations you use. This documentation expands on the network description you studied in Chapter 4. You should list each area of the network that uses a different type of cable and termination. In addition, you should list any exceptions you made during an installation. These entries provide valuable information to people who may need to know which materials and standards were used during installation. Entries in this section may look like the following example:

- Patch panels:
  - Hubble CAT5e 568-A (floor 1 main distribution facility (MDF))
  - Otronics CAT5e 568-A (floor 1 intermediate distribution facility (IDF) and floor 3 IDF)
  - Siemon CAT5e 568-A (floor 2 IDF)
  - Punched down with Harris 110 punch-down tool
- Horizontal cabling:
  - Category 5e, blue, plenum-rated, Lucent
  - EIA/TIA-568-A termination
  - Verified to have a maximum of 0.5-inch untwist at termination point
  - Tested with Paladin LANpro Navigator to CAT5e standard

Using Cut Sheets

A **cut sheet** is a document, usually in tabular form, that lists each cable run. A cut sheet should include information on the connection made by the cable, the length of the run, the cable ID and type of cable, the patch-panel port you used, and an indication of whether the cable is currently in use. You should also document whether the cable run has been tested, and the test result. The cut sheet demonstrates that the network infrastructure is documented and tested, and that you know where everything is located.

The cut sheet lets you quickly see the points connected by every cable, and the cables' status. Cut sheets are key items in your documentation, so you must keep them accurate and up to date. For example, you can use a cut sheet to locate any unused cables in an area where you could add workstations or replace failed cable. Table 5-2 shows a typical cut sheet.

Table 5-2   Cut sheet for intermediate distribution facility on the third floor

Connection	Cable ID	Patch Panel/ Port	Length (feet)	Test Status	Use Status	Cable Type
IDF3 to Room 301	301-001	PP1-IDF3/15	77	OK	Used	CAT5e
IDF3 to Room 301	301-002	PP1-IDF3/26	72	OK	Used	CAT5e
IDF3 to Room 301	301-003	PP1-IDF3/11	79	OK	Used	CAT5e
IDF3 to Room 302	302-001	PP1-IDF3/17	129	OK	Used	CAT5e
IDF3 to Room 302	302-002	PP1-IDF3/29	137	Failed NEXT	Unused	CAT5e
IDF3 to Room 309	309-001	PP1-IDF3/21	114	OK	Used	CAT5e
IDF3 to MDF	IDF3 MDF-01	FP1-IDF3/01	229	OK	Used	MM-Fiber

Labeling

Label all cable runs, equipment, patch panels, and jacks with a name or number that clearly identifies them. Use a naming convention that conveys necessary information, then be consistent with your labeling throughout the network. Labels are like street signs and building addresses; they can help you locate any element of a network.

Labeling Cable Runs

You should always label cable runs on both ends of the cable, a few inches above its termination point. Typically, you label cable runs after terminating and testing them, to avoid having to replace labels. If you must redo a termination, you must remove more of the cable jacket, which could damage the label.

The least expensive way to label cables is to use a permanent marker. You can also use preprinted wire markers, which contain self-adhesive numbers. These are both proven methods, but if you have a lot of labeling to do, try a professional cable labeler. These handheld units print vinyl labels that adhere to cables, jacks, and patch panels.

To help you locate cables later, your labels should indicate the room where the cable is going. Always make sure that the label ID matches the cable ID on your cut sheet. If you use a cable tester that identifies, stores, and prints test results, you can identify the test result with the same ID you use for the cable label.

Labeling Patch Panels and Jacks

You should label each patch panel with a unique name or number, and then include these IDs in your documentation. Label jacks on their faceplates, and specify the ports to which their patch panels are connected.

Decide on a naming convention for the patch panels, then apply a label to each patch panel in the network. For example, an informative naming scheme for IDF patch panels on the third floor of a building might include IDs such as PP1-IDF3, PP2-IDF3, PP3-IDF3, and so on. Patch panels on the second floor might have such names as PP1-IDF2, PP2-IDF2, and so on. You must use a naming scheme that conveys necessary information and stays consistent throughout the network.

After you name the patch panels, you can label the jacks with associated patch panel and port information. For example, a jack on the third floor whose cable goes to the seventh port on patch panel 2 in IDF3 might be labeled PP2-IDF3/07. This information would appear in the Patch Panel/Port column of the cut sheet. Using this type of scheme makes it easier to connect, disconnect, and move the workstation plugged into a particular jack. Post a copy of each cut sheet in the appropriate IDF to help technicians determine where each port is connected on each patch panel.

Documenting Cable Test Results and Problems with the Cable Plant

Installing, testing, and labeling cable runs can be hot, difficult, tedious work. The best part of cable testing is hearing that satisfying tone from the testing device when a cable passes all its tests. You can then label the cable and move on to the next one.

If you have a cable tester that can store test results for later printing, take full advantage of it. It provides proof that cables were tested against applicable standards, and that they passed the tests. After you complete the testing, attach the tester to a PC serial port and import the results into a spreadsheet or similar document. You can then add this spreadsheet to your documentation manual.

If your cable tester does not have such capabilities, then document your test results the old-fashioned way—with pen and paper. When you record the results, include the cable ID, the time and date of the test, the equipment used, and the tester's name. Most testers also record the length of the cable so it can be transferred to the cut sheet. If your tester does not report the cable length, you can determine it yourself by calculating the difference between the footage markings at each end of the cable.

When you have concerns about the cable plant, or you know of specific problems, include them in the documentation. For example, you can describe any anomalies that may have occurred during installation or testing, such as a significant number (more than 1 percent) of failed cable tests. Later, you can investigate why the failure rate was so high. Perhaps the cabling was substandard, or maybe a number of cables were too close to a large EMI source; whatever the ultimate reason, you should note the problem in case it becomes an issue later.

DOCUMENTING EQUIPMENT ROOMS

You need to describe each equipment room in detail in your documentation. Include the room location and room dimensions, as well as the types of doorways, ceilings, walls, cooling, heating, and lighting used. The ANSI/EIA/TIA-569-A standard defines guidelines for designing and configuring equipment rooms. (Chapter 4 discusses this standard in more detail.)

Describing Cable Runs and Areas Served

In addition to describing the physical parameters of the equipment room, you should document all the cables in each equipment room and the building areas that each room serves. The following text shows some sample documentation:

> *"Entering the room through conduit 3 in the southeast corner is a bundle of 33 Category 5e cables that serve rooms 301, 302, 303, and 305. Conduit 2, in the center of the west wall, has a 24-strand multimode fiber cable that runs to the MDF. Four fiber strands are in use."*

This type of detailed information gives future readers sufficient knowledge to make any needed changes and additions with confidence. If building renovations are necessary, this information can help prevent cable breaks and other accidents.

Describing Devices and Their Location in Each Room

These descriptions are the most frequently used part of your equipment room documentation. Before you make additions or changes to the network, you need to know which devices are in each equipment room, and their capacities. Before you can add workstations in any area, you must determine whether the patch panels, hubs, or switches in the relevant equipment room have enough available ports to accommodate the additions. For example, Table 5-3 shows documentation for an IDF on the third floor of a building where you plan to add workstations.

Table 5-3   IDF3 equipment list

Device Type	Device Name	Location #	Ports/# Ports Free
Category 5e patch panel	PP1-IDF3	Rack 1	48/4
	PP2-IDF3	Rack 1	48/0
	PP3-IDF3	Rack 2	24/2
3Com 4005 Switch	MS1-IDF3	Rack 1	40/5
3Com Superstack 4300	H2-IDF3	Rack 1	48/6
	H3-IDF3	Rack 2	48/0

5

Documenting Power Considerations in Equipment Rooms

Many network devices require considerable power to operate, and some even have special electrical outlet requirements. Examine each equipment room to determine the type and number of available power outlets. After the equipment installation is complete, document the power budget, including how much total power is available to the room (in watts or volt-amps), and how much power is in use. This documentation helps you decide whether the equipment room can handle additional devices.

For the primary equipment room, you must also know how many power circuits are available. Most major equipment comes with redundant power supplies. You should plug each one into a different circuit so the equipment can continue to operate if one circuit loses power.

Most equipment rooms use an uninterruptible power supply (UPS) to power network devices in case of a power interruption. Your documentation should specify the type and number of UPSs in each equipment room, the number of outlets available, and the power budget for each UPS. Larger UPS models have significant current requirements, and some have special outlet requirements. You should include this information in your documentation.

Diagramming Equipment Racks and Installed Equipment

Provide detailed drawings of your equipment racks, with the installed devices shown and labeled. The drawings should show the physical location of the racks in the equipment room, or you can write a description of the location. These drawings are an excellent way for other readers of your documentation to learn about the network without having to visit each equipment room. At a minimum, you should include the rack name and location (e.g., Rack1-IDF3 west wall); the patch panel name, type, and ports (e.g., PP1-IDF3: 48-port CAT5e patch panel); the switch or hub name, type, and ports (e.g., SW1-IDF3: 24-port 10/100); the UPS name and type (e.g., UPS1-IDF3: Smart-UPS 1000); and the manufacturer, part number, and serial number.

Documenting Known Problems or Concerns with Equipment Rooms

In this section of the documentation, you include information about any rooms that do not meet specifications for cooling, power, or lighting. Also include any steps you plan or recommend to address these concerns. This documentation demonstrates that you recognize the concerns and have taken initial steps to resolve them.

CHAPTER SUMMARY

❑ Backbone distribution systems provide the interconnection between telecommunications rooms, equipment rooms, and entrance facilities. The two types of backbone distribution systems are the interbuilding system, which connects other buildings to the main cross-connect, and the intrabuilding system, which provides connections between the floors of a multistory building.

❑ The maximum recommended distances for backbone cables depend on their application. For example, the maximum distance for data applications is 90 meters (295 feet). For voice applications, the maximum distances vary among the different cross-connects.

❑ When planning multipair (backbone) cable spaces, you should stay as far away as possible from power cables, transformers, electrical motors, and fluorescent lighting.

❑ A typical fiber backbone installation consists of one fiber-optic cable, usually in counts of 6, 12, or 24 fibers, that runs between the main cross-connect and each TR.

❑ Backbone distribution systems usually employ a hierarchical star topology with one or more levels. Horizontal distribution systems use a simple star topology.

❑ The horizontal distribution is the part of the cabling system used to distribute, support, and provide access to the horizontal cabling. This cabling system provides the physical means for transporting signals between the telecommunications outlet/connector in the work area and the horizontal cross-connect in the TR. The cabling and its associated connecting hardware make up the content of the horizontal pathway and related spaces.

❑ Work area components for horizontal distribution include telephones, fax machines, data terminals, and computers, plus any other items located between these components and the telecommunications outlet.

❑ Your cable plant documentation includes all the cables and termination points in an installation, such as work area outlets, patch panels, and punch-down blocks. The cable plant information is probably the most useful and important component of your documentation—once cables are run through ceilings or floors and terminated, finding a particular cable that is causing problems can be almost impossible if you didn't label it.

❏ Describe each equipment room in detail in your documentation. Include information for all cable runs, devices, racks, power considerations, and known problems or concerns. This documentation makes additions and changes easier, provides port information to accommodate additions, and identifies all equipment and its locations.

KEY TERMS

backbone distribution system — The portion of the premises distribution system that provides connections among entrance facilities, equipment rooms, and telecommunications rooms.

binder group — A group of 25 twisted pairs in a large-pair-count cable. Each binder group is identified with a uniquely colored binder.

BIX — The trade name of a NORDX/CDT in-building termination and cross-connect system for unshielded twisted-pair (UTP) cables.

cable plant — All the cables and termination points in an installation, including work area outlets, patch panels, and punch-down blocks.

campus environment — A group of related buildings.

composite cable — A hybrid cable that contains both fiber-optic cable and copper conductors.

consolidation point — An intermediate interconnection point for horizontal cabling.

cross-connects — A group of wall- or rack-mounted connection points used to mechanically terminate and administer building wiring.

cut sheet — A document, usually in tabular form, that lists each cable run.

fiber-optic cable — An assembly of one or more optical fibers with strengthening material and an outer jacket.

horizontal cabling — The portion of a structured cabling system that connects the telecommunications room and the work area.

horizontal cross-connect (HC) — A method of connecting horizontal cabling to intrabuilding backbone cabling or equipment cable by using connection hardware and jumpers or patch cords.

hybrid cable — A telecommunications cable that contains two or more types of conductors, such as UTP and optical-fiber cable.

insulation displacement connections (IDCs) — Copper wire connected in a manner that makes it unnecessary to strip the insulation away from the wire, because the connecting hardware has receptacles that house a small piece of metal capable of piercing the insulation.

interbuilding backbone — A backbone network that provides communications between buildings.

intermediate cross-connect (IC) — A cross-connection between first- and second-level backbone.

intrabuilding backbone — A backbone network that provides communications within a building.

jumper — An unjacketed grouping of twisted pairs used between connection hardware to cross-connect backbones, equipment, and horizontal cabling.

main cross-connect (MC) — The primary connection and flexibility point for intrabuilding backbone cabling and equipment cables.

patch cord — A length of stranded copper wire or optical-fiber cable with connectors at each end to join telecommunications circuits at a cross-connect point.

Plastic Insulated Conductor (PIC) cable — Twisted-pair cable designed to ease cable-pair identification.

premises distribution system — A generic term that includes both backbone and horizontal cabling and all their components.

riser cable — Main distribution cable segments that run between floors or sections of a building. This cable is more correctly known as backbone cable.

splicing — The joining of two or more segments of wire to create one continuous wire.

star topology — A LAN configuration in which nodes are connected individually to one common point (or "hub"). The hub can be active when it regenerates signals, or passive when it does nothing except provide a physical connection between machines.

work area — An area where users operate workstations or PCs.

work area cables — The modular cords that connect the telecommunications outlet to the network interface card (NIC) in the work area.

REVIEW QUESTIONS

1. Backbone systems normally provide which of the following two types of connections?

   a. innerbuilding and extrabuilding

   b. interbuilding and intrabuilding

   c. intrabuilding and innerbuilding

   d. extrabuilding and intrabuilding

2. Design requirements for voice and data backbones are the same; both are stringent and very complex. True or False?

3. What are the two main topology options for designing intrabuilding backbone cabling?

   a. star and hierarchical star

   b. bus and star

   c. hierarchical ring and star

   d. hierarchical star and bus

4. The same telecommunications room can house connecting hardware to serve the function of intermediate and horizontal connections. True or False?

5. What is the ideal location for the main cross-connect?

   a. in the telecommunications rooms of every building

   b. near or in the main equipment room

   c. near or in the telecommunications room of the main building

   d. near or with the intermediate cross-connect system

6. What is the advantage of using a one-level hierarchical star for the interbuilding backbone?

   a. It allows easy maintenance and security against unauthorized access.

   b. It provides increased flexibility.

   c. It allows for the easy addition of future interbuilding backbones.

   d. all of the above

7. What are the most recognized cable types for backbone systems?

   a. single-mode optical fiber and 100-ohm twisted-pair

   b. 100-ohm twisted-pair and thin coaxial cable

   c. thin coaxial cable and single-mode optical fiber

   d. single-mode optical fiber and 80-ohm twisted-pair

8. When a single cable type does not satisfy all user requirements, you may use more than one medium in backbone wiring, as long as these media use different facility architecture and different locations for cross-connects. True or False?

9. Which of the following should you consider when choosing transmission media?

   a. required useful life of backbone wiring

   b. flexibility of the medium with respect to supported services

   c. site size and user population

   d. all of the above

10. The more uncertain the requirements are, the more flexible the backbone wiring system must be. True or False?

11. Using the same backbone cabling for voice and data is recommended for operations, administration, and maintenance. True or False?

12. When using optical fiber for a backbone, what can you do to satisfy present and future needs?

    a. Use only single-mode fiber.

    b. Use only multimode fiber.

    c. Use both multimode and single-mode fiber.

    d. Use a 12-fiber optical fiber.

13. The main cross-connect is the primary connection and flexibility point within a network, because it provides _____.

    a. a means of terminating and cross-connecting intrabuilding backbone cables

    b. a means of terminating and cross-connecting backbone cables from entrance facilities

    c. a means of terminating and cross-connecting interbuilding backbone cables and equipment cables at one common administration point

    d. all of the above

14. Which of the following considerations is important for the location of the equipment room?

    a. Locate it away from electromagnetic interference.

    b. Expansion of the equipment room should not be restricted by building components.

    c. It must be accessible for the delivery of large equipment.

    d. all of the above

15. What equipment is recommended to terminate riser cable pairs?

    a. a 66 cross-connect system and a 110 cross-connect system

    b. a 110 cross-connect system and a BIX cross-connect system

    c. a 14,000 cross-connect system and a BIX cross-connect system

    d. a BIX cross-connect system and a 66 cross-connect system

16. What is the recommended size of an optical fiber cross-connect, and where should it be installed?

    a. a 6-fiber cable for every telecommunications room

    b. a 24-fiber cable for the main cross-connect

    c. a 24-fiber cable for every telecommunications room

    d. a 12-fiber cable for every telecommunications room

17. Why are horizontal cabling systems needed?

    a. They provide the physical means for transporting telecommunications signals between the work area outlet and the horizontal cross-connect in the TR.

    b. They provide the cable and connecting hardware.

    c. They provide distribution support.

    d. They provide the pathway between the work area outlet and the TR.

18. Which of the following is NOT a topology rule you should follow for horizontal distribution?

    a. It must follow a star topology.

    b. You must connect the work area outlet to a horizontal cross-connect in a TR on a different floor.

    c. You must connect the work area outlet to a horizontal cross-connect in a TR on the same floor.

    d. Bridged taps and splices are not permitted.

19. What is the maximum distance allowed for horizontal distribution?

    a. 90 feet

    b. 100 feet

    c. 100 meters

    d. 90 meters

20. Which of the following is recommended for use as a distribution medium?

    a. four-pair, 100-ohm UTP

    b. two-fiber, 62.5-125 mm optical fiber

    c. two-pair, 150-ohm STP-A

    d. all of the above

21. Each work area must be equipped with _____.

    a. one outlet (one for voice and data)

    b. two outlets (one for voice and one for data)

    c. three outlets (one for voice and two for data)

    d. four outlets (two for voice and two for data)

22. Which of the following is NOT considered a work area component?

    a. telephones

    b. computers

    c. fax machines

    d. typewriters

23. How are 4-pair, 100-ohm, twisted-pair cables terminated in the work area?

    a. on a 66 connector

    b. on a four-position modular jack

    c. on an eight-position modular jack

    d. on a six-position modular jack

5

24. What are the configurations of pin/pair assignments for 100-ohm UTP?

    a. T-556-A and T-556-B

    b. T-568-A and T-568-B

    c. IEC 60603-7 and IDC

    d. 568A–ISDN and 568B–ALT

25. Every floor should have at least one telecommunications room. Additional rooms should be provided when the total floor area served exceeds _____, or the maximum horizontal cable run exceeds _____.

    a. 10,000 meters, 90 feet

    b. 1000 meters, 100 feet

    c. 1000 square meters, 100 meters

    d. 1000 square meters, 90 meters

HANDS-ON PROJECTS

Project 5-1

Being able to design the backbone system for your building(s) will be an important part of your job. In this exercise, you will design and draw the layout for a backbone system in a four-story office building.

1. Using a workstation that has Visio installed, start Visio and select a new drawing.

2. Design and draw the backbone cabling system between the building's main and horizontal cross-connects, using a star topology.

3. Print your drawing and save it as **Four-story Star**.

4. Open a new drawing in Visio.

5. Design and draw the same backbone cabling system, this time using a hierarchical star topology.

6. Print your drawing and save it as **Hierarchical Star**.

Project 5-2

For this exercise, refer to the two drawings you created in Project 5-1.

1. Explain how you created each topology design.

2. Explain why you created each topology in the manner you did.

3. Which topology design would you choose for the building, and why?

Project 5-3

In this exercise, design and draw the layout of a backbone system for a small, local college. The college has the following five buildings, which need to be part of the same network: Administration (which includes the main equipment room), Networking, Electronics, the library, and labs. Each building has a telecommunications room (TR).

1. Using a workstation that has Visio installed, start Visio and open a new drawing.

2. Design and draw the Administration building. Show the location of the main equipment room.

3. Design and draw the other four buildings, including the location of each TR.

4. In your drawing, show the location of the main cross-connect and indicate how you would connect each building to it.

Project 5-4

Describe the basic star topology and its options. Discuss when and why you would use each option.

Project 5-5

The local college for which you designed a backbone system in Project 5-3 has received a grant from the state and will be expanding. The expansion includes a new building next to Administration for Student Services, two new buildings behind the Networking building, one new building behind Electronics for the Electronics lab, one building next to Electronics for multimedia, and one building next to the library for an open lab.

College administrators were so pleased with your original design that they have asked you to design the backbone system for the expansion. The equipment room will remain in Administration. The main cross-connect will remain where it was in your previous project. Each new building will have its own TR. Design and draw the entire campus in Visio. Show how all cabling is being run, and label all TRs, intermediate cross-connects, and horizontal cross-connects.

Project 5-6

The local college is again happy with your work, and now wants you to create a design specification for the work areas in each of the new buildings. Each building has two stories, and all of the buildings have the same floor plan: 16 classrooms (eight on each side of the corridor), men's and women's lavatories, a storage closet, and a TR. Each classroom must accommodate 30 workstations, 10 dial-up modems (one for every three workstations), and 15 telephone outlets (one for every two workstations).

Draw a design of a basic building floor plan and a basic classroom within the building. Show all cable runs, including where and how they will be run, and their uses.

CASE PROJECTS

Case Project 1

For the new design you created in Project 5-3, write a summary of your design specifications. Include the approximate size of each building, the distance from each building to the main cross-connect, the cable type(s), hardware, and topology you are using, and the number of pairs that will be available for the horizontal cross-connects and backbone system. Explain your reasons for each choice.

Case Project 2

For the new design you created in Project 5-5, write a summary of your design specifications. Include the approximate size of each building, the distance from each building to the main cross-connect, the cable type(s), hardware, and topology you are using, and the number of pairs that will be available for the horizontal cross-connects and backbone system. Explain your reasons for each choice.

Case Project 3

For the new design you created in Project 5-6, write a summary of your design specifications. Include the approximate size of the room, the distance from the room to the intermediate cross-connect, the cable type(s) and topology you are using, the number of cables per workstation, and the workstation hardware you are using. Explain your reasons for each choice.

Case Project 4

The design specification summaries you completed in the three preceding cases provide a foundation for building a complete documentation manual. Use the documentation sections from the first five chapters and your summaries from the three cases to create a documentation manual for the college's network.

6

CABLE TERMINATION AND SPLICING

After reading this chapter and completing the exercises, you will be able to:

- Name the various locations for cable termination
- Splice wire and cable
- Discuss the "tools of the trade" for cable termination
- Understand the color codes and wiring schemes used for cable termination
- Terminate cable
- Document network hardware

The process of connecting cables to workstation outlets, connecting blocks, and cable connectors is called cable termination. This chapter discusses the various locations where you terminate cable, the connecting devices and tools you need, and the steps required for termination. You will also have opportunities to use the tools and practice terminating cable.

In addition, you sometimes need to splice cables if they are damaged or need to be extended. This chapter covers splicing in detail.

LOCATIONS FOR TERMINATING CABLE

After you complete your system design, select and run your cable, and implement all necessary grounding and bonding, you need to terminate your cables so the system will operate. One important place where cables are terminated is called the **network interface**, the **demarcation point**, or the demarc for short. At the demarc, control or ownership of the communications facilities changes from the external service provider's equipment to the customer's. (The external service provider is usually the local telephone company, or "Telco.") Cables must also be terminated in the equipment room, the telecommunications rooms, and the work areas. The way you terminate the cable depends on its location and type; each of these locations requires different equipment and tools for termination, as you will see in the following sections.

Everywhere you terminate cables, you must test them for faults such as shorts, opens, and reversals. You must also ensure that the cables comply with appropriate standards. See Chapter 8 for more details.

Network Interface Devices and Demarcation Points

Demarcation points are defined in Section 68.3 of Federal Communications Commission Rule 68. **Network interface devices**, the equipment used to terminate cable at demarcation points, are required by the same rule. Rule 68 was designed to ensure that customer equipment and wiring could be connected to the Telco network without causing harm. Network interface devices also permit all customer equipment and wiring to be disconnected from the Telco wiring for testing and maintenance. When the equipment and wiring are disconnected, direct access to the Telco network is provided through an industry-registered jack of a type specified in Rule 68.

The number of pairs you use in the Telco and customer cables is the primary factor in selecting equipment for cable termination at the demarc. Several network interface devices are available for use at the demarcation point; each device is designed to accommodate a maximum number of cable pairs.

Network interface devices generally fall into one of two categories: those used for small systems and those used for large systems. Small systems include residences and small businesses that have one to six telephone lines or cable pairs. Large systems include large companies and commercial buildings with multiple tenants; these buildings and companies can have several hundred telephone lines or cable pairs. The following sections describe each system in more detail.

Small Systems

Network interface devices for small systems come in several sizes and types. The device shown in Figure 6-1 is one of the most commonly used types for small systems; it can accommodate one to six cable pairs.

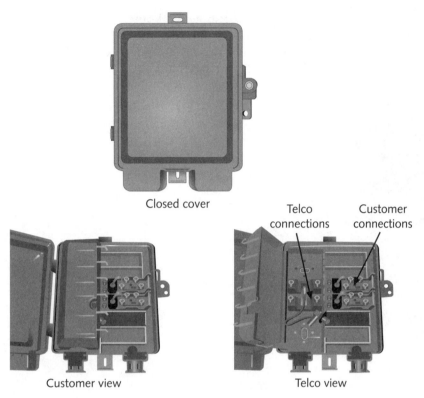

Closed cover

Telco connections   Customer connections

Customer view   Telco view

Figure 6-1   Small-system network interface device

The network interface device for these small systems is a box that is usually made of high-impact, waterproof plastic. The box is divided into two sections. One section is used to terminate the Telco cables; it includes a connecting block with two screw terminals, a standard modular jack, an earth ground connection, and a **protector**, a series of fuses that protect lines and cables from lightning and power surges. There is one screw terminal, protector, and modular jack per cable pair.

The other section of the box is used for terminating customer wiring. The customer section is designed with a **terminal strip**, which is a piece of metal with attached screws for connecting the wire pair. This section also includes a standard modular plug, which is wired to the terminal strip and plugs into the jack wired to the Telco section. Each cable pair has one terminal strip and modular plug.

Large Systems

Network interface devices for large systems are quite different from those for smaller systems. Using terminal strips with screws and modular plugs to terminate cable for large systems—especially a system with more than 10 or 15 cable pairs—would be tedious, untidy work for a technician.

A primary component of the large-system network interface device is a **punch-down block**, a rectangular block of plastic with metal connectors that are split through their center and embedded in the plastic. The two most common types of punch-down blocks are 50-pair 66-types and 50-pair M110-types; both are shown in Figure 6-2.

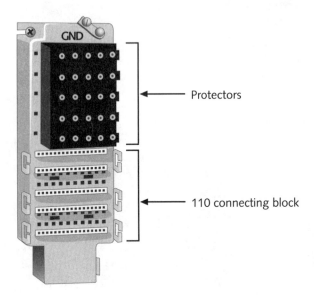

Figure 6-2   Large-system network interface device with protector

BIX and Krone also offer termination devices (Figure 6-3), although they are rarely used because of their proprietary designs and higher prices.

Other components in a network interface device for large systems include protectors and a wood backboard for indoor installations (Figure 6-4), or an enclosed, metal wall-terminal box for outdoor installations, as shown in Figure 6-5. When working with large systems, you will often find the demarcation point indoors, in the entrance room or equipment room.

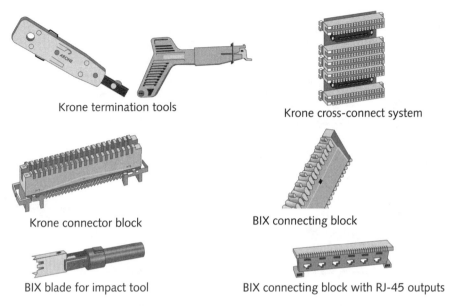

Figure 6-3   BIX and Krone connectors and termination equipment

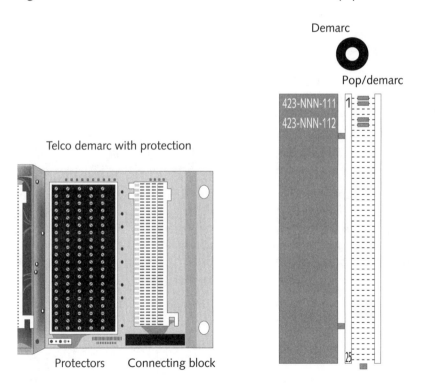

Figure 6-4   Indoor entrance facility demarc with protector

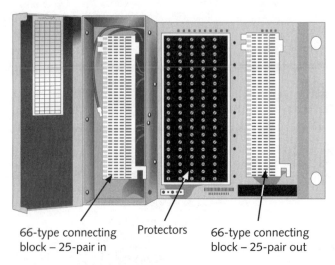

66-type connecting   Protectors   66-type connecting
block – 25-pair in   block – 25-pair out

Figure 6-5   Outside wall terminal demarc with protector

Equipment Rooms and Telecommunications Rooms

Whether you terminate cables in equipment rooms or telecommunications rooms, you use the same types of termination equipment. In equipment rooms, you usually have backbone cabling to terminate and cross-connect to your telecommunications equipment. Sometimes this cabling is also the demarcation point for your building, so you need to terminate these cables as well, and cross-connect them to your telecommunications system. In the telecommunications rooms, you generally need to terminate and cross-connect only the horizontal and backbone cables.

Two common methods are used for terminating cables in these rooms. The first method is to terminate the cables on punch-down blocks that are wall-mounted on wood panels. A typical wall-mounting arrangement for punch-down blocks is shown in Figure 6-6.

The second method is to terminate the cable on rack-mounted patch panels. The patch panels have punch-down blocks on the back for cables and modular receptacles on the front for plugging in patch cords, as shown in Figure 6-7. When using patch panels, you must use one set of panels for horizontal cables and another set of panels for backbone cable. When all the cables are terminated on the patch panels, you can use the patch cords to cross-connect the horizontal cables to the backbone.

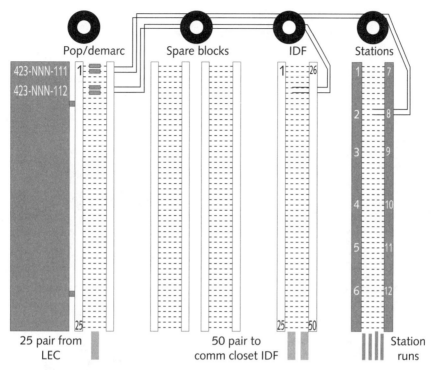

Figure 6-6   Wall-mounted system in equipment rooms and telecommunications rooms

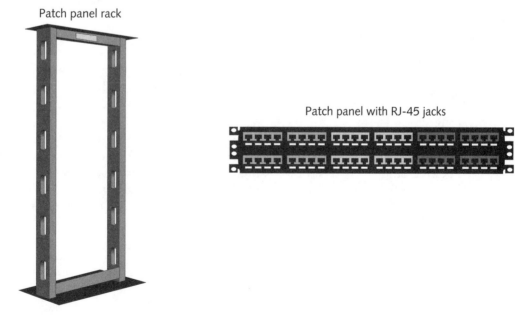

Figure 6-7   Rack and patch panel

An additional termination method, wire wrapping, is used primarily on distribution frames in Telco central offices. You make a wire wrap connection by coiling the wire around the sharp corners of a square terminal post under mechanical tension supplied by a wrap tool. The terminal post must be square, because its corners dig into the wire to form a gas-tight connection. Figure 6-8 shows wire wrap terminal blocks and wire-wrapping tools.

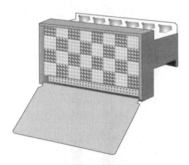

Wire wrap block

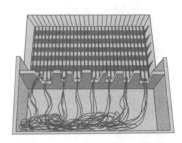

Wire wrap block with wiring completed

Mechanical wire wrap gun

Electric wire wrap gun

Figure 6-8   Wire wrap terminal blocks and tools

Work Areas

Cable termination in the work area requires terminating the horizontal cable to a telecommunications outlet (jack), which provides connectivity between the telecommunications equipment and the cables (Figure 6-9). A telecommunications cord provides the interface between a piece of telecommunications equipment and a telecommunications outlet. There are literally thousands of telecommunications outlets from which to choose. When you take a closer look, however, you find that the biggest difference is the color of the jacks.

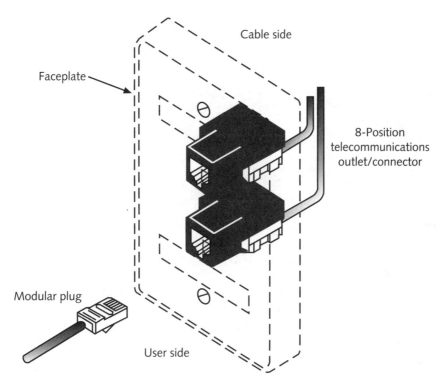

Figure 6-9   Telecommunications outlet

Telecommunications Outlets

Telecommunications outlets are available in configurations of 2-pair (4-position/RJ-11), 3-pair (6-position/RJ-25), and 4-pair (8-position/RJ-45). All of the jacks are available in two designs: a flat-plate, or flush-mount, jack and a box, or biscuit or surface-mount, jack. A flush-mount jack is a flat, rectangular jack plate with the cable-connecting interface on the back and a female receptacle for the telecommunications cord on the front; the plate is attached to an outlet box in the wall.

A surface-mount jack is a covered square or rectangular plastic box; the cable-connecting interface is inside the box, and a female receptacle is on one outside edge. The box is usually attached directly to a wall that does not have an outlet box. Occasionally you see surface-mount jacks on the backs of desks, on credenzas or bookcases, or in a safe location on the floor, like under a desk. None of these locations is recommended.

The cable-connecting interface (connector) for telecommunications jacks is available in three styles. The oldest design has screw terminals for connecting your wires. Using this type of jack requires you to remove some of the insulation from the wire pairs so the bare copper can be placed under the screws for termination, as shown in Figure 6-10.

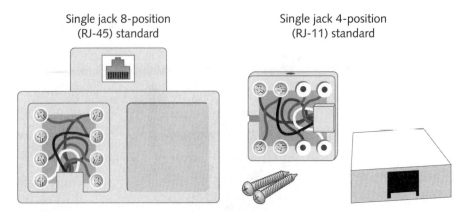

Figure 6-10   Surface-mount jacks with screw terminals

The other two designs use the M110-type of connector, but the wires are connected to the device differently in each design. One of the M110-type connectors requires that the wires be connected using a punch-down tool with an M110 blade. A **punch-down tool** is an impact tool that you push against the wire to force it into the center split in the metal and cut the excess wire off. This method does not require the insulation to be removed from the wires, because M110 connectors are the IDC type, as shown in Figure 6-11.

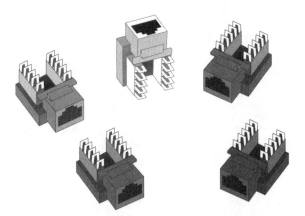

Figure 6-11   Flush-mount jacks with 110-type punch-down terminals

The second M110-type of connector comes with hard plastic caps that fit over the cable connector grooves (wire guides). All you need to do is lay the wires in the grooves, place the cap over the top, and press down until it snaps into place. Like the previous method, this method does not require removing the insulation from the cable; the caps perform a similar function as the punch-down tool, as Figure 6-12 shows.

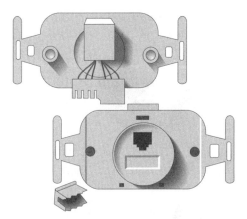

Figure 6-12 Flush-mount jack with 110-type toolless terminals

The jacks used for fiber-optic cable are similar to those used for copper. Multimode fiber is more commonly used than single-mode fiber; however, the jacks for both types are almost identical.

Telecommunications Cords

Telecommunications cords provide connectivity between the telecommunications equipment and the telecommunications outlet. These cords, also called silver satin cords, are typically made of filament-like strands of copper wires that are twisted together around a cotton-like material. Each of these wires is insulated in a different color and laid flat, side by side and in a particular color order, depending on the application and use. Then all the wires are wrapped, still lying flat, in another coat of silver-colored insulation. Usually, each end of the cord has a modular male plug attached. This plug connects to the female receptacle in both the telecommunications outlet and the telecommunications equipment.

When you use fiber, the termination plugs have a different construction of fiber-optic connectors than those used for copper wire. In addition, you must connect the fiber-optic cable to an optical transmitter and an optical receiver before making any connections to the telecommunications equipment. A typical fiber-optic connector and jack are shown in Figure 6-13.

6

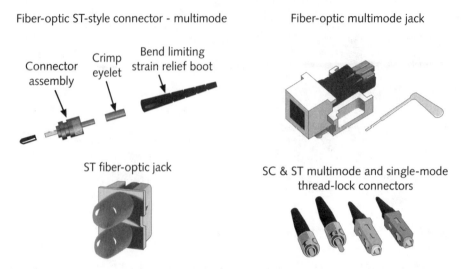

Fiber-optic ST-style connector - multimode

Fiber-optic multimode jack

Connector assembly

Crimp eyelet

Bend limiting strain relief boot

ST fiber-optic jack

SC & ST multimode and single-mode thread-lock connectors

Figure 6-13   Fiber-optic connector plugs and jacks

SPLICING WIRE AND CABLE

In the simplest sense, a **splice** is the connection of two wires, fibers, or cables. You can use splicing to solve a cabling problem during or after installation. You can splice cables when the distance of the run requires extension of the cable, or to repair a cable that has been cut or broken. The equipment and tools you can use for splicing depend on the location of the splice and the cable, and the type of cable being spliced.

Although there are hundreds of splicing options, vast amounts of available equipment, and many implementations for splicing, this discussion focuses on the most common splicing methods for copper and fiber-optic cable. The discussion also includes information about the equipment and tools you need for each of these methods.

Splicing Copper

Most of your splicing work will involve copper wire inside commercial buildings. The three primary methods of splicing copper wires are soldering, single-wire solderless crimping, and multiwire solderless connecting.

For many years, soldering was practically the only approved way to connect wires. It is still used for splicing, but the advent of easier, faster methods has made soldering much less popular. To splice wires using solder, you first strip about ½ inch of the insulation from each wire, then match each wire from one cable to the corresponding wire in the other cable. Next, you hold the two wires so the bare copper from each is touching the other, side by side. Then, you heat the wires with a soldering iron, apply solder to completely cover all bare copper, and wrap the solder splice completely with electrical tape or other insulating material. Repeat the process until all wires are spliced, then wrap all the splices together with an insulated covering or place them in an enclosure.

To make solderless, single-wire splice connections, use **B-wire connectors**, also known as "beanies" (Figure 6-14). Because of the beanie's construction, there is no need to strip or twist the wires. The outer portion of the beanie is a hard plastic, usually white, cylinder that is slightly wider at one end to allow the insertion of wires for splicing. Inside is a strip of metal that is almost twice as long as the outer casing; the metal's surface has small, needle-like projections that penetrate the wire's insulation when crimped, thus making contact. When you insert the strip of metal into the outer casing, it is bent in half so the needles face each other.

6

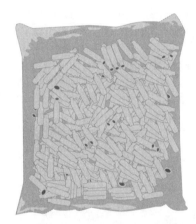

Figure 6-14   B-wire connectors

To make solderless, single-wire splice connections with a beanie:

1. Insert the wires you want to splice into the beanie's opening.

2. Hold the wires together so that an even amount of each wire (about 1 inch) is inside the beanie.

3. Using a wire-crimping tool or needle-nose pliers, crimp the beanie by squeezing it flat. When the casing is flat, the inner, needle-like projections pierce the wire insulation to complete the connection.

4. When you finish crimping the beanie, give it a few light tugs to make sure the wires are securely held inside and won't come loose.

Several manufacturers offer single-wire, solderless wire splices, although their installations are all similar and they work in the same way. In addition to the beanie, Scotchlok™ splices are popular. These splices are shown in Figure 6-15 with the necessary crimping tool.

Figure 6-15   Scotchlok splice and crimper

Beanies and Scotchlok splices save time and are easy to use, but they can't splice cables that have hundreds of pairs. For these cables, you need a multiwire splice connector that can splice 25 pairs at a time. This device is very similar to the 110 punch-down block, which uses an **insulation displacement connector (IDC)**. This device connects copper wires by piercing their insulation to make contact when you insert them into the IDC with an impact insertion tool. A typical 25-pair splice module and impact insertion tool are shown in Figure 6-16. You can use the splice module by itself or with any number of additional modules. You must house and protect 25-pair splice connectors in boxes, cases, or cabinets called **splice enclosures**, which are usually made of steel or metal (Figure 6-17).

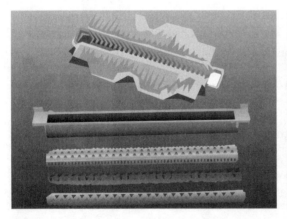
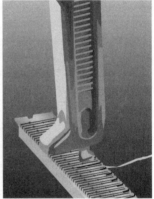

Figure 6-16   25-pair splice module and impact insertion tool

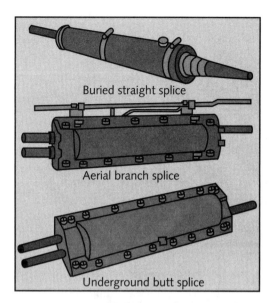

Buried straight splice

Aerial branch splice

Underground butt splice

Figure 6-17   Splice enclosures

A final method of splicing copper is a stopgap measure called "twist and tape." It is not defined by any code or standard; use it only in emergencies when extended system downtime could have dire consequences. Imagine receiving a frantic call from a nearby customer whose voice and data services are down because someone inadvertently cut the main feed cable from the demarc. To splice the 25-pair UTP cable properly, you would need equipment from a supplier that is more than one hour away, but the customer cannot afford another two to three hours of downtime. By going directly to the customer's premises, you can survey the damage, order necessary equipment from the supplier, and perform an emergency splice job to quickly restore the customer's service.

The "twist and tape" method consists of removing approximately 1 inch of insulation from each wire, then matching a wire from one side of the cut cable to the same wire on the other side. While holding the wires together, twist the bare copper ends around each other like a twist tie, making sure there are sufficient twists to hold the wires together. Then, wrap the wire with electrical tape, making sure that the tape completely covers the bare copper and extends down the wire's insulation about ½ inch. Repeat this procedure with each wire until all wire pairs are "spliced." The customer's services are thus restored in less than an hour, and you have time to go to the supplier, get the needed equipment, and return to the customer's location to make the proper splices.

Splicing Fiber

Fiber-optic splicing is the joining of two fiber cables, generally as a permanent solution. Although termination is the more common method of joining fibers, splicing typically results in lower light loss and back reflection. For these reasons, splicing is preferable when cable runs are too long for a single length of fiber, when you need to restore a severed cable, or when you need to join two different types of fiber cables, such as a 48-fiber cable and a 12-fiber cable.

 Before you try the following fiber-splicing procedures, you must read "Fiber-optic Safety" at the end of this section.

You can use one of two methods to splice fiber-optic cables: mechanical splicing or fusion splicing. **Mechanical splicing** uses simple alignment devices that hold the two fiber ends together precisely, enabling light to pass between fibers with losses as low as 0.3 dB. A typical mechanical splice and its related tools are shown in Figure 6-18.

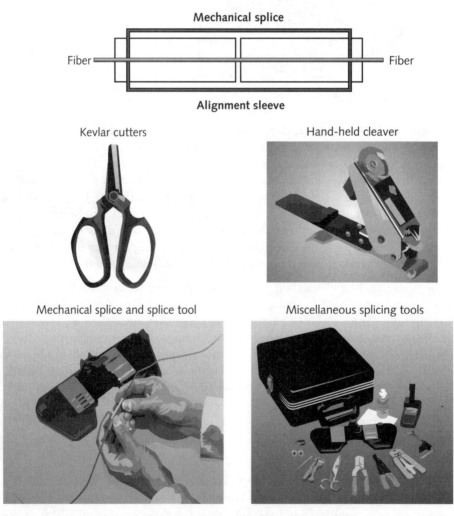

Figure 6-18 Mechanical splice and tools for fiber

Fusion splicing uses a machine that precisely aligns the two fiber ends, and then welds them together using heat or an electric arc. The resulting continuous connection between the fibers enables light transmissions with losses as low as 0.1 dB. Figure 6-19 shows a typical fusion splice and splice unit.

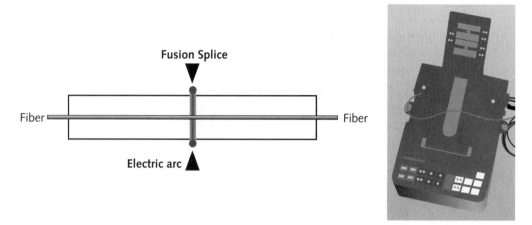

Figure 6-19 Fusion splice and splicing tool for fiber

Prices play a key role in choosing a splicing method. Mechanical splicing requires a fairly low initial investment ($1000 to $2000), but the cost per splice is significantly higher—from $12 to $40. By contrast, the cost per splice for fusion splicing ranges from $0.50 to $1.50, while the initial investment for fusion-splicing equipment is $15,000 to $50,000, depending on its accuracy and added features. Splicing equipment becomes more expensive as the precision and accuracy improve.

A cleaver is your most valuable tool for fiber splicing. For mechanical splices, you need a proper angle to ensure that light does not escape into the air gaps between the two fibers. A good cleaver for mechanical splicing costs $200 to $1000. Fusion splicing requires even more precise cleaving to achieve its exceptionally low losses; these cleavers cost $1000 to $4000. By following proper maintenance and operating procedures, you can ensure that your cleaver will last for years and splice fibers properly on every job.

The splicing method you choose also depends on whether you use single-mode or multi-mode cable, and on the particular needs of your industry. Fusion splices are used primarily with single-mode cable, while mechanical splices are used with both single-mode and multimode cable. The telecommunications and CATV industries generally use both types—fusion splices for long-haul, single-mode networks, and mechanical splices for shorter, local cable runs. However, both industries use fusion splicing for local cable runs when transmitting analog video. These signals require minimal reflection for optimal performance, so fusion splicing is the preferred method.

The following procedure explains the four required steps for proper fusion splicing:

1. Prepare the fibers by stripping off the protective coatings, jackets, tubes, and strength members, leaving only the bare fiber showing. Ensure that the fibers and all tools are clean.

2. Cleave the fibers. **Cleaving** is the process of nicking the fiber and then pulling or flexing it to cause a clean break. A good fiber cleaver is essential to successful fusion splicing. A proper splice requires the cleaved end to be mirror-smooth and perpendicular to the fiber's axis. Good cleavers can consistently produce a cleave angle of 0.5°.

3. Fuse the fibers. **Fusing** is the process of aligning the fibers and then heating them. Alignment can be manual or automatic, depending on your equipment. Remember, the more expensive equipment has more features and provides more accurate alignment. When the fibers are properly aligned, the fusion splice unit uses an electric arc to permanently weld the two fibers.

4. Protect your fiber from excessive bending and tensile forces, to ensure that the splice will not break. A typical fusion splice has a tensile strength from 0.5 to 1.5 pounds, and will not break during normal handling, but it still requires protection from excessive bending and pulling forces. If the splice is outdoors, you can use heat-shrink tubing, silicone gel, or mechanical crimp protectors to protect the splice from outside elements.

Mechanical splices are optical junctions where two fibers are precisely aligned and held in place by a self-contained assembly. Mechanical splices are not considered a permanent bond; the goal of the process is to align the two fiber ends to a common centerline, so their cores can pass light to each other. The following procedure explains the steps for mechanical splicing:

1. Prepare and cleave the fiber as you did in the preceding fusion-splicing procedure. Keep in mind that cleave precision is not as critical in mechanical splicing.

2. Mechanically join the fibers by positioning their ends together inside the mechanical splice unit. No heat is used in mechanical splicing. Instead, the **index matching gel** inside the mechanical splice helps to couple the light from one fiber to the other. This gel works like the epoxy that held cores together in older splices.

   The completed mechanical splice provides its own protection, so no additional measures are necessary.

As you create mechanical splices or fusion splices, observe the following guidelines to ensure their quality:

- When working with fiber, keep in mind that invisible particles can accumulate on your tools and cause problems. Clean your tools and the fiber frequently and thoroughly; it can save you time and money.

- If you notice a problem while performing a fusion splice, first check your splicing equipment for dirt. If dirt is not the problem, check the machine parameters. The two key parameters in fusion splicing are fusion time and fusion current. Different combinations of these two parameters can produce the same results—for example, high time and low current settings can be the same as high current and low time settings. Change only one setting at a time until you find the correct parameters for your fiber. Make any necessary adjustments slowly and methodically; sweeping changes could make you lose the desired settings.

Fiber-Optic Safety

Before you install, maintain, or repair fiber cable, you should attend fiber-optic safety training. Fiber can be dangerous; you must know its potential dangers and how to avoid them. Always make safety your first priority and use common sense when working with fiber.

Observe the following guidelines to avoid injuries and accidents when using fiber-optic cable:

- **Laser safety** — Although lasers can be harmful, their dangers are easy to prevent. Always assume that every fiber is active and that it uses laser technology. The laser's infrared light is invisible, but it can damage your eyes if you look directly into it. To avoid danger, always keep the ends of the fiber pointed away from you while splicing. For more information on laser safety, see ANSI z136.2-1988 or the *OSHA Technical Manual*, Section 11, Chapter 6.

- **Connector microscope** — When you inspect connectors with a connector microscope, the fiber end is pointed directly at your eye from a close distance for extended periods of time. The fiber's infrared light poses a danger. Most high-powered microscopes (300x) have built-in infrared filters as a safeguard, but less expensive, low-powered microscopes (100x) may not. No matter which model you use, always deactivate a fiber before viewing it under the microscope.

- **Ultraviolet (UV) light** — UV light is sometimes used to cure adhesives in splices and connectors. The light is invisible, but the rays can damage your eyes. For protection, use safety glasses that attenuate infrared and UV light. Make sure that the glasses block the correct wavelengths.

- **Bare and exposed fibers** — A **bare fiber** has had all of its primary coatings removed, exposing the jagged glass surface. During the fiber-cleaning process, hundreds of tiny scraps are generated; every one must be accounted for and disposed of properly. The end of a bare fiber looks harmless to the naked eye, but when viewed under a microscope, it resembles a group of harpoons. Bare fiber can easily penetrate the skin and then break off, creating an injury that is difficult to treat. The tiny scraps also break off when you try to extract them. Fiber scraps can cause skin infections, serious eye injuries, or internal injuries if ingested. Do everything you can to avoid losing any scraps.

- **Clothing** — If fiber scraps get on your clothing, do not try to wipe them off. Shake them off instead.

- **Tape** — Transparent tape and electrical tape are safe and excellent tools for picking up fiber scraps. Avoid the impulse to pick up scraps with your bare hands, or to drag them to the edge of a surface to get a grip. The scraps will end up in your lap or in your finger. Instead, use the sticky side of the tape to pick up the fiber. Use electrical tape that is at least 2 inches wide, which provides sufficient area to ensure that fiber ends are not left exposed. Using black electrical tape makes the scraps stand out, and helps you pick them up and dispose of them safely.

- **Disposal** — Proper disposal requires fiber scrap containers, fiber "trash cans," and tape. You can buy a fiber trash can that has proper labeling and built-in spill protection, or you can make your own, as long as you apply a label indicating that the container holds dangerous fiber scraps. To safely dispose of fiber-filled electrical tape, layer it on both sides with strips of 2-inch-wide masking tape to form an envelope. Place the tape envelope in a double layer of trash bags and discard it in the fiber trash can. To safely dispose of the fiber trash can, tape the lid shut with duct tape and throw the container into a large trash bin.

- **Other safety precautions** — Never take food or beverages into a fiber work area; you could accidentally ingest fiber scraps. When working with fiber, never rub your eyes or use the bathroom without washing your hands first. Whenever possible, try to use work surfaces and work areas that have dark colors, which make the glass fibers easier to see. Smooth vinyl or leather coverings for chairs make it easier to spot stray fibers. When making splices, always use proper lighting and a magnifier, sit at a comfortable work height, and make sure all your tools and supplies are within reach.

THE TOOLS OF THE TRADE

Many technicians in service industries use common tools such as screwdrivers, pliers, wrenches, and drills in their everyday work. However, these tools cannot trace cable pairs, terminate wires on a punch-down block, make the connections in a telecommunications outlet, or install a modular plug on a telephone cord. These tasks require tools that are specifically designed for a telecommunications specialist.

You need to know everything about these tools, including the tasks for which they were designed, where to find them, their proper names, and, of course, how to use them. Most of these tools often come together in toolkits, complete with carrying cases. A number of companies manufacture these tools, both separately and in prepackaged toolkits, including Harris Corporation, Klein Tools, Ideal, Paladin, and Siemon. Most of these manufacturers publish product catalogs on their Web sites, and include information for where you can purchase the products, because most of the manufacturers use distributors. These distributors also supply tools and parts to the electrical industry, because telecommunications professionals and electricians use similar tools.

This section helps you identify specialized industry tools and understand how to use them.

The **telephone line tester**, also called a "**butt set**" in the trade, is used for testing lines, jacks, and circuits. It is a fully functioning phone in a portable, impact–resistant handset case. It has a cord with two angled beds of nail clips on the end that provide easy connection to the metal clips of punch-down blocks, to screw terminals, and even to wire pairs for testing. A typical butt set is shown in Figure 6-20.

Figure 6-20   Telephone line tester (butt set)

An **impact tool**, also known as a punch-down tool, is used for connecting wires to 66-type or 110-type terminals. The punch-down tool provides torque and impact to push the wires into the terminals. Both the 66 and 110 blades have a cutting edge for cleanly removing any excess wire that extends below the bottom of the connecting terminal (Figure 6–21).

66-type punch-down blade   110-type punch-down blade

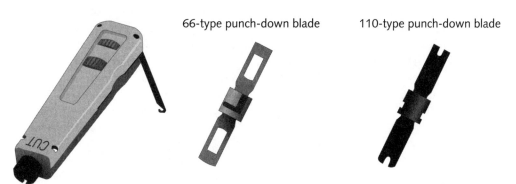

Figure 6-21   Impact tool (punch-down) with 66 and 110 blades

The **tone generator** and **inductive amplifier** are two of the most helpful tools in your toolkit. (These tools are also known as a toner and tracer, respectively, or the fox and hound, after a manufacturer in the field.) Picture yourself in a building that has over 1000 telecommunications devices installed. You need to locate the cable for a device that is not working properly, and you think the problem is the cable. You have no wiring plan, and neither the cables nor jacks have any type of identifying information. How do you locate the cable you need? The tone generator, when connected to a pair of wires, emits a sound you can hear through the speaker of the inductive amplifier when the probe tip passes over the wires (Figure 6-22).

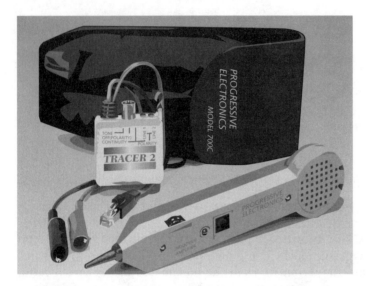

Figure 6-22 Tone generator and inductive amplifier

Use the cable stripper and the crimp tool to put plugs on cables. Figure 6-23 shows a typical cable stripper and crimp tool. Use the **cable stripper** to remove the cable sheath and expose the wires inside. It is designed to never remove too much of the cable sheath, if you use it according to the manufacturer's instructions. Use the **crimp tool** to squeeze the contacts in the modular plug so they make permanent contact with the wires and secure the plug onto the cable.

Cable stripper

Telephone ratchet crimp tool

Figure 6-23 Cable stripper and crimp tool

The next two items, bridging clips and cable ties, are not technically tools, but they should always be in your toolkit. **Bridging clips** are small metal clips that are used on a 66-type punch-down block to connect the punch-downs on the left side to those on the right side. You use **cable ties** to secure cables to racks, poles, or even to each other to create a neat bundle. Figure 6-24 shows a section of a 66-type punch-down block with bridging clips and a single bridging clip.

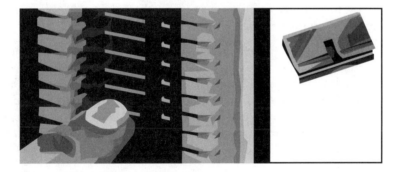

Figure 6-24 Bridging clips

The additional tools in the following list should already be familiar to you. Carry them in your toolkit as well, because you will use them on a regular basis.

- Screwdrivers in a variety of sizes and tips
- Diagonal cutters or wire cutters
- Needle-nose pliers
- Hex key set

- Pocket flashlight (with spare batteries)

- Cable tester

- Magnetic extractors

- Soldering iron, solder, and solder wick

- Screws and anchors in a variety of sizes

- Permanent marker

- Electrical tape

- Sponge

COLOR CODES AND WIRING SCHEMES USED FOR CABLE TERMINATION

So far, you have learned where cables are terminated, the equipment available for termination, and the tools you need to terminate cable. In this section, you will learn why color codes are used for termination. Then, in the next section, you will learn the actual steps for terminating cable.

Every wire in every cable you use has a color. These wire colors are collectively referred to as the color code; 25 color designations define how cables are connected. Just as a road map shows you how to get from point to point, the color code tells you how and where to terminate each wire, depending on its color.

There is only one color code; however, different wiring applications use only certain portions of the color code, and in a variety of ways. If you know the color code well, you can always apply it to any configuration that your application requires. This is why Western Electric used to devote the first two full days of its weeklong training class to making students memorize the color code. Some of the students might have considered such emphasis excessive, not to mention boring. But they have probably never forgotten the color code, and it undoubtedly has helped them numerous times over the years.

Because wiring is always done in pairs, the color code is separated into two parts, one for each wire in the pair. The two parts are called the tip and the ring. This terminology, and the color code itself, come from the telephone industry—every telephone line is a circuit, and thus requires a pair of wires, one with voltage and the other a ground. The **tip** wire is the ground or common wire, and the **ring** wire provides the voltage. The first part of the color code designates the color of the tip wires, and the second part designates the color of the ring wires. The wires are not usually solid colors; most often they are striped along the length of the wire.

You can tell the tip wire from the ring wire by the color of the thicker stripe. The predominant color or stripe of tip wires is always white, red, black, yellow, or violet. The predominant color or stripe of ring wires is blue, orange, green, brown, or slate.

The Color Code for 25-Pair and Larger Cable

Large cables use all 10 colors in the color code. Table 6-1 explains how these 10 colors can be combined to create 25-pair color designations.

Table 6-1   Color code chart for 25-pair and larger cables

Wire/Color Code	Tip/Ring	Pair #	Block Position
White/Blue	T	1	1
Blue/White	R		2
White/Orange	T	2	3
Orange/White	R		4
White/Green	T	3	5
Green/White	R		6
White/Brown	T	4	7
Brown/White	R		8
White/Slate	T	5	9
Slate/White	R		10
Red/Blue	T	6	11
Blue/Red	R		12
Red/Orange	T	7	13
Orange/Red	R		14
Red/Green	T	8	15
Green/Red	R		16
Red/Brown	T	9	17
Brown/Red	R		18
Red/Slate	T	10	19
Slate/Red	R		20
Black/Blue	T	11	21
Blue/Black	R		22
Black/Orange	T	12	23
Orange/Black	R		24
Black/Green	T	13	25
Green/Black	R		26
Black/Brown	T	14	27
Brown/Black	R		28
Black/Slate	T	15	29
Slate/Black	R		30
Yellow/Blue	T	16	31
Blue/Yellow	R		32
Yellow/Orange	T	17	33
Orange/Yellow	R		34
Yellow/Green	T	18	35
Green/Yellow	R		36

6

Table 6-1   Color code chart for 25-pair and larger cables (continued)

Wire/Color Code	Tip/Ring	Pair #	Block Position
Yellow/Brown	T	19	37
Brown/Yellow	R		38
Yellow/Slate	T	20	39
Slate/Yellow	R		40
Violet/Blue	T	21	41
Blue/Violet	R		42
Violet/Orange	T	22	43
Orange/Violet	R		44
Violet/Green	T	23	45
Green/Violet	R		46
Violet/Brown	T	24	47
Brown/Violet	R		48
Violet/Slate	T	25	49
Slate/Violet	R		50

The table shows you how 10 colors can combine to create 25 pair colors (50 colors), but you also need to know how to work with larger cable. Every group of 25 pairs has a colored piece of plastic or string wound around it, called a **binder**. The colors of the binders also follow the color code, allowing you to always know which group of 25 pairs to use, and in which order. When you add the colored binders, you can designate up to 625 pairs; however, the slate color of the ring wires is rarely used as a binder, because when the size of the cable exceeds 100 pairs, it generally increases in multiples of 100 pairs. If you only need to separate 100 pairs, then you would use only the blue, orange, green, and brown binders with each of the five color binders of the tip wires. Again, every 100 pairs are wound in binders that also follow the color code. As long as you know the color code, you can always tell which bundle of cable you need to use and the order to use it, no matter how many pairs are in the cable.

Wiring Schemes

As you learned earlier, some applications use only a portion of the color code, and require termination in a particular order. The standards organizations have worked hard to help keep cabling and wiring uniform. For example, the EIA/TIA created 568-A and 568-B standards to define the wiring configurations for 4-pair Category 5 cable terminated in RJ-45 modular plugs (Figure 6-25).

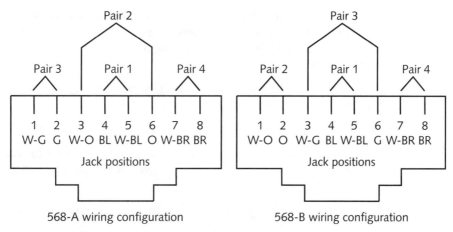

Figure 6-25   EIA/TIA 568-A and 568-B wiring configurations

EIA/TIA-568-A and 568-B are the two most common wiring schemes for Category 5 cable in the telecommunications industry. However, they are not the only schemes. In the past, some telecommunications equipment manufacturers developed their own proprietary wiring schemes, then certified a limited number of technicians to work on their systems. As standards and codes became more important, nonstandard wiring schemes began to disappear. Some of these systems are still in use, however, so be aware of their existence and use caution if you work on one.

TERMINATING CABLE

So far you have learned the principles of cable termination. Now it is time to try it yourself. This section provides basic instructions and guidelines for preparing and terminating various cables, and step-by-step instructions to guide you through the actual process.

As you terminate wires in the following sections, don't worry if some of your connections don't work properly the first time—you will get better. Many people suddenly acquire 10 thumbs when they try to terminate cable for the first time, and break the wires repeatedly. Or, they might punch down a 50-pair cable, only to discover too late that they reversed the two cables on the blocks. Keep practicing until you get the hang of it.

Terminating Demarc Cables

The first step in cable termination is to connect the cable(s) at the network interface, or demarc. The following procedures show you how to terminate cables in both small-system and large-system network interface devices.

To prepare and terminate your cable in a small-system network interface device, you need a Phillips-head screwdriver, a slotted screwdriver, a cable stripper, a butt set, diagonal cutters, and needle-nose pliers. When you have the proper tools, take the following steps to terminate the cable:

1. Pull your cable up into the network interface box through the plastic hole cover in the bottom.

2. Using your cable strippers, remove approximately 6 inches of the cable sheath.

3. After the cable sheath is removed, separate the pairs you need to terminate in the box. If any pairs are left over, bundle them neatly and place them in the box under your cable.

4. Inside the box on the terminal strips, loosen the screws that you need to use.

5. Take the first pair of wires (the white/blue pair) and remove approximately 1 inch of insulation.

6. When the insulation is removed, wrap the bare copper wire once around the screw connected to the green wire of the modular plug. Begin wrapping from the left side of the screw and wrap clockwise under the screw. Tighten the screw when you finish.

7. Repeat Step 6 with the blue/white wire, but place it under the screw connected to the red wire of the modular plug. Tighten the screw when you finish.

8. If you have more lines to connect, repeat Steps 4 through 7, substituting the next pair in the color code chart for the white/blue and so on. Continue until you have connected all the lines.

9. When all the wires are connected, use your butt set to test for dial tone.

10. When you finish terminating the wires, make a neat bundle of any slack that remains, keep the bundle inside the box, close the cover, and tighten the screw.

A large-system network interface device is usually a 66-type punch-down block with 50 rows of four connecting terminals in each row. The two connecting terminals on the right side in each row are common with each other, as are the two terminals on the left side. This is why these blocks are referred to as Split 66 blocks. For this type of termination, you need your impact (punch-down) tool with the 66 blade, diagonal cutters, cable strippers, bridging clips, and cable ties. When you have the proper tools, take the following steps to terminate the cable:

1. Locate the 66 block, which is mounted on brackets that stand 2 inches away from the wall. Next, insert the cable behind the block from either the top or the bottom, depending on the direction the cable is running. Feed the cable out the right side of the block, between the wall and the back of the block. The Telco typically uses the left side of the block.

2. Using the cable strippers, remove about 12 inches of the cable sheath.

3. Tie-wrap the cable to the top or bottom leg of the block's bracket, and fan out the cable so you can separate it into color groups. Because it is easier to punch cables down from the bottom of the block up, take out the violet group and neatly push the other groups out of your way.

4. Split the violet/slate pair, then pull the slate/violet wire all the way through the bottom wire guide. As you pull the wire tight in a slight downward motion, hook it over the groove on the 66 terminal.

5. Keep some tension on the wire by holding it several inches below the terminal. Then, with the impact tool held cutting side down, push the blade over the terminal and wire. This movement pushes the wire into the terminal and cuts it off neatly underneath.

6. Follow the same procedure with the violet/slate wire and then with the rest of the wires from bottom to top.

7. When all wires are terminated, place the bridging clips on the middle two terminals in each row. If there are fewer than 25 lines, you only need to place the bridging clips on the number of pairs that are needed for the lines being connected.

8. Use your butt set to clip on the appropriate terminals for each line on the right side of the block. Next, use the butt set to test for dial tone.

Terminating Cable in Equipment Rooms and Telecommunications Rooms

When terminating cable in the equipment rooms and telecommunications rooms, you use many of the same tools and equipment you used for the large-system network interface device, with the addition of a cable tester. The only other difference is that your blocks and any patch panels use the 110-type of terminals instead of the 66-type of punch-down block. Although the 66-type is sufficient for voice terminations, it is not recommended for terminating data and computer network cables. In these cases, the higher density of the 110-type punch-down block makes it a better choice.

The 110-type punch-down blocks usually mount vertically, as opposed to the 66-type, which mounts horizontally. The 110-type punch-down block and the patch panels both have wire guides for laying in the wires. With this type of termination, you usually bring the cable to the block from the side and use the block channels to guide the cables to the terminal for connection.

The 110-type block does not need bridging clips, but it only has one set of terminals for the wires. To cross-connect two blocks, such as backbone to horizontal or horizontal cables to the horizontal cross-connect, you use 110-type connecting blocks, as shown in Figure 6-26. Place the 110-type connecting blocks (available in four, five, and eight pairs) over the existing terminals on each block, then push them straight down on top. The metal feet on the connecting block will make contact with the metal contacts in the original block where the cable is punched down. After all the connecting blocks are in place, terminate your jumpers on the appropriate pairs of each block.

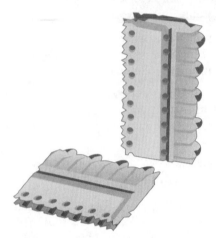

Figure 6-26   110-type connecting blocks (4-pair and 5-pair)

If you are using patch panels in any of these rooms, you need a sufficient number of patch cables. These cables are commercially available, but you also can make them yourself. You need a cable stripper, crimp tool, diagonal cutters, CAT5 cable cut into appropriate lengths, and two RJ-45 modular plugs for each patch cord. Once you have the appropriate tools, take the following steps to make your own cables:

1. Use the cable stripper to remove approximately 1 inch of the cable sheath from each end of your cables.

2. Separate the four cable pairs, but do not untwist them.

3. Select the required wiring scheme for your system. Separate the individual wire pairs by untwisting them, but do not untwist more than ¼ inch of the wires. While holding the wires, put them in the appropriate color sequence.

4. When all the wires are lined up in the correct order, trim their tops off to ½ inch so they are neat and even. Next, gently but firmly push them all the way into the RJ-45 plug, ensuring that the top ⅛ inch of the cable sheath is also completely inside the plug.

5. Take the crimping tool, insert the RJ-45 plug into the appropriate receptacle, and squeeze the handles of the tool together firmly.

6. Remove the modular plug and repeat the process until all the terminations are complete.

7. Use the cable tester to ensure that each of your patch cords is in good working order.

Having completed the terminations in the equipment rooms, telecommunications rooms, and the demarc, and having used most of the tools of your trade, you are well on your way to becoming a telecommunications technician.

Terminating Cable in Work Areas

Terminating cables in the work area is the last stop in connecting your system. Work area termination requires telecommunications outlets (jacks), and might require telecommunications cords. You also need diagonal cutters, an impact tool, a cable stripper, a Phillips screwdriver, and possibly a crimp tool and modular plugs.

The way you terminate work area cables to jacks depends on the type of jack you select. The following paragraphs briefly explain how to terminate cables on the three types of jacks discussed earlier in this chapter.

- Terminating cable on jacks with screw terminals is very similar to cable termination for a small-system network interface device. To help you make a good connection between the copper wire and screw terminal, always make sure that the insulation is completely removed from the wire. Also, make sure there are no nicks or cuts in the copper wire from the cutters. Wrap the copper wire firmly for one turn under the screw, beginning from the left side of the screw and wrapping clockwise as close to the top of the insulation as possible.

- You can also use the 110-type punch-down connecting blocks for work area termination. Connect the wires to these blocks in the same way you terminated cable previously in equipment rooms and telecommunications rooms with 110-type terminations.

- The preferred and recommended type of jack for use in the work area is the toolless 110-type connecting block. You place the wires in the connecting block in the same way as with all other 110-type connectors, but you do not use a punch-down tool. Instead, the connecting block has small plastic caps that you place over the tops of the terminals. Push each cap down firmly until you hear it click into place. When it clicks, the termination is complete. If any excess wire protrudes from the opposite side of the terminal, use your cutters to remove it.

Terminating Fiber-Optic Cable

Terminating fiber-optic cable is different from terminating copper cable. You can terminate fiber in two ways: either use connectors that can mate two fibers to create a temporary joint or connect the fiber to a piece of equipment, or use splices that create a permanent joint between two fibers, as discussed earlier in this chapter. Manufacturers have designed more than 80 styles of fiber-optic connectors, but most applications use the common types shown in Figure 6-27.

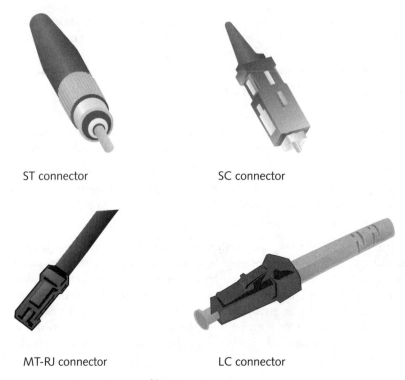

ST connector   SC connector

MT-RJ connector   LC connector

Figure 6-27   Common fiber-optic connectors

The most popular fiber-optic connectors are the ST and SC connectors. However, the relatively new small form factor (SFF) connectors are quickly gaining ground. The new EIA/TIA-568-B standard opened the door for SFF connectors; 568-B allows the use of any fiber-optic connector, as long as it has a FOCIS (Fiber Optic Connector Intermateability Standard) document behind it. The following list describes popular fiber connectors in more detail.

- **ST connector** — This trademarked product of AT&T is the most popular connector in multimode networks because it is inexpensive and easy to install. It has a bayonet mount and a long cylindrical ferrule to hold the fiber. Most ferrules are ceramic, but some are metal or plastic. These connectors are spring-loaded, so you should always make sure they are seated properly.

- **SC connector** — This snap-in connector is widely used in single-mode systems because of its excellent performance. It was specified as a standard by EIA/TIA-568-A, but its high cost and difficulty of installation limited its popularity for years. However, newer SC connectors are improved in both areas. The snap-in connector latches with a simple push-pull motion; it is also available in a duplex configuration.

■ **LC connector** — This new SFF connector uses a 1.25-mm ferrule, which is half the size of the ST connector. Otherwise, it is a standard, ceramic ferrule connector that is easily terminated with any adhesive. It performs well, and is used with single-mode fiber.

■ **MT-RJ connector** — This SFF duplex connector is used for multimode fiber. Both fibers are housed in a single polymer ferrule. The connector uses pins for alignment, and comes in both male and female versions.

DOCUMENTING NETWORK HARDWARE

So far in this book, you have learned why good documentation is important. You have read overviews of the items that need to be documented, and learned how to document the cable plant and equipment rooms. The next part of your documentation manual should cover all the hardware in your network, including internetworking devices, servers, and workstations.

Documenting Internetworking Devices

The documentation of internetworking devices includes hubs, switches, routers, and advanced features on these devices, such as chassis-based switches, VLANs on switches, and configuration files for switches and routers. Your documentation should include the manufacturer, model, and serial number of each internetworking device. It should also include physical and logical addresses, port usage information, device locations, the areas served by devices, connections to other devices, and firmware versions, if applicable.

This documentation plays a key role in network troubleshooting and support. You can record the information in a spreadsheet, in a database, or in narrative form. Table 6-2 is an example of a spreadsheet you might develop for hubs and switches. Your own devices and features might require different column headings.

Table 6-2   Hubs and switches spreadsheet

Device Type/Label	Model and Serial #	Loc.	Loc. Served	Interconnection/ Port Number	IP Address	MAC Address	Ports/ Free
Managed Hub/ MH1-IDF1	Synoptics 2814, 324343657	IDF1	Room 202	H2-IDF1/BP, SW1-MDF/P1	192.168.1.240	0000cab3546	16/0
Hub/ H2-IDF1	Synoptics 2803, 324234658	IDF1	Room 202	MH1-IDF1/BP, H3-IDF1/BP	N/A	0000cab3305	16/0
Hub/ H3-IDF1	Synoptics 2803, 324234659	IDF1	Room 202	H2-IDF1/BP	N/A	0000cab3254	16/10
Switch/ SW1-MDF	Cat4000, 8443901224	MDF	Campus	MH1-IDF1/P1, SW1-24-IDF2/P2	192.168.2.245		

Be sure to provide a key of abbreviations and other terms that may not be obvious to readers of your documentation. For example, "Loc." in the preceding table stands for "Location." Also, some columns may require further explanation. The Interconnection/Port Number column refers to other internetworking devices to which the device is connected. For example, the first device, Hub MH1-IDF1, has a connection to Hub H2-IDF1 through port BP. "BP" stands for backplane; this tells you that the hub has a special backplane connector to stack other hubs. MH1-IDF1 has another connection to a switch labeled SW1-MDF, which goes through the hub's port 1.

Using a spreadsheet or database allows you to sort information by column heading and find information easily. For example, you could sort by location to obtain a quick reference of all the internetworking devices in an equipment room. You could sort by model number to determine the quantities of particular models and devices on the network.

Advanced features of network devices can be difficult to document in a spreadsheet or database, so you should include a written description instead. Explain the important features of each installed device, including port speed, supported duplex modes, and SNMP capabilities. Create separate sections to document each device. For example, you might document a switch labeled Cat4000-IDF3 with the following information:

Cat4000-IDF3 (Device model: Cisco Catalyst 4000; Number of slots: 3)

Installed modules:

- Slot 1: Supervisory Module/29489-8a
- Slot 2: Catalyst 4000 E/FE/GE Module/29489-1a
- Slot 3: Catalyst 4000 10100 Auto Module/29489-3a

Configuration of three VLANs:

- VLAN01: Ports 1–12, Slot 2–192.168.1.0
- VLAN02: Ports 13–24, Slot 2–192.168.2.0
- VLAN03: Ports 1–24, Slot 3–192.168.3.0
- Configuration file: (Insert the configuration file from the switch, excluding passwords.)

Documenting Servers

To maintain a reliable and secure network, you must have accurate and updated server documentation. You can then find needed information in a hurry, and you can drastically reduce the time spent training new employees to manage the servers. The server documentation should describe the server's hardware configuration and operating system, available services, resource configurations and limitations, administrative contacts, and server documentation tools.

Describing the Server

Include a general description of the server's purpose, the primary services it provides on the network, and the users who benefit from the service. For example, you might describe a server named SAL-SRV1 with the following text:

SAL-SRV1

A Windows 2000 server that provides Sales Department document sharing and print services, along with Internet Information Server Web services for the Sales intranet. SAL-SRV1 serves about 30 employees in the main office on the third floor. This server is configured as a member server in the LB-Corp domain.

You can include other useful details, but note that more specific information and technical data appear later in the documentation.

Server Hardware Configuration and Operating System

When documenting the server's hardware configuration, you should start with the manufacturer, model number, and serial number. The operating system information should list the version number and any installed updates or patches. If you have several servers, document them uniformly.

Include the most pertinent information about hardware configuration, so that upgrades and repairs can be made easily. Information that you do not use as frequently, such as the type of installed memory, number of free slots, and BIOS version, can be available through hyperlinks if your documentation is electronic. For example, you can make the model description a hyperlink, then create a detailed specification sheet for the server that you access via the link.

List all critical information in one location. For example, include the MAC address and IP address with the NIC information. Table 6-3 shows an example of how you might summarize your server hardware configuration and operating system.

Table 6-3   Server hardware configuration and operating system

Server: SAL-SRV1				
Model: Dell PowerEdge 500SC Location: IDF1		Serial #: DCS-50049443		
Operating System: Windows 2000 Server		Patches: SP2, IE5.5 SP1, code Red Virus Cleaner		
CPU (#/Speed)	**RAM (Amount/ Type/Free Slots)**	**Bus Slots (Type/Free)**	**Drives (Type/Size)**	**NIC/MAC/IP**
Pentium III 1/1 GHz	512 MB/ECC SDRAM/ 2 DIMM	PCI-32/1 PCI-64/2	EIDE/30 GB HD EIDE/CD-ROM SCSI-2/8 GB DAT	Intel 10/100 04AB33126900 192.168.1.33
I/O Ports	**Additional Information**		**Drive Bays**	**Modem**
Two USBs, two serial ports, one parallel port	Phoenix BIOS version 4.4, 250W ATX power supply, tower chassis, PS/2 keyboard and mouse		Two 5.25-inch, Two 3.5-inch	3Com-56 K

6

Available Services on the Server

List all available services on the server, along with their purpose. This information helps you understand the ramifications of a server failure, and helps you configure security appropriately. Services can include file and printing, Web services, and FTP, as well as DNS, DHCP, Active Directory, backup, Telnet, database, e-mail, and terminal services. Numerous other services may be possible, depending on the operating system. You can place this information in a table, if necessary.

Server Resource Configuration and Limitations

This section of the documentation describes how the hard drives are configured and lists the limits of their storage capacity and memory. Use this section to specify how the drives are partitioned and formatted. Document the size of each partition, the amount of free space available after installation, the least amount of free space allowed before the drive must be upgraded, whether the drives are configured for redundancy, and the maximum number of drives that the server can support.

The section on memory configuration should include the total amount of memory on the server, as well as the amounts of available free memory and virtual memory when the server is running. Determine the minimum allowable amount of free memory before a memory upgrade is required. Specify the maximum amount of memory supported by each server.

You should also document the maximum number of users each server is designed to support. If you use a Web server, include the maximum number of transactions the server is designed to handle per minute. This information helps you determine when to make network upgrades or design changes.

Administrative Contacts for Servers

This section of the server documentation should list contact information for all the people who handle various support issues. Different people might be assigned to create user accounts, set security permissions, make changes to services, and perform software or hardware upgrades.

Server Documentation Tools

Collecting information about your servers can take time, so take advantage of tools that can help automate the task. For example, the System Information utility comes with any Windows 98 server or later. For each machine, the utility creates a text file of configurations that you can print or save to disk. Other third-party utilities are available to help you manage and view information for networked computers and servers.

Documenting Workstations

Documentation for workstations should be similar to your server documentation. Always include hardware configurations, addresses, and available services, when applicable. Document the primary users and installed applications on each workstation, as well as any policies or restrictions that apply to it. You can automate data collection for workstations using the tools described in the previous section, "Server Documentation Tools."

CHAPTER SUMMARY

6

- ❏ Cable termination is the process of connecting cables to workstation outlets, connecting blocks, and cable connectors. Several locations in every telecommunications system require cable termination, including the network interface, or demarcation point, the equipment rooms and telecommunications rooms, and the work areas. The connecting devices and tools you use to terminate cable depend on the cable's location and type.

- ❏ The demarcation point is where control or ownership of the communications facilities changes from the Telco equipment to the customer-provided equipment. Federal Communications Commission Rule 68 requires demarcation points to ensure that customer equipment and wiring can be connected to the Telco without causing harm. Network interface devices, the equipment used to terminate cable at demarcation points, permit all customer equipment and wiring to be disconnected from the Telco wiring for testing and maintenance.

- ❏ Network interface devices generally fall into one of two categories: those used for small systems and those used for large systems. Small systems include residences and small businesses that have one to six telephone lines or cable pairs. Large systems include large companies and commercial buildings with multiple tenants; these buildings and companies can have several hundred telephone lines or cable pairs.

- ❏ Equipment rooms and telecommunications rooms require termination of backbone, horizontal cross-connect, and horizontal cabling. The termination methods are similar for all three types of cabling; only the actual equipment and required tools may differ, depending on the media type being terminated. In these rooms, you can terminate cables by mounting the equipment on walls or by using racks and patch panels.

- ❏ Work area terminations involve wiring the horizontal cabling to the telecommunications outlets (jacks).

- ❏ Splicing is the process of making permanent connections between wires, cables, or fibers. Splicing is commonly used to extend the length of a cable or to repair a break or cut.

- ❏ Telecommunications professionals use a variety of specialized tools, including telephone line testers (butt sets), impact tools, cable strippers, cable-crimping tools, tone generators and inductive amplifiers (toners and tracers), and bridging clips.

❐ The color code is crucial information for a telecommunications professional. Every type of wiring and termination is based on the color code.

❐ Network hardware documentation includes the servers and workstations in a network, as well as all internetworking equipment such as hubs, switches, and routers. Complete hardware documentation makes troubleshooting easier and helps you determine when upgrades and design changes are necessary.

KEY TERMS

B-wire connectors — Solderless, single-wire splice connections, also known as "beanies."

bare fiber — A fiber that has had all of its primary coatings removed, exposing the glass surface. Bare fiber can be dangerous if you do not follow safety procedures when working with it.

binder — A colored piece of plastic or string wound around a group of cables for identification.

bridging clips — Small metal clips used on 66-type punch-down blocks to connect the wires that are terminated on the left and right sides of a block.

butt set — *See* telephone line tester.

cable stripper — A tool that removes a portion of the cable sheath to expose the wires inside.

cable ties — Devices used for securing cables.

cleaving — The process of nicking a fiber and then pulling or flexing it to cause a clean break.

crimp tool — A tool that creates a secure, permanent contact between a modular plug and a cable.

demarcation point (demarc) — The point at which control or ownership of the communications facilities changes from the Telco equipment to the customer's equipment.

fusing — The process of aligning and then heating fibers.

fusion splicing — A splicing method that uses a machine to precisely align two fiber ends and weld them together using heat or an electric arc. The resulting continuous connection between the fibers enables light transmissions with losses as low as 0.1 dB.

impact tool — A tool that provides torque and impact for connecting wires to both 66-type and 110-type punch-down blocks.

index matching gel — Material inside a mechanical splice that helps to couple the light from one fiber to another.

inductive amplifier (tracer) — A tool used to find and identify cables by locating the sound emitted by a tone generator.

insulation displacement connector (IDC) — A device that connects copper wires by piercing their insulation to make contact when you insert them into the IDC with an impact insertion tool.

mechanical splicing — A splicing method that uses simple alignment devices to hold two fiber ends together precisely, enabling light to pass between the fibers with losses as low as 0.3 dB.

network interface — *See* demarcation point.

network interface device — Equipment used to terminate cable at the demarc.

protector — Fuses that protect lines and cables from lightning and power surges.

punch-down block — A solid plastic block with imbedded metal connectors, for terminating wires from larger cables (more than six pairs).

punch-down tool — *See* impact tool.

ring — The voltage half of a cable pair.

splice — The connection of two wires, fibers, or cables.

splice enclosure — A box, case, or cabinet, usually made of steel or metal, that houses and protects cable splices.

telephone line tester (butt set) — A tool used for testing lines, jacks, and circuits. It can easily connect to the metal terminals on punch-down blocks, to screw terminals, and directly to a cable pair.

terminal strip — A piece of metal with attached screws that allow wires to be connected. Terminal strips are usually found in small-system network interface devices.

tip — The ground or common half of a cable pair.

tone generator (toner) — A device that connects to one end of a pair of wires, then sends a sound throughout the cable so it can be located and identified on the other end.

REVIEW QUESTIONS

1. At which location does cable termination usually take place?

   a. demarc

   b. telecommunications room

   c. workstation area

   d. all of the above

2. In which two situations would you splice a cable? (Choose the two that apply.)

   a. when you need more cable pairs

   b. when the cable is damaged

   c. when you need to extend the length of a cable

   d. when you make a mistake

3. In which section of the Federal Communications Commission rules is a demarcation point defined?

    a. 86.3

    b. 63.8

    c. 68.3

    d. 83.8

4. Why are demarcation points required?

    a. to ensure that the customer's equipment and wiring can be connected to the Telco network without causing harm

    b. to ensure that the customer network can be connected to the equipment without causing harm

    c. to ensure that the Telco equipment and wiring can be connected to the FCC without causing harm

    d. to connect equipment to a network

5. How many pairs can a small-system network interface device accommodate?

    a. 2 to 4

    b. 1 to 6

    c. 1 or 2

    d. 1 to 5

6. Which piece of terminating equipment is used in large systems and can save time during installation?

    a. punch-down tool

    b. tone generator

    c. protector

    d. punch-down block

7. The demarcation point for large systems is always in the entrance facility or equipment room. True or False?

8. Which two common methods are used for terminating cables in equipment rooms and telecommunications rooms? (Choose the two that apply.)

    a. punch-down block

    b. telecommunications outlet

    c. patch panel

    d. backbone cables

9. The telecommunications outlet provides the connection between the horizontal cable and the telecommunications equipment. True or False?

10. Which of the following is the standard pair configuration for telecommunications outlets?

a. 2

b. 4

c. 3

d. all of the above

11. The biggest difference between connecting copper cables and fiber-optic cables is that fiber-optic cables require connection to an analog transmitter and digital receiver. True or False?

12. What names are given to the two parts in a pair of wires?

a. tip and tap

b. top and bottom

c. tip and ring

d. tap and ring

13. According to the color code, what are the predominant colors of the tip wires?

a. white, red, blue, green, and violet

b. white, red, yellow, orange, and black

c. blue, orange, green, brown, and white

d. white, red, black, yellow, and violet

14. According to the color code, what are the predominant colors of the ring wires?

a. blue, orange, green, brown, and slate

b. blue, orange, red, yellow, and brown

c. green, white, violet, black, and yellow

d. red, blue, orange, black, and brown

15. In larger cables, colored binders are used to separate groups of cable. True or False?

16. Which wiring configurations define the color code for 4-pair CAT5 cable terminated in an RJ-45 jack?

a. EIA/TIA-586-A and 586-B

b. EIA/TIA-586-B and 586-C

c. EIA/TIA-568-A and 568-B

d. EIA/TIA-568 and 586

6

17. Which wire pair is the first to be terminated at the small-system network interface on line 1?

    a. white/orange

    b. violet/slate

    c. white/blue

    d. violet/blue

18. The piece of hardware that connects the right and left sides of a split 66-type punch-down block is called a bridging adapter. True or False?

19. When terminating cable on a 66-type punch-down block, it is always a good idea to start at the bottom of the block with the violet/slate pair. True or False?

20. When using 110-type punch-down blocks, what piece of equipment is needed so cross-connects can be run from one block to another?

    a. 110-type bridging clips

    b. 110-type connecting clip

    c. 110-type connecting block

    d. 110-type bridging block

21. Match the item in the left column with the description in the right column.

    a. bridging clips

    b. telephone line tester

    c. cable ties

    d. impact tool

    e. cable stripper

    f. tone generator/
       inductive amplifier

    g. crimp tool

    1. connects wires to terminals

    2. used to remove cable sheath

    3. must be connected to a fiber-optic cable to enable it to function

    4. squeezes the contacts together in a modular plug

    5. portable phone used for testing lines, jacks, and circuits

    6. used to secure cables

    7. connects the left and right sides of a punch-down block

    8. connects the telecommunications equipment and the cable

    9. used to locate a cable by emitting and finding a tone

HANDS-ON PROJECTS

6

Project 6-1

For this project, find information about all the tools you think should be in the toolkit of a telecommunications professional. For each type of tool, research products from at least three manufacturers. Obtain the following information about each tool: brand name, number of different models available, price, special features, and any specific advantages or disadvantages. Create a report that compares the tools and analyzes your findings. List all your sources of information in the report.

Project 6-2

Based on your research in Project 6-1, design your own complete, reasonably priced dream toolkit. Develop a report that lists all the items in the toolkit and explains your criteria for each selection.

Project 6-3

For this exercise, determine the advantages and disadvantages of several types of jacks.

1. Determine the advantages and disadvantages of screw terminal jacks, M110-type punch-down jacks, and M110-type toolless jacks.

2. Determine the advantages and disadvantages of surface-mount and flush-mount jacks.

3. Determine the advantages and disadvantages of the 66-type punch-down block and the M110-type punch-down block.

4. Write a report that details the information you gathered about these three groups of hardware. For each group, indicate the item you prefer and why. List all your sources of information in the report.

Project 6-4

1. Create diagrams that explain how cables terminate on 2-pair, 3-pair, and 4-pair jacks. For each jack, identify where the wires from each cable would appear in the color code chart. Label the diagrams clearly and explain all information as necessary.

2. Create a diagram that explains how 40 pairs of cable terminate on both a 66-type punch-down block and an M110-type punch-down block. Identify where all 40 pairs would appear in the color code chart. Label the diagram clearly and explain all information as necessary.

3. Print your diagrams and any supporting explanations you need to submit to your instructor.

Project 6-5

In this exercise, perform several cable terminations using screwdrivers, an impact tool with both 66 and 110 blades, cutters, strippers, a crimp tool, and tie wraps. Perform complete cable terminations on the following equipment:

- ❑ A 25-pair cable to a 66-type punch–down block
- ❑ A 25-pair cable to an M110-type punch–down block
- ❑ Two pairs of a 4-pair cable on a screw terminal jack
- ❑ A 4-pair cable on an M110-type punch–down jack
- ❑ A 4-pair cable on an M110-type toolless jack
- ❑ A 4-pair CAT5 cable with modular plugs that conforms to EIA/TIA-568-A
- ❑ A 4-pair CAT5 cable with modular plugs that conforms to EIA/TIA-568-B

When you complete your terminations, test the ones you can test and submit your work to the instructor.

Project 6-6

In this exercise, create a report that explains why you should not mount jacks on the backs of desks, credenzas, and bookcases, or place them in a safe location on the floor. Provide one or more recommendations for relocating these jacks.

CASE PROJECTS

Case Project 1

The requirement for network interface devices is defined in Federal Communications Commission Rule 68. Research this requirement, and then write an explanation of why these devices are important. List all your sources of information.

Case Project 2

Write a report that explains the importance of uniform cabling and wiring standards. Include your own opinions about the importance of these standards. List all your sources of information in the report.

Case Project 3

Write a brief report that explains the possible negative implications of terminating and cross-connecting a cable without using the proper color code. List all your sources of information in the report.

Case Project 4

Your manager has selected you to design and implement a complete telecommunications system for your company. You will design the system, choose the topology, select the appropriate cable, and select each type of termination device. Using a computer in your lab that has Visio installed, create a drawing of your system that identifies all cable runs, the equipment rooms and telecommunications rooms, the demarcation point, and each workstation in all work areas. Account for the following information in your design:

❏ The building has one story.

❏ It includes a front office/reception area that is staffed by one person.

❏ There are six private offices.

❏ There are two work areas, each with 10 full-time workstations.

❏ One additional workstation in each work area is designated for use by subcontractors.

❏ The Finance Department has three full-time employees and two part-time employees. From November through May, three more people work in the department full-time and three work part-time.

After you create your design, prepare a report that details the choices you made, including those for cable, topology, termination equipment, and any other items you included.

6

7

FIRESTOPPING AND COMPREHENSIVE FIRE PREVENTION SYSTEMS

After reading this chapter and completing the exercises, you will be able to:

♦ Identify the elements of a comprehensive fire protection system

♦ Understand firestopping and its role in fire protection

♦ Discuss the different products and materials used in firestopping

♦ Select the appropriate firestopping system for your application

♦ List installation guidelines for firestopping systems

♦ Document network addresses, changes, procedures, and logging

Fires take lives and destroy property every day. Everyone learns about fire prevention and protection at an early age, but no matter what steps we take, fires still occur. That is why extensive knowledge of fire protection is so important, and why building codes have such stringent construction requirements for fire prevention and protection.

A comprehensive fire protection system is one of the most important safety measures in building construction. This system consists of fire detection, containment, and suppression subsystems. Firestopping is the key element of containment, and is the main subject of this chapter. Although your job as a telecommunications professional focuses on firestopping and its role in fire protection, you also need to understand how firestopping fits within the entire fire protection system.

FIRE PROTECTION SYSTEMS

When dealing with fire, your primary goal is its prevention. Because total prevention has yet to be achieved, however, fire protection becomes the next priority. In existing buildings and new construction, you can protect against fire in a number of ways. For example, you can review all building plans to ensure that fire protection is addressed, institute and enforce building codes to enhance protection, and perform regular building inspections. The more efficiently you employ these fire protection techniques, the closer you get to the goal of total fire prevention.

A comprehensive fire protection system that meets or exceeds building code requirements is one of the best defenses against fire. This system is a combination of three smaller systems:

- Detection systems provide early warning signals that can prevent losses to fire.

- Suppression systems are used to extinguish fires.

- Containment systems reduce the rapid spread of fire and toxic fumes from their point of origin.

The following sections describe each of these systems in detail. As a telecommunications professional, you are responsible for the integrity of fire containment systems. However, you must have a working knowledge of the other two systems to truly understand the containment system and its role in fire protection.

Fire Detection Systems

Detection systems provide early warning signals that can prevent fire losses. At one time, these systems were only provided if they were required by code. Today, more and more building owners and managers install fire detection systems whether the code requires them or not. Attitudes began to change as companies' equipment and records became more valuable, and as a more fundamental focus on building safety and security increased the demand for fire detection systems. In addition, fire codes are constantly being upgraded with more stringent requirements and new standards, which have significantly changed approaches to detection system design and installation.

Safe and fast detection is essential to reliable fire protection—the earlier a fire is detected, the less significant its dangers and damages will be. Several elements work together to form a fire detection system. For example, control panels work with detectors and alarms to enable fast reaction in case of fire. The following sections describe the primary elements of detection systems and how they work.

Detectors

Many types of smoke and fire detectors are available; they are designed for different burning characteristics and have different responses. In many cases a mixed system provides the most effective protection.

Figure 7-1 shows various detection devices you might consider. The following list describes these detectors and several others.

Gas

Optical

Spark and flame

Heat

Ionization

Figure 7-1   Fire detection devices

- Optical smoke detectors react to the scattered light caused by smoke aerosols. Their response to visual smoke is especially good, and they are an ideal solution for dealing with **cold smoke** (nonglowing, smoldering fires).

- Differential maximum heat detectors respond to a maximum temperature or a defined temperature rise within a certain period of time. These detectors are good for use in hotel kitchens and workshops, where traditional smoke detectors are not recommended.

- Ionization smoke detectors respond to the smallest visible smoke particles and invisible particles. These detectors are best used in areas where glowing or open flames are expected at an early stage of a fire.

- Spark and flame detectors react to optical radiation and select only small areas of the light spectrum for detection. They are the right choice for areas where open flames are expected to develop quickly.

- High-sensitivity smoke detectors are 1000 times more sensitive to highly diluted smoke and other heat by-products than conventional smoke detectors. These detectors are also equipped with an active airflow sampling network to provide the earliest possible recognition of fire. High-sensitivity smoke detectors are designed for areas where conventional smoke detectors will not work, such as clean rooms, computer rooms, atriums, high-bay warehouses, and nuclear facilities.

- Bypass detectors are elements in both fire detection and containment systems. They constantly monitor exhaust air and climatic ducts. When changes occur, indicating fire, protection flaps are released or air-conditioning systems are shut down to prevent the spread of fire and smoke.

- Multifunctional detectors are combined measuring-chamber systems that can respond to different burning characteristics at the same time.

- Gas detectors monitor for the presence of hydrogen chloride (HCl). HCl is emitted by the thermal decomposition of **polyvinyl chloride (PVC)**, material found in the insulation of most wire and cable, and in most plastic conduit. When HCl mixes with water vapor in the air, it forms hydrochloric acid, which can cause significant damage to printed circuit boards and other sensitive electronic equipment. When electronic equipment or cables begin to fail, the resulting heat buildup causes the decomposition of PVC, which in turn produces HCl emissions. The presence of HCl occurs when the temperature reaches 250°C, long before the temperature is sufficient to produce heat or flames.

Control Panels, Alarms, and Annunciators

Although detectors are a significant part of the fire detection structure, they are complemented by other elements, including fire control panels, alarms, and annunciators. **Fire control panels** provide supervision and coordination among the various elements of a detection system. Alarms provide the necessary signals for rescue and timely firefighting, and **annunciators** provide graphic displays to pinpoint alarms quickly.

Fire control panels are available in many sizes, from compact small-scale panels to demanding large-scale panels. A typical fire control panel is shown in Figure 7-2. Regardless of their size, control panels allow you to supervise and coordinate the other elements in the system. Most control panels are capable of multizone configurations that provide a wide range of controls for both detection and suppression systems. When properly configured, control panels can operate early-warning smoke and flame detectors, provide sprinkler supervision services, set water flow alarms, and control automatic extinguishing system releases, including deluge sprinkler systems. Control panels must conform to all applicable requirements for local and auxiliary protective signal systems, as defined by National Fire Protection Association (NFPA) Code 72.

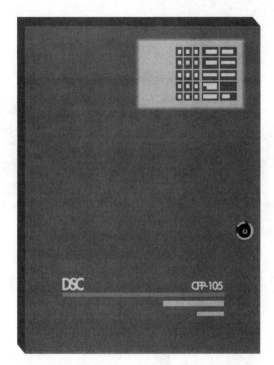

Figure 7-2 Fire control panel

Alarms, also referred to as notification appliances, are important in fire rescue and timely firefighting (Figure 7-3). The three main categories of alarms are:

- Manual fire alarm stations, the little red boxes with white lettering. These alarms are common in commercial buildings. You activate the alarm by breaking a piece of glass and pulling down on a lever.

- Audible alarms emit a distinctive sound to signify the presence of fire.

- Optical alarms signal fire with blinking lights, flashing lights, or strobe lights.

Visual strobe signal   Multitone signal with strobe

Horn   Horn with strobe   Amplified speaker

Bell   Manual station

Figure 7-3   Notification appliances

Annunciators like the ones shown in Figure 7-4 provide graphic displays that help to pinpoint alarms quickly. They are designed to quickly identify and locate fires and other related events on a custom floor-plan display. Light-emitting diodes (LEDs) provide remote indications of individual alarms throughout the fire detection system.

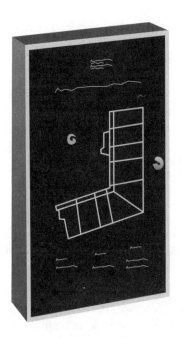

Figure 7-4   Annunciators

Fire Suppression Systems

A fire requires three ingredients: a heat source for ignition and burning; a sufficient quantity of oxygen, usually from the surrounding air; and a source of combustion, which is any solid, liquid, or gas fuel that will burn. If any of these three ingredients is missing, combustion cannot occur.

The main responsibility of a **suppression system** is to extinguish fire; its secondary goal is to help reduce damage. Fire suppression systems extinguish fires by removing either the heat, the oxygen, or the source of combustion.

The **extinguishant**, the substance used to put out a fire, is the primary component in a fire suppression system. The extinguishant you select determines which extinguishing method you use.

Extinguishants

In this section you will examine several common extinguishants, their characteristics, and the methods they use for fire suppression.

Water is mainly used for Class A (glowing substance) fires. Its extinguishing effect is mainly based on its heat-binding capabilities. Its cooling effect disturbs thermal reactions, hinders the further processing of flammable substances, and interrupts the formation of gases and vapors. In simple terms, water extinguishes by cooling, or removing heat.

Extinguishing foam and aqueous solutions are a highly effective combination of water, a foaming agent, and air, used to put out Class A and Class B fires. A percentage of a stable foaming agent is added to the water flow, and the mixture is foamed with air in foam generators. The degree of foaming depends on the capacity of the generator, the foaming agent, and the air intake. Low air intake produces a wet, heavy foam, or low-expansion foam. Increasing the air intake produces drier and lighter, medium- and high-expansion foam. Air foam uses different extinguishing effects, including cooling (removing the heat), suffocating and covering (removing the oxygen), separating and displacing (removing the source of combustion), and restraining. You can use these extinguishing effects separately or in combination to successfully put out a fire.

You can also extinguish fires with **clean agents**, electrically nonconductive materials that leave no residue and help protect sensitive electronic equipment. Clean agents include FM-200, which extinguishes flames by absorbing their heat upon impact, and inert gases such as argon, nitrogen, and carbon dioxide, which displace or remove the atmospheric oxygen. This suffocation effect occurs if the oxygen value necessary for combustion falls below a specific limit.

Clean agents have been used since the 1950s, when halon gases were found to be effective extinguishing agents, especially for protecting sensitive electronic equipment. Unfortunately, halon gases have a chlorofluorocarbon (CFC) base, and CFC gases have the highest ozone-depleting potential of any chemicals in common use. As a result, the manufacture of new halon was banned in 1993. Then, in 2000, European Regulation EC 2037/2000 prohibited new halon from being used to refill existing systems. In addition, the use of recovered, recycled, or reclaimed halon was banned after 2002. All halon systems must be decommissioned before December 31, 2003.

Besides halon, however, several other clean extinguishing agents are available:

- FM-200, a hydrofluorocarbon, is considered an acceptable alternative to halon in occupied and unoccupied areas. FM-200 is becoming more popular because its relatively fast natural degradation does not reduce stratospheric ozone. It is also safe for human exposure, and leaves no residue.

- Argon (Ar) is a noble gas obtained from ambient air. Argon is heavier than air, with a density ratio to air of 1.38:1. In its gaseous form, argon is compressed and stored in high-pressure steel cylinders. It is nontoxic; however, during the buildup of gas concentrations needed for extinguishing fires, a dangerous situation could arise from the combination of fire gases and an oxygen deficiency.

- Nitrogen (N_2) is a colorless, inodorous, and tasteless gas found in the atmosphere. It is lighter than air, with a density ratio to air of 0.967:1. In its gaseous form, nitrogen is compressed and stored in high-pressure steel cylinders. It is nontoxic, but its gas buildup creates the same danger as that for argon.

- Carbon dioxide (CO_2) is also found in the atmosphere. It is heavier than air, with a density ratio of 1.53:1. Carbon dioxide is liquefied under pressure and stored in high-pressure steel cylinders or large, low-pressure vessels. Because it is liquid and requires less space, you can store significantly larger quantities of it. High concentrations of carbon dioxide are unhealthy, and trade associations require specific protection measures when specific limits are exceeded. Due to its physical characteristics, carbon dioxide is the only gas used in hand-held fire extinguishers.

Although all of these gas extinguishants provide efficient, clean fire suppression, particularly for sensitive electronic equipment, they still have disadvantages and hazards:

- **Enclosure integrity** — If a space is not gas-tight, system integrity can be compromised, reducing the ability to suppress fire.

- **Lack of cooling** — Most inert gases cannot cool hot gases or surfaces.

- **Lack of smoke scrubbing (cleaning)** — Inert gas systems cannot remove dangerous and toxic smoke particles produced by fire. Smoke can often cause great damage to sensitive electronics.

- **Dangers of accidental discharge or discharge during fire** — In a fire, some inert gases can produce toxic by-products such as hydrogen fluoride, which can be harmful to people and sensitive equipment. CO_2 can be lethal when discharged in an occupied space, either by accident or in a fire.

Another extinguishant, known as extinguishing powder, quickly and effectively puts out a fire by removing the oxygen from it—in other words, by suffocating it. The powder creates melting layers on glowing embers of the combustible material, and prevents the diffusion of atmospheric oxygen around the fire. Once the powder has extinguished a fire, it cannot start again. Extinguishing powders consist mainly of nonpoisonous, inorganic salts that are mixed with waterproofing and pouring agents.

Fire Containment Systems

A fire **containment system** is designed to reduce the rapid spread of fire and toxic fumes from their point of origin. These systems are considered **passive** because they are nonmechanical and nonelectrical, and require no human intervention or moving parts. The system functions to contain a fire within the area where it started, and prevents loss of life by keeping combustion products such as smoke, hot gases, and flames from spreading throughout a building.

A fire containment system uses walls and floors that comply with **fire resistance ratings (fire ratings)**. These ratings refer to the ability to withstand fire and continue to perform a structural function, as determined by the ASTM E-119 standard, "Standard Test Methods for Fire Tests of Building Construction and Materials." The system also uses **penetrations**, voids or holes in a building's construction through which pipes, conduits, and cable trays may pass. Finally, the system uses joint seals and other passive features to compartmentalize a structure into discrete, isolated units that confine a fire and its toxic by-products to the point of origin.

A fire containment system includes three main components:

- **Fireblocking** consists of subdividing barriers that resist or block the spread of fire within the concealed small spaces of stud walls, at soffits and drop ceilings, and at the top and bottom of stair stringers.

- **Draftstopping** consists of similar barriers that block the spread of fire within the large concealed spaces of flooring, attics, and crawlspaces.

- **Firestopping** is a method of passive protection that helps contain fire and toxic gases to the area of origin by sealing around penetrations and construction joints in fire-rated floors and walls. Firestopping is the primary component in the fire containment system, and is the focus of the rest of this chapter.

A typical fire stop for penetrations is shown in Figure 7-5, and a typical construction joint is shown in Figure 7-6.

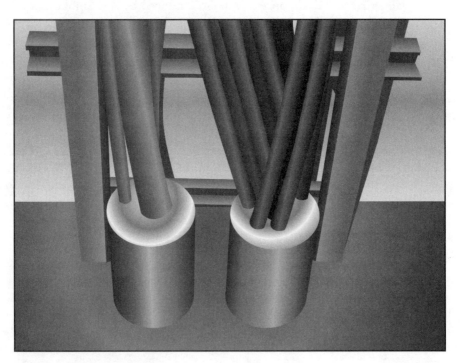

Figure 7-5   Typical fire stop

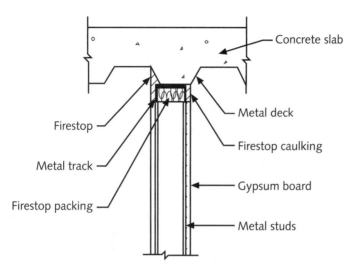

Figure 7-6   Typical construction joint

Debates have raged for many years about the need for passive fire containment systems if a building has an active fire suppression system, such as automatic **sprinklers**. These devices apply water directly onto flames and heat to cool combustion and prevent ignition of adjacent combustible materials. In 1998, however, more than 8 million sprinkler systems were recalled, and testing revealed that more than 20 percent of the systems were defective. This major recall dramatized the vulnerability of active systems to malfunctions or human error, and the risk of depending on these systems exclusively instead of balancing them with passive components. The practice of installing and using both active and passive systems is referred to as **redundancy**. With both types of protection in place, there is greater assurance that building occupants will have time to exit before hot gases, smoke, and fire spread throughout the building. If the active system should fail, as sometimes happens, the passive system is still in place for safety.

FIRESTOPPING AND ITS ROLE IN FIRE PROTECTION

As the key component in any fire containment system, firestopping plays an important role in comprehensive fire protection. Firestopping systems include fire resistance-rated walls, floors, or ceilings; penetration items such as pipes, cable, or conduit; and listed materials to seal penetrations or construction joints.

The containment of fire has been proven to reduce danger and provide time for people to safely exit a building. This measure of protection has played a major role in the adoption and enforcement of firestopping systems by major building codes.

In 1975, a potentially disastrous fire spread through cable trays at the Browns Ferry Nuclear Power Plant. The fire heightened awareness of the need for specific materials to protect through-penetrations. Eight years later, the **American Society for Testing and Materials** (now called **ASTM International**) completed ASTM E-814: "Standard Test Method for Fire Tests of Through-Penetration Fire Stops." This standard established performance criteria for materials used to protect penetrations that pass through fire resistance-rated assemblies. The firestop assemblies are tested to indicate how well they protect against fire, hot gases, temperature rise, and air (smoke) leakage.

To ensure that fire stops provide proper protection and meet code requirements, ASTM E-814 and other codes require assemblies to have an **FT rating**. The F indicates the number of hours that a fire-resistant barrier can withstand fire before allowing the flames to pass through an opening; the T indicates how many hours it takes temperatures on the non-fire side of a fire-rated assembly to exceed 325°F above the ambient temperature. FT ratings are expressed as the lower of the F and T measurements. For example, if a firestopping system has an F rating of two hours and a T rating of 15 minutes, the assembly has an FT rating of 15 minutes. FT ratings are required for any firestop assembly that penetrates a **firewall**, a type of fire protection that subdivides a building or separates adjoining buildings. They are also required for any horizontal **fire separation** assemblies that act as a barrier against the spread of fire.

Besides FT ratings, several other tests are designed to rate the performance of firestopping products:

- **ASTM E-84** — "Standard Test Method for Surface Burning Characteristics of Building Materials," which evaluates the spread of fire along the surface of the material. This is not a fire resistance test.

- **ASTM E-119** — "Standard Test Methods for Fire Tests of Building Construction and Materials," which evaluates fire-resistant constructions that contain through-penetration or construction joints. This test measures time and temperature requirements.

- **ASTM E-814** — This standard was mentioned earlier in this section. Firestopping systems that are tested to this standard are subjected to fire exposure, then to a hose stream test to establish the F rating, and finally the thermal conductivity is recorded to establish the T rating.

FIRESTOPPING PRODUCTS AND MATERIALS

Many firestopping products are available to meet the needs of any application. These products must be tested and listed by an independent testing laboratory such as Underwriters Laboratories, and should display the approving agency's classification mark on the package or container. This classification mark does not approve the product for use in all firestopping applications, but only for the application for which it was designed and tested. Because so many products are available, you must match your application with an appropriately listed firestopping system.

The most common firestopping method is the use of **sealants** to seal openings around penetrations and construction joints. Sealants are categorized into two groups:

- **Intumescent** products are designed to expand at a predetermined temperature range. These products are commonly approved for use around insulated and noninsulated metal pipes, combustible and glass pipes, cables, cable bundles, electrical buses, and nondampered HVAC ducts. Intumescent sealants typically provide the widest range of through-penetration applications.

- **Nonintumescent sealants** are most commonly used in construction joints and some through-penetration applications (Figure 7-7). They are well suited to construction-joint applications where movement of the joint is expected. There are generally two types of nonintumescent seal: acrylic-based, which cleans up easily with water and can be painted to provide a finished look in exposed areas; and silicone-based, which works well for applications that may be exposed to weather and ultraviolet rays. All nonintumescent sealant remains flexible when cured and allows for movement. It comes in various forms, from caulk-gun grade to self-leveling forms that require no additional tooling once applied. Other forms are sprayable mastics for joint applications, where speed and ease of application are most desirable (for example, top-of-wall applications). Sprayable mastics can be applied quickly using industrial, airless spray equipment, and are good for applications where large joint runs exist and for joints where maximum movement is needed. Most sprayable mastics clean up easily with water.

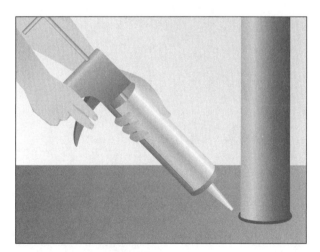

Figure 7-7 Typical sealant

Because vented plastic pipes are combustible, they present a far more challenging fire hazard than metal pipes or conduits. If they are not properly firestopped, the pipes can melt or burn, leaving a passage for fire to spread quickly to adjoining rooms or the floor above. The penetration itself has a natural flammability, and intumescent materials installed around these pipes need to be capable of closing down and sealing the opening when the penetration burns away. Fortunately, several products are available to address these problems.

Very large, combustible pipes exceed the capabilities of intumescent seals to properly seal the opening and maintain the desired fire rating. Therefore, intumescent collars and wrap strips are used on these pipes to maintain their rating. A common pipe collar and wrap strip are shown in Figure 7-8. Intumescent **collars** are usually constructed of galvanized steel bands with specially designed intumescent material inlaid in the band. They have fixed or adjustable mounting tabs for attachment to the wall or floor assembly. Intumescent collars come in many sizes, to handle the various sizes and schedules of combustible pipes. Most collar systems incorporate a smoke seal using a sealant material within the **annular space**, the distance between the penetrating item and the surrounding opening of the penetration.

Intumescent **wrap strips** are long strips of a highly intumescent material that are available in various widths (usually 1 to 2 inches), and are wrapped around the penetration a certain number of times. With the wrap strip in place, the penetration is slid into the annular space within the floor or wall assembly, or held in place with a prefabricated steel band or retaining collar.

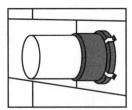

Intumescent pipe collar

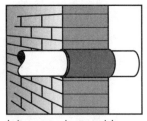

Intumescent wrap strip

Figure 7-8   Intumescent pipe collar and wrap strip

Very large openings or openings with multiple penetrations present a real challenge to firestopping. The materials used in such applications should be designed and tested to function properly with many types of penetrations. Large, multiple-penetration openings can contain combustible penetrations such as plastic pipes and cables, insulated pipes, cables and cable bundles, cable trays, and a variety of metal penetrations. The following list describes firestopping products you can use for these applications:

- **Fire blocks** are designed to form a barrier to fire and smoke. They are used in walls and are ideal for computer rooms under raised or access floors.

- Intumescent **fire pillows** are made of a specially treated glass cloth filled with a mixture of mineral fiber and reactive expansion agents. Upon exposure to fire, a fire pillow first expands and then hardens to provide a complete and durable seal. Figure 7-9 shows one way to use fire pillows. They are good for sealing cable trays and ducts, and for use in areas where services are continually modified, such as telecommunications areas and computer rooms.

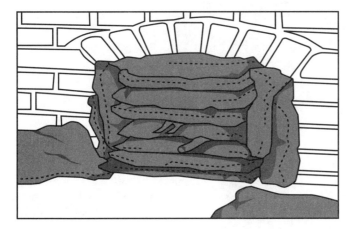

Figure 7-9   Fire pillows

- Intumescent **mortar** is a gypsum-based, fire-resistant material that expands when activated by water, and sets to form an excellent seal. Figure 7-10 shows how mortar is typically used. You can easily reactivate it by adding more water for up to 45 minutes after it is mixed. Also, you can easily add more services through the mortar and then reseal them with more mortar.

- **Fire-rated foam** is a one-component polyurethane foam that expands to fill and seal gaps. Foam is rated, but is not intumescent. It cures quickly through the absorption of moisture from the atmosphere, and has excellent adhesive properties. When set, the foam forms a strong bond to most building materials. Cured foam has a substantially closed cell structure, so it hardens to a semirigid form, making it both firm and yielding. These products were developed to seal single and multiple penetrations that have limited access, due to close annular spacing or other obstructions that prohibit the use of traditional firestopping methods. Fire-rated foam typically requires access from only one side of the assembly being penetrated.

Figure 7-10 Fire-rated mortar

Most products in the previous list allow you to create additional penetrations in the opening or remove penetrations that have been taken out of service. You can then reshape these materials to form a new seal. This flexibility is extremely beneficial in telecommunications, where new cable installation is an ongoing process. The following paragraphs describe several other firestopping products you might find useful.

Intumescent **putty** is a nonhardening and noncuring firestopping product. It is commonly used around penetrations for electrical cable, telecommunications cable, and metallic pipes (Figure 7-11). You can reaccess the putty to add or remove cables or pipes. Intumescent putty expands under heat to form a hard **char** material, a grayish-black crust created when organic sealants are burned, which restricts the passage of heated toxic gases and flames. Intumescent putties are easy to mold and install around penetrations of various shapes and sizes, and they adhere well to most common building materials.

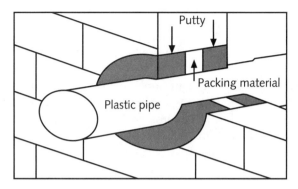

Figure 7-11 Putty

Cast-in devices incorporate firestopping with the insertion of a durable cylindrical device through a penetration, which allows another pipe to be inserted through it. These cylindrical devices are known as **sleeving**. During the early stages of new construction, before the concrete is poured, cast-in firestopping devices are installed in place of the traditional pipe sleeves. The firestop material is already contained within the cast-in device. Once the concrete is poured, the last step of the firestopping process is to pass the penetrations through the cast-in device. Because these devices usually incorporate a built-in smoke and water seal, additional steps are generally not required for firestopping. A major benefit of cast-in devices is the labor savings; one person can complete the sleeve and firestopping process in one easy step. Cast-in devices also simplify the inspection of proper firestopping.

Fire seals are small pieces of rubberlike, flexible, fire-retardant material. They adhere tightly to cable trays, conduits, and cables, allowing them to move within the penetration. These seals not only confine the hazards of fire, smoke, and toxic fumes, they effectively seal out dust, water, and other contaminants. Joint seals, one of the numerous types of seals, are shown in Figure 7-12.

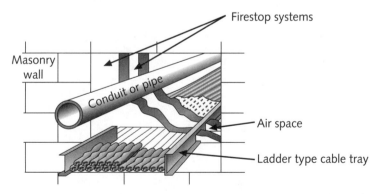

Figure 7-12 Fire seals

SELECTING THE RIGHT FIRESTOPPING SYSTEM

So many firestopping products are available that you might find it difficult to know how to select the right ones for your application. Fortunately, plenty of educational resources can help you find the appropriate products. For example, many top manufacturers provide on-site technical consultation and engineering support to answer your questions and help you select firestopping products and listed systems. Engineering support is especially helpful with complicated applications. The manufacturers can also provide professional installers to take over the problems and liabilities associated with proper firestopping.

Of course, you might prefer to handle the entire firestopping process yourself. You will still have access to the same educational resources. In addition, you can determine that you have made the correct firestopping selections by answering the following questions and reviewing the building schematics and suggestions in Figure 7-13.

- What hourly rating is required?

- What type of construction is involved?

- What are the types and designs of the fire resistance-rated items (for example, gypsum board, concrete block, masonry)?

- What are the sizes of the holes or openings?

- What type of penetrants will be used?

- How big is the annular space?

- If the penetrants are conduit, are they metallic or nonmetallic, and how many are there?

- If the penetrants are piping, how large are the pipes, and are they vented or closed?

- If the penetrants are cables, what type(s) of cable will be used, and how many?

- Are there other considerations, such as movement or vibration in the area?

- Has any unusual contraction or expansion been observed?

- Will penetrants need to be modified frequently?

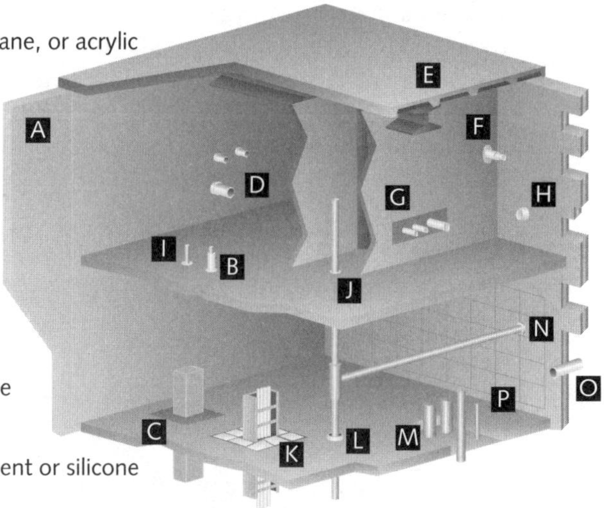

A. Expansion joint using silicone, urethane, or acrylic joint sealant

B. Insulated metal pipe using intumescent sealant

C. Bus duct using silicone sealant

D. PVC, CPVC, and polypropylene pipes using intumescent devices

E. Top-of-wall joint between concrete-steel fluted decking and gypsum walls using acrylic or silicone sealant, or acrylic spray

F. Insulated metal pipe using intumescent or silicone sealant

G. Multiple metal pipe using ceramic or silicone sealant, or mortar

H. Insulated cables using intumescent, silicone, or ceramic sealant

I. PVC pipe using intumescent devices (positioned at ceiling level) and intumescent sealant (floor level)

J. Metal pipe using silicone, acrylic, ceramic, or intumescent sealant

K. Cable tray using intumescent pillows

L. PVC or CPVC pipe using cast-in place intumescent devices

M. Metal pipe, PVC, and insulated metal pipe using intumescent wrap strip and intumescent sealant

N. Small PVC or CPVC pipe using intumescent sealant

O. PVC pipe using prefabricated intumescent devices for walls

P. Expansion joint using silicone, urethane, or acrylic joint sealant

Figure 7-13   Suggested firestopping locations and materials

INSTALLATION GUIDELINES FOR FIRESTOPPING SYSTEMS

Traditionally, cable installers have shown a blatant disregard for firestopping materials and firewalls. Firewalls are designed to save lives and property in case of fire; properly firestopped penetrations keep a fire, its smoke, and its toxic gases from spreading.

Because a firestopping system must be tested and listed, it must also be installed according to appropriately tested and listed system parameters. One missed or even partially missed parameter could cause death, property damage, or interruption of a company's operations—and the liability lies with you, the installer. If you install a firestopping system, you need to consider it a "**zero tolerance**" system, meaning there is no room for error.

To ensure that your system installation meets zero-tolerance requirements, you can follow the basic recommendations of the Firestop Contractors International Association (FCIA) and Factory Mutual Research (part of FM Global), in their new joint standard, FM 4991: "Standard for Approval of Fire Stop Contractors." These basic recommendations are:

- Select the right products.

- Install the system properly.

- Inspect the installation.

- Provide documentation that the installation was performed properly.

Until the FM 4991 standard was developed, the only qualifications for firestopping system installers were published as one or two lines in specifications. A line might simply read "contractor approved by the manufacturer," or "contractor with experience in the type and size of work specified," or "with a reference project that can be visited for inspection." The impetus for firestopping installation training has come primarily from product manufacturers, who spend time and money teaching contractors to install products according to all codes and specifications.

In addition to FM 4991, future standards will most likely require specific training for installers in proper firestopping practices. This training will probably avoid naming specific vendors so it can encompass the wide array of available equipment. Training will probably also require continuing education, to help installers keep pace with fast-changing product and testing criteria. Besides using FM 4991, you can take the following steps to ensure a zero-tolerant firestopping system:

- Check with the building inspector and fire marshal in your area to ensure that you know the local fire codes, and that you are in complete compliance. Also, be familiar with the requirements for your specific application, as defined by the National Electrical Code (NEC), NFPA, and the ANSI/EIA/TIA 569-A standard (firestopping section).

- Make sure that all firestopping procedures explicitly follow the manufacturer's installation instructions for each product you use. Some products have limitations that are not found on the product packaging. Know these limitations and do not exceed them, or your system may fail inspection.

- If your company does not have a standard operating procedure for firestopping tasks, you need to establish one. If you have one, review it periodically for updating.

- Any time you use a firestopping product, you must ensure that all materials and assemblies are approved by a nationally recognized testing facility such as Underwriters Laboratories.

- Do not run new cables through existing fire barriers that violate code. Some building inspectors blame code violations on the last person to do work in the area, even if the person did not commit the violations.

- To protect yourself from the possibility that other companies might open your firestopping assembly and perform work that would violate the fire code, document your installation by recording your company name, the date, and the number of cables penetrating the fire barrier. Use indelible ink at the penetration, then take pictures of it and the information you recorded.

- Remember, intumescent materials expand to fill a sleeve when it is exposed to heat, so never exceed the fill capacity of a sleeve. If it is near capacity with a fill level of 59 percent, install a new sleeve.

- Never use regular insulation for packing. Use only **mineral wool batt insulation**, a nonflammable, noncombustible material made from spun rock or slag from steel, copper, or lead.

Mineral wool can withstand temperatures of more than 1000°C without melting. This resistance enables it to act as a shield against fire when incorporated into the structure of a building. Mineral wool has other advantages as well. For example, it is a natural resource, which makes it safe and environmentally friendly. It is a better thermal insulator in normal weather than other fibers, due to its ability to absorb and exude moisture from the air. It can absorb sound and thus reduce noise levels. It is a healthy alternative because it is not carcinogenic. Also, it can efficiently absorb and permanently retain indoor air pollutants, such as formaldehyde emitted by common building materials and furniture, and nitrogen dioxide and sulfur dioxide by-products from gas stoves and heaters.

DOCUMENTING NETWORK ADDRESSES, CHANGES, PROCEDURES, AND LOGGING

Effective network documentation requires a current list of MAC and IP addresses, and a detailed record of network changes. Every change you make to the network requires a written procedure and logging in a separate journal.

Documenting MAC and IP Addresses

Next to cable plant documentation, a current and accurate list of all network MAC and IP addresses is the most important documentation you can have. MAC is short for Media Access Control, and IP stands for Internet Protocol. You can use a searchable database to include the MAC and IP address of every server, workstation, managed hub, switch, and router on your network. Besides the MAC and IP addresses, you should also record the name and location of each network device. You can even skip the IP addresses if they all are assigned using DHCP (Dynamic Host Configuration Protocol). This TCP/IP standard allows a workstation to request its TCP/IP configurations from a DHCP server. For example, if you use a simple modem and telephone line at home to connect to your Internet service, a DHCP server provides your IP address and TCP/IP configurations.

A database of MAC and IP addresses can come in handy during troubleshooting. For example, you might see an unusually high number of error packets from a particular MAC address during a network monitoring session. If your database is up to date, you can simply enter the MAC address to locate the machine. In this situation, the problem might be a faulty network interface card (NIC) that needs replacement. (Don't forget that replacing the NIC changes the MAC address, and requires an update to the database.)

A MAC address database can also be useful in conjunction with a NetWare environment that lets you set up login parameters to enhance network security. By establishing intruder detection and intruder lockout settings, you give users a certain number of attempts to log in with a correct password before the system locks out the account. These settings make your network more secure and increase your chances of catching intruders. When a login attempt fails and lockout occurs, a server log records the event and the device's MAC and IP addresses. You can enter the MAC address into your database to try to find the offending machine. If the MAC address is not part of your network, you know that the intruder is external, and that you need to search further using the recorded IP address.

Documenting Additions, Moves, and Changes

Your documentation must allow you to determine what has changed in your network, in case a change causes a problem with the network's performance. This documentation also lets you keep track of all network users and devices. Your work is incomplete until you document it.

This part of your documentation should consist of two sections: the first should provide detailed procedures for all additions, moves, and changes to the network, and the second section should be a detailed log of all actions taken.

Documenting Procedures for Changes

Every change you make to the network requires a detailed, written procedure to ensure that all changes are consistent and documented. For example, if a user moves her workstation to a different location, the written procedure must specify all the actions required to complete the move successfully. The procedure may look like Table 7-1.

Table 7-1 Sample procedure for moving a workstation

Action Taken at Old Location	Action Taken at New Location
Remove the patch cable from the hub/patch panel.	Install the patch cable in a new patch panel/hub.
Update the cut sheet.	Update the cut sheet.
Update the hub documentation to reflect a new free port.	Update the hub documentation to reflect one less free port.
Update the MAC address database to show the workstation's new location, and enter information about the move in the workstation log.	

You should rigorously follow a philosophy of documenting every type of change in your network. If you don't, your documentation will become hopelessly outdated, and all your hard work will be wasted. You should document procedures for installing new applications on servers and workstations, for hardware and software upgrades, and for address changes. This part of the documentation could easily be a separate booklet that you could give to all new technicians.

Logging Additions, Moves, and Changes

You should log network changes in one or more separate journals, rather than in your documentation manual. A good rule of thumb is to keep a journal for each server, for each equipment room, and for each workstation area of your network. The information in the journal should include the device that was changed, the type of change made, and the reason for the change. It should also include the time, date, and location of the change, and the name of the technician who made it.

The journal can be a simple notebook with hand-drawn columns to hold information. A well-kept journal can provide a running history of all work done on the network. If your network begins to have problems, the information in the journal can help you determine if any recent modifications may have played a role.

CHAPTER SUMMARY

- Fires take lives and destroy property every day, which is why building codes have such stringent requirements for fire protection. A comprehensive fire protection system is one of the most important safety measures in building construction.

- A fire protection system should include three separate subsystems for fire detection, fire suppression, and fire containment. The fire detection system provides early warning signals with detectors, fire control panels, alarms, and annunciators that help you locate alarms. The fire suppression system extinguishes the fire and helps reduce damage, by removing either the heat, the oxygen, or the combustion source. The fire containment system reduces the spread of fire.

❐ Firestopping, the key element of a fire containment system, is the method used to contain fire and toxic gases to the area of origin by sealing around penetrations and construction joints in fire-rated floors and walls. A firestopping system includes fire resistance-rated walls, floors, or ceilings; penetration items such as pipes, cable, or conduit; and listed materials to be used for sealing.

❐ Firestopping products come in a variety of types to meet the needs of any application. All firestopping products must be tested and listed. Products are approved only for the application for which they were designed and tested, not for all firestopping applications. Sealants are the most widely used firestopping products. Other products include collars, wrap strips, fire blocks, fire pillows, mortar, foam, putty, caulk, cast-in devices, and fire seals.

❐ Many top manufacturers of firestopping products provide on-site technical consultation and engineering support to answer your questions and help you make the proper selections for firestopping products and listed systems. The engineering support can help you work with complicated applications.

❐ To help ensure that your firestopping installations are "zero tolerance" systems, obtain proper information from the manufacturer of each product you use, and follow their installation instructions explicitly. You can also obtain information through FM 4991, "Standard for Approval of Fire Stop Contractors."

❐ Your network documentation must include a section for listing MAC and IP addresses of all the nodes on your network. Documentation must also include detailed procedures for any network additions, moves, and changes. Log all changes in a set of journals to maintain a running history of all work done on the network. These procedures and documentation help you eliminate and troubleshoot network problems.

Key Terms

annular space — The distance between the penetrating item and the surrounding opening of the penetration.

annunciators — Units that provide graphic displays to pinpoint alarms quickly.

ASTM International (formerly the American Society for Testing and Materials) — An independent volunteer group that generates testing standards.

cast-in device — A device that incorporates the sleeving process and firestopping into one simple step.

char — A grayish-black crust that forms when organic sealants are burned.

clean agents — Electrically nonconductive materials that leave no residue and help protect sensitive electronic equipment.

cold smoke — A nonglowing, smoldering fire.

collars — Usually galvanized steel bands with inlaid intumescent material and adjustable mounting tabs for attachment to a wall or floor assembly.

containment system — The fire protection system responsible for reducing the rapid spread of fire and toxic fumes from their point of origin.

detection system — The fire protection system responsible for providing early warning signals of fire.

draftstopping — Installing barriers that block the spread of fire within the large concealed spaces of flooring, attics, and crawlspaces.

extinguishant — The substance used to put out a fire.

extinguishing foam — A highly effective combination of water, a foaming agent, and air, used to extinguish Class A and Class B fires.

fire block — Fire-resistant material designed to form a barrier in walls and under raised or access floors.

fire control panels — Devices that provide supervision and coordination among the various elements of a fire detection system.

fire pillow — A specially treated glass cloth filled with a mixture of mineral fiber and reactive expansion agents. Fire pillows expand when exposed to heat, and then harden to provide a complete and durable seal.

fire resistance rating (fire rating) — A rating that determines the ability of a wall or floor to withstand fire and continue to perform its structural function, as determined by the ASTM E-119 standard.

fire seals — Small pieces of rubberlike, flexible, fire-retardant material that adhere tightly to cable trays, conduits, and cables, allowing them to move within the penetration.

fire separation — A type of construction assembly that acts as a barrier against the spread of fire.

fire-rated foam — A one-component polyurethane foam that expands to fill and seal gaps around single and multiple penetrations that have limited access.

fireblocking — Installing barriers that block the spread of fire within the concealed small spaces of stud walls, at soffits and drop ceilings, and at the top and bottom of stair stringers.

firestopping — A method of passive fire protection that helps contain fire and toxic gases to the area of origin by sealing around penetrations and construction joints in fire-rated floors and walls.

firewall — A type of fire protection that subdivides a building or separates adjoining buildings.

FT rating — The combination of an F rating (the number of hours that a fire-resistant barrier can withstand fire before allowing the flames to pass through an opening) and a T rating (the number of hours it takes temperatures on the non-fire side of a fire-rated assembly to exceed 325°F above the ambient temperature). The FT rating is always the lower of the two measurements.

intumescent — Designed to expand at a predetermined temperature range.

mineral wool batt insulation — Nonflammable, noncombustible insulation made from spun rock or slag.

mortar — A gypsum-based, fire-resistant material that expands when activated by water and sets to form an excellent seal.

nonintumescent sealant — An acrylic-based or silicone-based sealant that remains flexible when cured to allow movement.

passive system — A nonmechanical, nonelectrical fire containment system that requires no human intervention or moving parts.

penetration — A void or hole in a building's construction through which pipes, conduits, and cable trays may pass.

polyvinyl chloride (PVC) — Material found in the insulation of most wire and cable, and in most plastic conduit.

putty — A nonhardening, noncuring firestopping product that expands when heated.

redundancy — The practice of installing and using multiple systems for protection against system failure.

sealant — Material used to seal openings around penetrations and construction joints.

sleeving — The insertion of a durable cylindrical device through a penetration so that another pipe can be inserted through it.

sprinklers — Devices that apply water directly onto flames and heat to cool combustion and prevent ignition of adjacent combustible materials.

suppression system — The fire protection system responsible for extinguishing fires.

wrap strips — Long strips of intumescent material, usually 1 or 2 inches wide, that are wrapped around a penetration a certain number of times.

zero tolerance — A term for a system that allows no margin for error.

REVIEW QUESTIONS

1. What are the three elements of a comprehensive fire protection system?

   a. detection, suppression, and comprehension

   b. containment, detection, and extinguishants

   c. detection, suppression, and containment

   d. suppression, prevention, and detection

2. As a telecommunications specialist, you have the greatest direct involvement with which element of the fire protection system?

   a. protection

   b. suppression

   c. firestopping

   d. containment

3. Which of the following actions can enhance fire protection in a building?

   a. reviewing building plans

   b. instituting and enforcing building codes and standards

   c. performing regular building inspections

   d. all of the above

4. Which agency and code define the requirements for fire control panels?

   a. National Fire Protection Association, 72

   b. NEC, 72-2

   c. National Fire Protection Association, 76

   d. NEC, 72

5. Which of the following two factors have contributed to changing attitudes concerning fire protection systems?

   a. code requirements

   b. increased value and importance of equipment and records

   c. a more fundamental focus on building safety and security

   d. slow response of fire departments

6. The primary goal and responsibility of a fire suppression system is _____.

   a. to prevent fires from spreading

   b. to identify the fire's location

   c. to remove the heat from the fire

   d. to extinguish the fire

7. The secondary goal of a fire suppression system is _____.

   a. to remove the oxygen fueling the fire

   b. to keep the fire from spreading

   c. to help reduce damage caused by fire

   d. to extinguish the fire

8. What are the three main types of fire alarms?

   a. manual fire alarm stations, audible, and optical

   b. control panel, detection, and LED

   c. annunciators, fire extinguishers, and manual fire alarms

   d. audible, optical, and annunciators

9. The primary component of a fire suppression system is an extinguishant. True or False?

7

10. Match each extinguishant with its suppression property.

a. water

b. extinguishing foam

c. inert gases

d. FM-200 gas

e. extinguishing powder

1. Depending on density, it can remove heat, oxygen, and source of combustion.

2. It removes heat by cooling.

3. It removes oxygen by the creation of melting layers.

4. It removes heat in Class A fires.

5. Suffocation occurs when oxygen values fall below a certain combustion limit.

11. The three inert gases used in fire suppression are _____.

a. argon, nitrogen, and carbon dioxide

b. nitrogen, oxygen, and helium

c. argon, carbon, and neon

d. carbon dioxide, argon, and oxygen

12. Which extinguishing gas is gaining in popularity because it does not reduce stratospheric ozone?

a. cyanide

b. nitrous oxide

c. FM-200

d. ammonia sulfate

13. The primary reason that FM-200 does not reduce stratospheric ozone is its relatively slow degradation rate. True or False?

14. The purpose of a fire containment system is to confine a fire, its smoke, and its toxic by-products to a limited area and prevent it from spreading. True or False?

15. Fire containment systems are considered to be _____.

a. passive/aggressive systems

b. aggressive systems

c. nonmechanical systems

d. passive systems

16. Fire resistance-rated walls and floors are assemblies that can withstand fire and continue to perform their structural functions. True or False?

17. Which two of the following qualities make a fire containment system passive?

a. the fire resistance rating of the structure

b. being nonmechanical and nonelectrical

c. being mechanical with moving electrical parts

d. no human intervention or moving parts

18. Fire containment systems include _____.

    a. fireblocking, draftstopping, and firestopping

    b. draftstopping, extinguishants, and annunciators

    c. fireblocking, firestopping, and fire resistance

    d. none of the above

19. The agency and code that establish fire resistance ratings for materials used to protect penetrations that pass through fire resistance-rated assemblies are _____.

    a. ASTM, E-714

    b. Fire Protection Agency, E-811

    c. American Society for Testing and Materials, E-814

    d. NEC, E-814

20. Why is redundancy needed in fire protection systems?

    a. in case an active system malfunctions due to human error

    b. to provide time for building occupants to safely evacuate the area

    c. because of the vulnerability of active systems to mechanical malfunction

    d. all of the above

21. What are the components of a firestopping system? (Choose all that apply.)

    a. the listed materials used for sealing penetrations and construction joints

    b. tested sprinkler systems

    c. fire resistance-rated walls, floors, or ceilings

    d. penetration items such as pipes, cables, or conduits

22. The FT rating of a firestopping system is calculated by adding the F and T ratings. True or False?

23. Which of the following subdivides a building or separates adjoining buildings?

    a. fire separation

    b. firewall

    c. annular space

    d. fire block

24. Which device incorporates firestopping and sleeving in one simple step?

    a. fire foam products

    b. zero tolerance

    c. fire blocks

    d. cast-in device

7

25. Firestopping products are tested and listed by an independent testing laboratory, which places its classification mark on the product's package or container upon approval. What does this classification mark signify?

   a. The product has been approved for the application for which it was designed and tested.

   b. The product has been approved for use with all firestopping applications.

   c. The product cannot be used until it is tested further.

   d. The product can only be used if the FT rating is greater than 15 hours.

HANDS-ON PROJECTS

HANDS-ON PROJECTS

Project 7-1

One of your customers has hired you to design and install their new fire protection system. The following information describes the customer's building space and equipment:

- The building is a single-level structure.

- The reception area has one phone, one networked computer, one printer, and one fax machine.

- Adjacent to the reception area is a copy room that also serves as storage for office supplies. The wall separating the reception area and copy room is fire resistance-rated.

- There are eight private offices, each with a phone and a computer attached to the network. Two of the offices have their own printers; everyone else prints to the network printer in the copy room.

- There is an open work area with 10 desks; each desk has a phone and a networked computer. The wall between the private office area and the open work area is fire resistance-rated.

- Your customer stores all the cleaning supplies and party decorations in a telecommunications closet. The ceiling and all walls are fire resistance-rated.

- The building has two restrooms and an employee lounge that is furnished with a table and chairs, a refrigerator, a microwave oven, a coffee maker, some vending machines, and one telephone.

- The building currently has no fire protection system, although there is one smoke detector installed in the reception area.

   1. For the new fire protection system, create a list of all equipment you plan to install. The list should include the types and quantities of each item you plan to use. Explain why you selected each item and how you decided on its location.

2. Using a computer that has Visio installed, create a floor plan of the existing office space. Make sure you include the locations of all equipment, furniture, and network cables. Describe the type of network cables used and their routes from the server in the telecommunications room to each workstation. Include the locations of all other telecommunications equipment, their cables, the type used, their routes from the telecommunications room to each workstation, and their function (e.g., telephone or modem).

3. From the list you created, add all the new fire protection equipment to your floor plan. Show the routes and types of any additional cables you need.

4. Print your floor plan and list to turn in to your instructor.

Project 7-2

In this exercise, list the three methods of extinguishing a fire. Include two or three examples of when and how you might use each method.

Project 7-3

For this exercise, refer to the list of extinguishants in your text and select the best one for extinguishing the following types of fires. Explain each of your selections.

❏ Fire in an indoor trash can that contains paper, food scraps, metal cans, aluminum foil, and plastic wrap

❏ Fire in an outdoor garbage bin that contains grass, leaves, wood, paint cans, aerosol cans, rusted metal, and small bits of rubber

❏ Kitchen grease fire

❏ Car fire with the motor running

❏ Fire in a warehouse that stocks computer equipment, other electronics, and electrical parts

❏ Fire in a warehouse that stocks industrial cleaning solutions and pesticides

Project 7-4

Many applications offer multiple choices for firestopping materials. In this exercise, select the most appropriate firestopping material for each of the following scenarios. Explain your reasons for each selection.

❏ You ran a large amount of CAT5 cable to a section of a building that had not been used before. The amount of cable you used required a large, vented-plastic pipe.

❏ Your customer has built a new work area. You need to run cables to this work area to accommodate 50 workstations now; however, you know that additional large amounts of cable will be added in the near future. The location of the new work area prevents you from using any of the existing cable trays. You add a new cable tray that penetrates a fire resistance–rated wall.

❑ Your customer is the local hospital. The operating-room area was recently remodeled, and now the telephones and computers are not easy to access. You have been asked to relocate these units.

❑ The demarcation point is on the wall outside your customer's building. You need to provide a cable from the demarc to the equipment room inside the building, which requires running the cable through a firewall with a large opening that accommodates multiple metal pipes.

Project 7-5

Use your textbook, libraries, and the Internet to define the following three terms, which are used primarily by Underwriters Laboratories (UL). As part of your definitions, explain how each term is used by UL. Include your source(s) for each definition.

❑ Classification

❑ Listing

❑ Recognition

Project 7-6

Use your textbook, libraries, and the Internet to define the following terms as they relate to fire protection. Include your source(s) for each definition.

❑ Passive

❑ Active

❑ Redundancy

❑ Draftstopping

❑ Fireblocking

Project 7-7

Use your textbook, libraries, and the Internet to define the following terms as they relate to fire codes, fire protection standards, and fire testing. Include your source(s) for each definition.

❑ Thermal conductivity

❑ Fire-resistant

❑ Tested

❑ Listed

❏ Approved

❏ Zero tolerance

Project 7-8

The telecommunications company you work for does not have a current standard operating procedure (SOP) for installing firestopping systems. You and a co-worker have been assigned to update the SOP. Research the current firestopping requirements, rules, laws, codes, and standards. Once you have obtained this information, update the SOP.

CASE PROJECTS

Case Project 1

A number of detectors are available for today's fire protection systems. For each of the following detectors, write an explanation of what it does, how it works, and its most likely commercial and residential applications. Use your textbook, libraries, the Internet, or any other resources to research these detectors, and identify these resources in your explanation.

❏ Optical smoke detectors

❏ Differential maximum heat detectors

❏ Ionization smoke detectors

❏ Spark and flame detectors

❏ High-sensitivity smoke detectors

❏ Bypass detectors

❏ Multifunctional detectors

❏ Gas detectors

Case Project 2

For this project, contact the offices of your local building inspector and fire marshal, and get the current building and fire safety codes for your city or town. Next, find the building and fire safety codes for your state, and then find the national codes. After you have all the code information, write a summary of your findings. Your summary should also include answers to the following questions:

❏ Are there any differences among the sets of codes? If so, what are they?

❏ If there are differences, which code takes precedence?

❏ Besides your local building inspector and fire marshal, what were your sources of information for each set of codes?

Case Project 3

On October 14, 1998, the U.S. Consumer Product Safety Commission and Central Sprinkler Company announced the recall of more than 8 million Omega Sprinklers, manufactured by Central Sprinkler. For this project, search for information about the recall and the company. Use the Internet, old newspaper articles, or any other resources you prefer.

When you finish, write a summary of what you learned. Include answers to the following questions: Was one factor responsible for the recall, or was there more than one? What were the results of the recall? What was the problem with the sprinklers? What did Central Sprinkler do, if anything, about the recalled equipment? How did the recall affect Central Sprinkler, its customers, the general public, and the fire protection industry? Explain why you answered the way you did, and list the resources you used for the project. If necessary, use the following Web sites to get started:

❑ *www.cpsc.gov/cpscpub/prerel/prhtml99/99008.html*

❑ *www.cpsc.gov/cpscpub/prerel/prhtml01/01201.html*

❑ *www.sprinklernet.org/technical/recall.html*

Case Project 4

You should only use firestopping products that have been tested and approved for your application. You know that "independent laboratories" administer these tests and certify the equipment, but what do you know about these laboratories or their testing?

For this project, you will research one of the best-known laboratories, Underwriters Laboratories (UL). Using a computer with Internet access, go to the certification section of UL's Web site (*www.ul.com*). Search for UL 1479: Test Standard for Through-Penetration Fire Stops, and UL 2079: Tests for Fire Resistance of Building Joint Systems. You can perform more Web searches for additional information.

When you finish, write a summary of each standard. Describe the parameters of the standard and explain what it measures or tests. Also, explain the types of tests UL performs and its criteria for determining whether an item passes its tests. Include any other information you think is important.

Case Project 5

On March 22, 1975, Browns Ferry Nuclear Plant suffered a devastating fire, which played a key role in the development of the ASTM E-814 standard. For this project, use a computer with Internet access to research the Browns Ferry fire. When you finish, write a summary of the fire, including how it started, what could have prevented it, and what made it so serious. Next, write a brief fire protection plan for Browns Ferry, as if you were in charge of the plant and the fire had not yet happened.

8

TESTING AND
TROUBLESHOOTING

**After reading this chapter and completing the exercises,
you will be able to:**

♦ Understand the necessity for testing your cable system

♦ Define and perform tests on copper and fiber media

♦ Understand troubleshooting methods and general techniques

♦ Identify and use testing and troubleshooting tools

♦ Design a disaster avoidance plan

♦ Manage your documentation

In the previous chapters you learned about various media types, decided which ones were appropriate for your application, and learned the proper methods for cable installation. You also studied various topologies, termination methods, proper grounding and bonding procedures, firestopping procedures, and the codes and standards that apply to your installation.

After you've taken all these steps, your installation is complete. Or is it? How do you know everything will work when you plug it in, or that it will perform according to specifications? How do you know your connections are correctly wired, or that no wires are broken? In short, if you find a problem, how do you identify and fix it? The answer is to test the newly installed system and to know the proper troubleshooting methods and techniques.

This chapter provides you with tools and information for testing your cable and network, and ensuring their proper performance after installation. The chapter explains troubleshooting methods and techniques, and provides several opportunities for practice. This chapter also discusses how to splice various types of cable, and explains basic principles of effective disaster avoidance.

TESTING YOUR CABLING SYSTEM

After you finish running your cable and making the necessary terminations, a final important step remains in the installation: testing the system. By testing your installation before activating the service, you can guarantee that the entire system is operating properly. Testing also confirms that all installed components meet the customer's performance specifications, as well as those in the applicable codes and standards. Finally, you test the cable to make sure your installation is acceptable to the customer.

These three types of cable testing—operational, performance, and acceptance—are discussed in the following sections. Some tests are designed with only one of these three criteria in mind, while other tests encompass all of them.

Operational Testing

To ensure that a system is working properly, you need to know some basic testing procedures:

- Check all cables for **continuity**, the uninterrupted connection or pathway from the beginning to the end of a cable. Continuity enables **connectivity**, the live connection between two endpoints.

- Perform a **polarity test** of cable pairs to confirm that their positive and negative wires are not crossed.

- Run a **connectivity test**, which ensures that all terminations are transmitting signals.

- You can test cables for **shorts**, unwanted contact between two wires that stops transmission signals.

- You can also test for **opens**. These breaks in a wire result in an incomplete circuit and inhibit the continuous flow of transmission signals.

These procedures are the basis for testing various types of media. Each media type comes with additional testing requirements, which are covered later in this chapter.

Performance Testing

Performance testing is designed to ensure that a system complies with all applicable codes and standards. In a telecommunications system, you primarily test for cable performance. This chapter discusses specific tests for each media type, and the testing criteria that identify compliance with codes and standards.

Acceptance Testing

Acceptance testing is designed to demonstrate functionality, prove conformity to specifications, and ensure performance based on the customer's measurement criteria, called **parameters**. These tests generally serve to satisfy the contract between you and your customer. Acceptance tests verify that workmanship is acceptable and confirm that installation methods and equipment meet customer specifications.

The customer's requirements and specifications for system installation are defined in the contract. The following list summarizes typical contract requirements:

- The types of cable to use for each portion of the installation. The customer might also specify a brand name for the cable, and even the color of the cable jacket.

- The acceptable means for running the cables

- Various types of termination equipment. Again, the customer might specify a brand name for the terminations.

- The performance expected from each type of cable, and the testing parameters. These parameters are generally the same as those defined by ANSI/EIA/TIA standards, although some customers have more stringent requirements.

- Verification that installation personnel are certified to test the type of cable being installed

- Verification that all testing equipment is approved, certified, and compliant with applicable codes and standards

- Complete documentation of the installation and test results, including labeled floor plans with all cables numbered for identification. A separate bound document contains all test results for each cable.

8

TESTING COPPER AND FIBER MEDIA

Each media type has its own specific tests, but this section focuses on testing procedures for fiber-optic media and copper, primarily UTP. Although these tests are designed to ensure that your cables comply with applicable ANSI/EIA/TIA standards, you can also use the results to guarantee cable operation, performance, and acceptance.

Hybrid and composite cables have not been discussed previously, but they are gaining in popularity, especially in the residential market. A **hybrid cable** is fiber-optic, and has two or more different types of cable within the same jacket. A **composite cable** also contains two or more different types of cable within the same jacket. In 1998 these definitions were made official; however, the terms were used interchangeably for years. When testing hybrid or composite cables, you must perform all applicable tests for each type of cable within the jacket.

Testing Copper UTP Cable

You should always test UTP cable systems in accordance with the TIA TSB-67 standard, which specifies methods, parameters, and minimum requirements for testing installed Category 3, 4, and 5 cabling with a hand-held instrument. TSB-67 defines performance requirements for UTP cabling links, consistent with the three categories of UTP cable and connecting hardware defined by the ANSI/EIA/TIA-568-A standard. TSB-67 also specifies the electrical characteristics and required accuracy of field testers, the difference between channel and basic link test configurations, and the required tests for determining the acceptance or failure of installed cabling. Although TSB-67 tests verify compliance with ANSI/EIA/TIA-568-A, they cannot guarantee how network equipment will work on the tested cable.

There are several benefits of testing and certifying your cable system according to TSB-67. You can verify that no faults occurred during the installation, and ensure that the system will perform according to the user's requirements. Also, if a problem occurs, the installer is protected from blame when it can be proven that the problem was not caused by faulty workmanship during installation.

TSB-67 defines two types of tests for UTP cable: the basic link test and the channel test. The **basic link** is the permanent part of a cable run that includes 90 meters of horizontal cable, the telecommunications outlet, and the first punch-down in the telecommunications room. The **channel** encompasses the basic link plus all patch cords and equipment cords. Figure 8-1 depicts a typical basic link and channel.

The channel and basic link tests are Category 5 certification tests; when checking your cable system, you should perform both tests to verify that the link and channel installations are correct. The tests are important in verifying proper workmanship, which has a direct impact on system performance. Your initial tests also provide a future reference for the system's proper state of operation or performance. This reference is called a **baseline**.

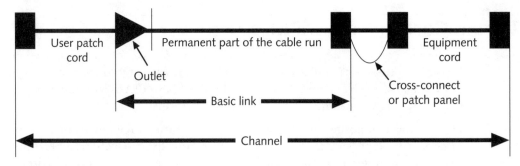

Figure 8-1   Basic link and channel diagram

TSB-67 defines four tests that all cables must pass to be considered compliant. These parameters and performance specifications are shown in Figure 8-2.

Test Parameters and Specifications for TSB-67

NEXT				Attenuation			
Channel		Basic link		Channel		Basic link	
MHz	dB	MHz	dB	MHz	dB	MHz	dB
1	60	1	60	1	2.5	1	2.3
4	50.6	4	51.8	4	4.5	4	4
8	45.6	8	47.1	8	6.3	8	5.7
10	44	10	45.5	10	7	10	6.3
16	40.6	16	42.3	16	9.2	16	8.2
20	39	20	40.7	20	10.3	20	9.2
25	37.4	25	39.1	25	11.4	25	10.3
31.25	35.7	31.25	37.6	31.25	12.8	31.25	11.5
62.5	30.6	62.5	32.7	62.5	18.5	62.5	16.7
100	27.1	100	29.3	100	24	100	21.6

8

Maximum Cable Length	
Channel	100 meters (328 feet)
Basic link	94 meters (308 feet)

Wire Map
Same for channel & basic link
12345678s
12345678x

Figure 8-2   TSB-67 performance specifications

The following section describes each of these tests:

- Wire map test
- Length test
- Attenuation test
- NEXT (near-end crosstalk) test

TSB-67 Tests for Copper UTP Cable

The **wire map test** identifies wiring errors and checks connectivity. The correct connectivity for UTP cabling is defined in section 10.4.5 of the ANSI/EIA/TIA-568-A standard, and is shown in Figure 8-3.

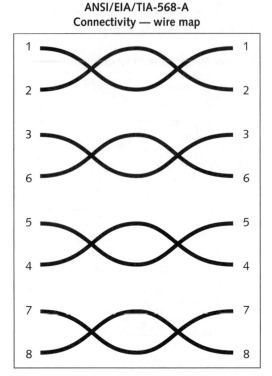

ANSI/EIA/TIA-568-A
Connectivity — wire map

Figure 8-3   ANSI/EIA/TIA-568-A connectivity diagram

The wire map test identifies the wiring errors shown in Figure 8-4 and described in the following list:

- **Opens and shorts** — These errors are described earlier in the chapter.

- **Crossed-pair** — This error occurs when one pair of wires is connected to different pins at each end of the cable. For example, pair 1 might be connected to pins 4 and 5 on one end of the cable, and to pins 1 and 2 at the other end.

- **Reversed-pair** — This error occurs when the two wires of a pair are connected to opposite pins at each end of the cable. For example, wires 1 and 2 might be on the correct pins at one end, while on the other end, wire 1 is on pin 2 and wire 2 is on pin 1. This problem is also called a polarity reversal or a tip and ring reversal.

- **Split-pair** — This error occurs when a wire from one pair is incorrectly connected to a wire from another pair, as if they were a pair. For example, the blue and white/orange wires might be on pins 4 and 5, and the white/blue and orange wires might be on pins 1 and 2.

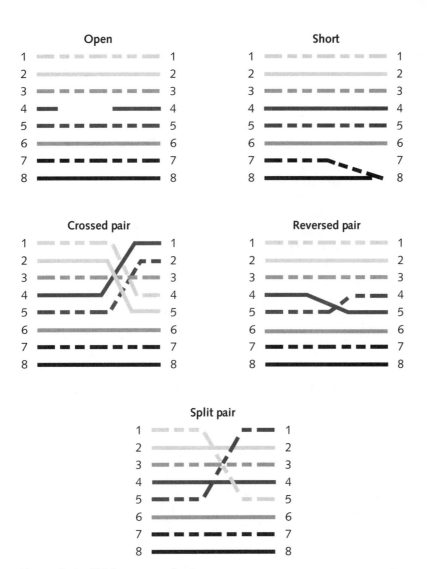

Figure 8-4   Wiring errors diagram

The **length test** verifies that the length of a cable is within the specifications for maximum allowable length. TSB-67 defines the maximum length for a basic link as 94 meters, including equipment cords, and the maximum length for a channel as 100 meters, including equipment and patch cords. You can determine the cable length either by measuring it with the length markings or with an electronic measuring tool. This tool reports the length of the longest pair, and estimates the length based on the electronic information. (Testing tools are discussed later in this chapter.)

The **attenuation** test measures a cable's signal loss from end to end. The farther signals travel on a cable, the weaker they become. Each interconnection on a cable reduces signal strength; also, high-frequency transmissions attenuate at a more rapid rate than lower-frequency transmissions. When performing attenuation tests, you must test all pairs in the cable. When you finish, compare the pair that had the worst performance reading to the allowable attenuation values defined in TSB-67 (shown earlier in Figure 8-2). If the pair with the worst reading surpasses the threshold value in TSB-67, your cable passes the attenuation test.

The **near-end crosstalk (NEXT)** test measures the signal coupling from one pair of wires to another pair within the same cable. When you talk on the telephone, you not only hear the other person through the handset, you hear your own voice. However, if your voice is amplified so loud that you cannot hear the other person, the line has unacceptable signal coupling and near-end crosstalk. To test for NEXT, you apply a balanced signal to a pair of wires at the near end of the connector, and then measure the signal on all pairs at the near end. If the measured NEXT loss is less than the worst-case values defined in TSB-67 (shown earlier in Figure 8-2), the cable passes the test. You must measure all pair combinations from both ends of the cable to ensure that the far-end connections also comply with TSB-67.

Proposed New Tests for Copper UTP Cable

ANSI/EIA/TIA committees are researching and defining additional performance guidelines for UTP cable at the time of this writing. These guidelines, known as TSB-95, provide additional specifications for transmission performance in Category 5, Category 5e, and Category 6 cable, but they are not yet approved or incorporated into ANSI/EIA/TIA-568-A. Figure 8-5 shows the TSB-95 performance specifications. These new guidelines include the following tests:

- **Propagation delay** — This test measures the amount of time it takes a signal to travel from one end of a cable to the other, in nanoseconds (nS). When testing your cable, you must test all pairs and then report the longest (worst-case) delay.

- **Delay skew** — The measurement of the time between the arrival, at the far end of a cable, of the first signal from one wire pair, and the arrival of subsequent signals from the remaining pairs.

- **Attenuation-to-crosstalk ratio (ACR)** — ACR is the calculated difference between the NEXT and attenuation measurements. It is an important measure of cable performance and usable bandwidth.

- **Power sum** — This measurement compares the crosstalk effects on all pairs in a cable. It is generally only used in combination with the ACR, NEXT, and ELFEXT tests.

- **Far-end crosstalk (FEXT)** — This test is similar to the NEXT test, except that the signal is sent from the local end of the cable and the crosstalk is measured from the far end of the cable.

- **ELFEXT** — This is a calculated result, not a measurement. It is derived by subtracting the attenuation of one cable pair from the FEXT that the pair induces in an adjacent pair.

- **Return loss** — This is a measurement of the signal that echoes or reflects back into the transmitter. Return loss is usually caused by an impedance mismatch, an imbalance in the cable, or a mismatch in connecting hardware.

8

Category 5e 100Ω											
Freq	NEXT		Attenuation		Return Loss		ELFEXT		PSNEXT		PSELFEXT	
MHz	Channel	Basic link	Channel	Basic link	Channel	Basic link	Channel	Basic link	Channel	Basic link	Channel	Basic link
1	60	60	3	3	17	17	57.4	58	57	57	54.4	55
4	53.6	54.8	4.5	4	17	17	45.3	48	50.9	52	42.4	45
8	48.6	50	6.3	5.7	17	17	39.3	41.9	45.7	47.1	36.3	38.9
10	47	48.5	7.1	6.4	17	17	37.4	40	44.1	45.6	34.4	37
16	43.6	45.2	9.1	8.1	17	17	33.3	35.9	40.6	42.2	30.3	32.9
20	42	43.7	10.2	9.1	17	17	31.4	34	39	40.7	28.4	31
25	40.4	42.1	11.4	10.3	16	16.3	29.9	32	37.3	39.1	26.4	29
31.25	38.7	40.6	12.9	11.6	15.1	15.6	27.5	30.1	35.7	37.5	24.5	27.1
62.5	33.6	35.7	18.6	16.7	12.1	13.5	21.5	24.1	30.6	32.6	18.5	21.1
100	30.1	32.3	24	21.6	10	12.1	17.4	20	27.1	29.3	14.4	17

Category 6 100Ω											
Freq	NEXT		Attenuation		Return Loss		ELFEXT		PSNEXT		PSELFEXT	
MHz	Channel	Basic link	Channel	Basic link	Channel	Basic link	Channel	Basic link	Channel	Basic link	Channel	Basic link
1	65	65	3	3	19	19	63.1	63.1	62	62	60.1	60.1
4	63.1	64.1	4	3.7	19	19	51.2	53.2	60.6	61.8	48.2	50.2
8	58.2	59.4	5.6	5.2	19	19	45.2	47.1	55.6	57	42.2	44.1
10	56.6	57.8	6.3	5.8	19	19	43.2	45.2	54	55.5	40.2	42.2
16	53.2	54.6	8	7.3	19	19	39.2	41.1	50.6	52.2	36.2	38.1
20	51.6	53.1	9	8.2	19	19	37.2	39.2	49	50.7	34.2	36.2
25	50	51.5	10.1	9.2	18	18.3	35.3	37.2	47.4	49.1	32.3	34.2
31.25	48.4	50	11.3	10.4	17.1	17.6	33.3	35.3	45.7	47.6	30.3	32.3
62.5	43.4	45.2	16.3	14.9	14.1	15.5	27.3	29.3	40.6	42.7	24.3	26.3
100	39.9	41.9	20.9	19.2	12	14.1	23.2	25.2	37.1	39.3	20.2	22.2
125	38.3	40.3	23.6	21.7	11	13.4	21.3	23.3	35.4	37.7	18.3	20.3
200	34.8	36.9	30.6	28.1	9	12	17.2	19.2	31.9	34.3	14.2	16.2
250	33.1	35.4	34.6	31.8	8	11.3	15.3	17.2	30.2	32.7	12.3	14.2

Figure 8-5   TSB-95 performance specifications

General Testing Rules for UTP Cable

You should always observe the following general testing rules for UTP cable, especially when the tests are used to certify your cable system:

- Do not move any cable or equipment during the testing period.

- In addition to recording pass/fail indications, always record the actual measured values and the date to indicate the frequency of testing.

- If you reconfigure any part of your system, always retest it.

- Always perform the NEXT tests and record the measurements from both ends of the cable.

- When performing channel tests, always test with the end-user cords and patch cords in place, and remember that the measurement values allow for 10 meters of equipment cords, patch cords, and jumpers.

- When attaching test instruments, only use qualified adapter cords. All UTP test leads and associated connecting hardware must be constructed of 0.5-mm (24 AWG) cable, and must meet or exceed the Category 5 cable requirements in ANSI/EIA/TIA-568-A.

- You can test 100-ohm, four-pair Category 3 or 5 cable while it is still on the reel, provided that the length is less than 100 meters.

- All field testers must meet TSB-67 accuracy requirements.

- If a cable run barely passes a test, you must record this marginal result in your written report of actual test measurements. Note a marginal cable run with an asterisk next to the measurement.

- Your written report is proof that the cabling system complies with ANSI/EIA/TIA-568-A and TSB-67. Figure 8-6 shows the items you should include in your written report.

Testing Fiber-Optic Cable

Test your fiber-optic cable installation to demonstrate that any exhibited loss does not exceed the acceptable limits defined by ANSI/EIA/TIA-568-B.3, the Optical Fiber Cabling Components standard. This standard specifies the components and transmission requirements of optical fiber cabling systems, including cable, connectors, and connecting hardware. The cables recognized for use by this standard are 50/125-μm and 62.5/125-μm multimode, and 8.3/125-μm single-mode fiber. Testing ensures that the cabling system meets the customer's attenuation specifications, and provides documentation of baseline (normal) readings, which are an essential gauge for future troubleshooting. When testing your installation, test the power levels on the transmitter and receiver to ensure that they are working properly, then document these results.

Cable Test Report						
Date of cable prep:		Date of test:		Media type:		
Project:			Contractor:			
Testing Equipment			Test Personnel			
Make:						
Model:						
Serial number:						
Date of last calibration:						
Cable number:		Cable type:	Pr/cond count:		Total serviceable prs:	

Individual pair/cond number	Number of cross-connects/ patches per pair	Results of wire map test	Results of length test	Results of attenuation test	Results of NEXT test	Results of propagation delay test

Figure 8-6   Sample report form for copper cable testing

To validate a fiber-optic cabling system, you must test for attenuation and bandwidth. Attenuation is a measure of signal loss through the cable as the signal travels from the transmitter to the receiver. A small amount of attenuation is unavoidable, acceptable, and not noticeable. Bandwidth is the measure of a cable's information-carrying capacity. Cable quality and length are two factors that determine bandwidth; the manufacturer generally provides a document or cable label that specifies the cable's proper bandwidth. Field testing for bandwidth is only necessary when the manufacturer's documentation is unavailable or insufficient for verifying compliance, or when the customer requires it.

After testing, be sure to include a written report of all test results in your documentation. You must include all the information shown in the sample report in Figure 8-7.

Cable Test Report					
Date of cable prep:		Date of test:		Media type:	
Project:			Contractor:		
Testing Equipment			Test Personnel		
Make:					
Model:					
Serial number:					
Date of last calibration:					
Cable number:		Cable type:	Fiber count:	Total serviceable prs:	
Individual fiber number	Connector type	Number of connectors/patches	Calculated minimum link loss	Length of run	Measured link loss per fiber

Figure 8-7   Sample testing report for fiber cable

Attenuation Testing of Fiber-Optic Cable

The number of splices and connections in a cable can adversely affect its performance, because more interruptions in the cable provide more opportunities for signal loss. Therefore, it is crucial that you test the attenuation in each cable of your system after installation. To ensure that your cabling system complies with ANSI/EIA/TIA-568-A, you must perform end-to-end attenuation tests and certify that the results conform to the standard. During attenuation testing, you must measure the cable in both directions and at both available wavelengths. A **wavelength** is the measure of the color of light, usually expressed in nanometers (nm).

Document all test results in writing. Spare fibers or unterminated fibers do not require attenuation testing, but you do need to test them for continuity.

Table 8-1 Performance parameters for optical fiber transmission

Optical Fiber Cable Type	Wavelength (nm)	Maximum Attenuation, in Decibels (dB)
50/125-µm multimode	850	3.5
	1300	1.5
62.5/125-µm multimode	850	3.5
	1300	1.5
8.3/125-µm single-mode inside plant	1310	1.0
	1550	1.0
8.3/125-µm single-mode outside plant	1310	0.5
	1550	0.5

Attenuation Testing of Link Segments

You should perform attenuation tests on every link segment of your cable. A **link segment** is composed of the cable, connectors, other connections, and splices between two fiber-optic termination units in your cabling system, including patch panels and work area outlets. You should test every terminated fiber within each segment. The measurement includes connectors at the termination interface on both ends of the link, but does not include attenuation associated with the active equipment interface.

There are three basic types of link segments:

- **Horizontal link** — A link that generally begins at the telecommunications (work area) outlet and ends at the horizontal cross-connect. The link may include **interconnections**, which are devices used to mate fiber-optic connectors or transition point splices.

- **Backbone link** — A link that begins at the main cross-connect and ends at the horizontal cross-connect.

- **Composite link** — A single point of administration architecture that eliminates the horizontal cross-connect. As a result, the horizontal and backbone cabling are combined.

When performing attenuation testing on a link segment, observe the following general guidelines:

- **Multimode horizontal link segment** — Perform the test in one direction only, and select only one wavelength, either 850 nm or 1300 nm.

- **Multimode backbone or composite link segment** — You perform the test in one direction only, but you must test both the 850-nm and 1300-nm wavelengths.

- **Single-mode horizontal link segment** — Perform the test in one direction only, and select only one wavelength, either 1310 nm or 1550 nm.

- **Single-mode backbone or composite link segment** — You perform the test in one direction only, but you must test both the 1310-nm and 1550-nm wavelengths.

To compute the acceptable attenuation value for any link segment, use the following general equation:

Acceptable link attenuation (dB) = cable attenuation (dB) + connector attenuation (dB) + splice attenuation (dB)

Tables 8-2, 8-3, and 8-4 contain computation factors for various attenuation measurements for each type of fiber-optic cable.

Table 8-2   Attenuation computation factors for 62.5/125-μm multimode fiber

Attenuation Type	Computation Factors
Cable attenuation	@ 850 nm – cable length (km) × 3.4 dB/km @ 1300 nm – cable length (km) × 1.0 dB/km
Connector attenuation ST/SC	(# of QL-ST/SC connectors × 0.40 dB) + (# of ST/SC connectors × 0.26 dB) + 0.38
Connector attenuation LC	(# of QL-LC connectors × 0.28 dB) + (# of LC connectors × 0.12 dB) + 0.23
Splice attenuation	# of splices × 0.14 dB

Table 8-3   Attenuation computation factors for 50/125-μm multimode fiber

Attenuation Type	Computation Factors
Cable attenuation	@ 850 nm – cable length (km) × 3.5 dB/km @ 1300 nm – cable length (km) × 1.5 dB/km
Connector attenuation ST/SC	(# of ST/SC connectors × 0.39 dB) + 0.42
Connector attenuation LC	(# of LC connectors × 0.22 dB) + 0.23
Splice attenuation	# of splices × 0.14 dB

Table 8-4   Attenuation computation factors for 8.3/125-μm single-mode fiber

Attenuation Type	Computation Factors
Cable attenuation	Cable length (km) × 0.5 dB/km
Connector attenuation ST/SC	(# of ST/SC connectors × 0.39 dB) + 0.42
Connector attenuation LC	(# of LC connectors × 0.24 dB) + 0.24
Splice attenuation	# of splices × 0.14 dB

All these computation factors and equations may appear complicated, but they are easier than they look. It helps to use the information in a couple of real-life situations. For example, suppose that you just finished installing a fiber-optic cabling system and are ready to start testing. The backbone link segment is 62.5/125-μm multimode fiber that links the main cross-connect and the horizontal cross-connect. The length of the cable run is 160 meters (0.160 km); the cable has one splice at mid-span and uses ST connectors. You need to calculate the acceptable link attenuation.

Because this is a backbone segment, however, you must test at both the 850-nm and 1300-nm wavelengths, which results in two separate computations. Use the computation factors shown in Table 8-2 and the following formula:

Acceptable link attenuation (dB) = cable attenuation (dB) + connector attenuation (dB) + splice attenuation (dB)

The answers are:

- Acceptable link attenuation @ 850 nm = [0.160 km × 3.4 dB/km] + [(2 × 0.26 dB) + 0.38 dB] + [1 × 0.14 dB], which equals 1.58 dB (0.54 + 0.90 + 0.14)

- Acceptable link attenuation @ 1300 nm = [0.160 km × 1.0 dB/km] + [(2 × 0.26 dB) + 0.38 dB] + [1 × 0.14 dB], which equals 1.20 dB (0.16 + 0.90 + 0.14)

As another example, suppose that you want to test a fiber-optic installation you just finished. You used a 12-fiber, 62.5/125-μm multimode fiber. The horizontal link you need to test is 75 meters (0.075 km) from the horizontal cross-connect to an interconnection in the open office area. From the interconnection point, four multimode, 15-meter, two-fiber cables are distributed to modular office furniture outlets, leaving four spare fibers of the horizontal cable for future use. All fibers are terminated with standard ST connectors, except at the outlets, where each fiber is terminated on a Quick-Light ST (QL-ST). You need to calculate the acceptable link attenuation of the horizontal link segments.

Because this is a horizontal link segment, you only need to test at one wavelength. You have chosen 850 nm. You must use two equations—one covers the distance from the horizontal cross-connect to the interconnection point, and the second covers the distance from the horizontal cross-connect to the outlets. Use the computation factors shown in Table 8-2 and the following formula:

Acceptable link attenuation (dB) = cable attenuation (dB) + connector attenuation (dB) + splice attenuation (dB)

The answers are:

- Acceptable link attenuation @ 850 nm (horizontal cross-connect to interconnection point) = [0.075 km × 3.4 dB/km] + [(2 × 0.26 dB) + 0.38 dB] + [0], which equals 1.16 dB (0.26 + 0.90)

- Acceptable link attenuation @ 850 nm (horizontal cross-connect to outlets) = [(0.075 + 0.015) km × 3.4 dB/km] + [(1 × 0.40 dB) + (2 × 0.26 dB) + 0.38 dB] + [1 × 0.14 dB], which equals 1.61 dB (0.31 + [0.92 + 0.38])

Try a few of these calculations on your own. You can use real-life situations from your own experience or make them up. Be sure that the cabling and equipment in your scenarios comply with all applicable standards and requirements.

Testing Optical Connectors, Adapters, and Cable Assemblies

In addition to link segment attenuation tests and performance parameters for optical fiber transmission, the ANSI/EIA/TIA-568-B.3 standard defines minimum performance standards for recognized optical-cable connectors, adapters, and cable assemblies. All of these devices must comply with the dimensional requirements of ANSI/EIA/TIA-604-3-1997, FOCIS 3, known as the Fiber Optic Connector Intermateability Standards. All multimode connectors, adapters, and cable assemblies must meet this standard when tested at wavelengths of 850 nm and 1300 nm ±30 nm. All single-mode connectors, adapters, and cable assemblies must meet this standard when tested at wavelengths of 1310 nm and 1550 nm ±30 nm. You must also perform all qualification testing in accordance with the 12 tests specified in the TIA Fiber Optic Testing Procedure (FOTP).

Before You Begin Testing

Perform the following basic procedures before you begin testing:

- Read the equipment manufacturer's testing instructions, which generally accompany every piece of testing equipment.

- Ensure that all connectors, jumpers, and adapters are properly cleaned.

- Ensure that your light source or optical time domain reflectometer (OTDR) operates within the range of 850 ±30 nm for multimode cable and 1300 ±20 nm for single-mode cable. Also, ensure that the power meter or OTDR is calibrated and traceable to the National Institute of Standards Technology. These are requirements for complying with EIA/TIA-526-14: Optical Power Loss Measurements. (OTDRs are explained later in this chapter.)

End-to-End Attenuation Testing Procedures

When testing for end-to-end attenuation in a fiber-optic system, you should use the procedures described in the following steps. These steps comply with the EIA/TIA-526 series of standards, which define fiber-optic testing.

1. Take a reference reading by connecting one test jumper from the power meter to the optical source. Set both the meter and the optical source to the same wavelength—850 nm and 1300 nm for multimode fiber, or 1310 nm and 1550 nm for single-mode fiber. Next, turn both units on and record the reading shown on the meter, in dB.

2. Take a check reading by connecting a second test jumper to the first test jumper with an interconnection sleeve. (The two jumpers must be the same size.) Turn on both the power meter and optical source, and record the power reading shown on the meter.

3. Subtract the reference reading from the check reading to ensure that the attenuation does not increase by more than 0.75 dB with the second jumper connected. ANSI/EIA/TIA-568-A defines the attenuation threshold as 0.75 dB.

4. If the attenuation is acceptable, proceed to Step 5. If the attenuation exceeds the threshold, clean all connectors except the optical source connection point, and then repeat Steps 2 and 3.

5. Take an official attenuation test reading by performing an end-to-end attenuation test. Connect the power meter and one jumper to one end of the cable being tested, then connect the optical source to the other end. Turn on both the power meter and optical source, and record the power meter reading.

6. To determine end-to-end attenuation, subtract the reference reading from the official attenuation test reading.

7. Document all of your readings.

NOTE

You must measure attenuation in both directions and at both applicable wavelengths, as shown in Step 1. You must document all attenuation measurements as well. Any fiber that is not terminated must be tested for continuity using an OTDR.

TROUBLESHOOTING METHODS AND GENERAL TECHNIQUES

Even if you only perform new installations, and you only use new cables and new connecting hardware, you still need to know how to troubleshoot your system. Problems occur during new installations just as often as they do with systems that have been in service for years.

To be a successful troubleshooter, you must be logical, methodical, and good at problem solving. Generally, you should perform the following troubleshooting steps in order. However, sometimes a problem might force you to try these steps in a different order, or to skip some steps entirely:

- Identify the symptoms.

- Verify user competency.

- Identify the scope of the problem.

- Recreate the problem and ensure that you can reproduce it reliably.

- Verify the physical integrity of all connections, beginning at the workstation, moving outward, and ending in the entrance facility.

- Consider whether recent system changes contributed to the problem.

- Determine a likely solution.

- Implement the solution.

- Test the solution.

Identifying the Symptoms

The first step in troubleshooting is to identify the symptoms of a problem, which can help you pinpoint its cause. The following questions may help you identify symptoms of a problem:

- Are system and network access affected?

- Are system and network performance affected?

- Is data affected? Are programs affected? Are both affected?

- Are all system services affected, or just some services?

- Is one workstation affected? Multiple workstations? The entire system?

- Are the symptoms consistent?

In addition to answering these questions, you must pay attention to the users, and to system and network behavior. Treat each symptom as unique, but potentially related to other symptoms. Above all, don't jump to conclusions about the symptoms. These tips help you avoid the risk of ignoring problems and causing even more as a result.

Verifying User Competency

To err is human. If you are troubleshooting a working system, one of your first steps should be to ensure that human error is not the problem. This step often saves you time, because problems caused by human error are usually simple to solve.

When diagnosing problems that may be due to user error, a powerful tool is patience. Watching users perform network functions is the best way to verify that they are doing the tasks correctly. Walk a user through various functions in order to replicate a problem, while gently providing training and tips for improvement, if necessary. If you use this methodical approach, you will catch any user-generated problems. Even if you discover that users did not cause a problem, you may have gained important information for future troubleshooting.

Identifying the Scope of the Problem

After you identify symptoms of the problem and rule out user error, you need to determine the scope of the problem. In other words, you need to know whether the problem affects one workstation, a group of workstations, a particular area within the system, or the entire system. For example, if a problem affects a group of workstations, you might deduce that the problem is with the cable segment serving the group. Or, if the symptoms are limited to one workstation, a single cable or the workstation itself might be causing the problem.

Answer the following questions to help you define the scope of a problem:

- How many workstations or segments are affected? Is it one, a group, a department, or the entire system?

- When did the problem begin? Has the system or workstation ever worked properly? Did the symptoms appear within the last hour or day? Are the symptoms intermittent? How long have intermittent problems been occurring? Do the symptoms only appear at certain times of the day, week, month, or year?

Defining the scope of a problem can eliminate some potential causes and point to more probable causes. In addition, narrowing both the geography and chronology of a problem can provide direction for subsequent troubleshooting steps.

Recreating the Problem

One of the best ways to determine the causes of a problem is to recreate its symptoms. If you cannot recreate the symptoms, the problem might have been caused by a one-time occurrence or a function that was performed incorrectly. The better you can reproduce the symptoms, the greater your chances are of solving the problem.

If the problem occurred on a working system and was reported by a user, you must follow the same steps that the person performed before reporting the symptoms to you. Otherwise, you could make an incorrect diagnosis or miss a crucial clue to solving the problem.

Verifying the Physical Integrity of Connections

A common cause of system problems is physical connectivity, which includes the cabling and all intermediate connections between the workstation and the main distribution frame. These problems are often easy to identify and fix. Answer the following questions to help you identify a problem with physical connectivity:

- Is the system device turned on?

- Is the device cable properly connected to both the device and the wall outlet?

- Are all grounds properly connected?

- Are all patch cables connected? Are they connected to the correct punch-down block or patch panel?

- Are the horizontal cross-connects properly connected to the backbone?

- Are all cables in good condition?

- Are all connectors in good condition and properly seated?

Besides verifying the connections between system devices and ground connections, verifying the soundness of the hardware used in these connections is also important. A sound connection means that cables are firmly inserted into their designated ports, punch-downs are firmly seated, connectors are not broken, and cables are not damaged. Intermittent problems are often the result of improperly connected grounds or unsound connections; these problems can be difficult to troubleshoot.

If the symptoms point to connectivity problems and you have verified the soundness of the cable, connectors, all connections, and hardware, then the problem might be that the length of a cable or segment exceeds the standards defined in IEEE 802. Ensure that these cable lengths are within the acceptable range.

Considering Recent Changes

Being aware of recent system changes is important, because changes can create problems if they are not carefully planned and implemented. System changes can include new cabling, connectivity devices, or connection hardware. Changes also include repairs of existing equipment, removal of equipment, or moving equipment.

To review system changes, refer to the system documentation. Any precise information you recorded about a change—including its purpose and the time and date it occurred—helps make your troubleshooting easier if you determine that the change caused the problem. You can either attempt to correct a problem that resulted from a change, or you can attempt to reverse the change and restore the system to its previous state. Both options have pros and cons, but reverting to a previous state is often less risky and time-consuming.

Determining a Likely Solution

At this point, you have gathered enough information to determine the most likely solution to the problem. In some cases there is only one solution; if so, making the determination is easy. Some problems are not as straightforward; however, by following the structured approach in the previous steps, you should be able to identify a probable solution.

Implementing the Solution

After you have found the problem and determined a likely solution, you can implement the solution. The solution might be easy, such as replacing a connector or patch cable, or it might be a much longer process, such as replacing an entire cable segment. No matter what the solution, however, you should thoroughly document it and the problem it solved.

As with identifying problems, implementing a solution requires foresight, patience, logic, and a methodical approach. Observe the following guidelines to implement an efficient, safe, and reliable solution:

- Have all documentation about the system, the problem, and the symptoms handy throughout the process.

- When the solution involves changing a piece of hardware, keep the old part, in case the solution doesn't work.

- Perform the change, replacement, move, or addition that you believe will solve the problem. Record your actions in detail in your official documentation.

- If your solution works, record details about the symptoms, the problem, and the solution in your official documentation.

- If you solved a significant problem, such as one that affected multiple connections, revisit the solution after a day or two. Verify that the problem has not recurred and that no additional problems have emerged.

- Clean up your work area.

Testing the Solution

Test your solution after implementing it. The type of testing you perform depends on your solution to the problem. For example, if you replaced a connector on a workstation cable, you should try to use the device that is connected to the cable. If the device functions as it should, the solution was successful. If the device does not work, you must consider other causes and solutions.

If the problem affected a system that has been used for some time, ask the person who reported the problem to assist you in the testing. This helps to ensure an objective assessment of the results.

TOOLS FOR TESTING AND TROUBLESHOOTING

You cannot diagnose all problems using the previous troubleshooting techniques, and some problems may take too long to diagnose using these techniques. In such cases, it is more efficient to use a tool that can analyze and isolate system problems. Many of the tools you use for everyday installation and maintenance are the same ones you use to test cables or troubleshoot problems.

Tools designed for testing and troubleshooting are divided into two categories: cable-testing tools and network monitors and analyzers. The tools you choose depend on the tests you need to perform, the problems you are investigating, and your network's characteristics.

Tools for Testing Copper Cable

Earlier in this chapter, you learned the different methods for testing UTP cable. Now you will learn about the associated tools for performing these tests. Such methods and tools are essential to cable installers and troubleshooters—for example, some experts estimate that almost 60 percent of all network problems are related to defective or improper wiring.

The tools for testing and troubleshooting UTP copper cable are divided into two categories: cable checkers, which perform a simple pass/fail test; and cable testers, which help you certify a cable's compliance with appropriate standards. The following list discusses these tools in more detail.

- **Multimeter** — A hand-held instrument that performs multiple tests on cable. For example, the ohmmeter can test for shorts (very low resistance) and opens (very high or infinite resistance). Other tests include continuity verification, attenuation measurement, and electrical outlet testing. A typical multimeter is shown in Figure 8-8.

Figure 8-8   Multimeter

- **Continuity tester** — A two-part test unit that consists of a base unit and a remote unit. Each unit connects to one end of a cable. The continuity tester can test for proper wire mapping, opens, shorts, reversed-pairs, and bad terminations. Figure 8-9 shows a typical continuity tester.

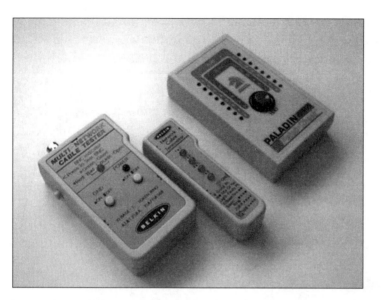

Figure 8-9 Continuity tester

- **Certified field tester** — Also called a performance tester, this device is required for performing ANSI/EIA/TIA tests that certify compliance of the cabling system. The device (Figure 8-10) tests all parameters required by TSB-67 and TSB-95. It is programmable and highly accurate.

Figure 8-10 Certified field tester

- **Time domain reflectometer (TDR)** — This tool works by transmitting a signal down the cable being tested and gathering information on the signal reflection that is returned. A TDR tests for line impedance, attenuation, opens, shorts, electrical interference (NEXT), cable distances, and connector or terminator problems. A typical TDR is shown in Figure 8-11.

Figure 8-11   Time domain reflectometer

NOTE

When you perform certification field tests to ensure compliance with applicable standards, you must use only equipment that meets the Test Accuracy Levels I or II defined by TSB-67. Level I testers were available before the adoption of TSB-67; they are not as accurate as Level II testers, which became available after TSB-67 was released. Level II testers are closer to lab grade, and are very accurate.

Tools for Testing Fiber-Optic Cable

Earlier in this chapter, you learned different methods for testing fiber-optic cable. In this section you examine tools for performing these tests and troubleshooting fiber-optic cable. Like the UTP cable tools, some fiber-optic testing tools are designed for a specific test, and some are designed to perform multiple tests. The tools you choose depend on the types of testing and troubleshooting you need to perform.

- **Power meter and optical light source** — These tools measure a cable's signal strength and attenuation, which is also known as insertion loss (Figure 8-12). The light source generates light waves along the cable that the power meter detects and measures. The light source can also determine leakage at connectors and bends.

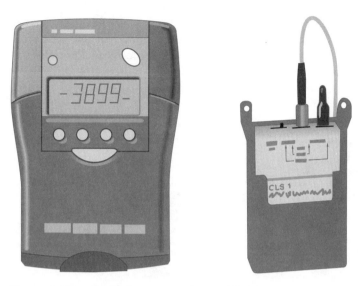

Figure 8-12   Optical power meter and light source

- **Optical time domain reflectometer (OTDR)** — This unit is very much like a TDR. It transmits light waves down the cable being tested, then measures the light waves reflected back to determine the cable's length and signal strength. A typical OTDR is shown in Figure 8-13.

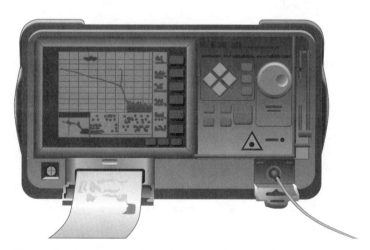

Figure 8-13   Optical time domain reflectometer

- **Jumpers** — These devices connect the power meter and the optical source. When you are ready to test, the jumpers also make the connection to the cable. Typical jumpers are shown in Figure 8-14.

8

- **Interconnection adapter** — This adapter is a circuit administration point, other than a cross-connect or information outlet, that provides access to a circuit and mates fiber-optic connectors. It typically makes connections with jacks and plugs. A typical interconnection adapter is shown in Figure 8-14.

Figure 8-14 Jumpers and interconnection adapters

Network Monitors and Analyzers

In addition to installing and maintaining cable, many telecommunications professionals maintain and troubleshoot networks. These duties require their own special tools, such as network monitors and network analyzers, that can perform more in-depth analysis than locating a simple user error or physical connectivity problem.

A network monitor is usually a software-based tool that continually watches network traffic from an attached server or workstation. Network monitors can determine which protocols are passed by each data packet, but cannot interpret the data inside a packet. A network monitor can capture network data traveling from one or many segments, capture frames sent by or to a specified node, reproduce network conditions by transmitting selected amounts and types of data, and generate statistics about network activity.

A network analyzer is a portable, hardware-based tool that helps you determine network problems. Network analyzers can typically interpret data at all layers of the OSI model. They can identify the protocol a packet uses, the type of information requested, where the packet came from, and where it is going. Network analyzers can also interpret the "payload" (data) portion of packets, translating it from binary or hexadecimal code into human-readable form. This capability allows analyzers to capture passwords traveling over a network, if the transmission is not encrypted. One type of network analyzer is a **sniffer**, a regular laptop PC equipped with a special network interface card (NIC) and specialized software to analyze network problems.

DISASTER AVOIDANCE

A disaster is an event that prevents a business from performing its critical functions. **Disaster avoidance**, or disaster prevention, is a series of measures designed to prevent, detect, or contain potentially calamitous incidents. Disaster avoidance is a component of **business continuity planning**, which stresses an organization's need to have its critical business services available at all times. This planning includes an organization's preparations for minimizing loss and continuing to operate in case of disaster.

Your first priority should always be to prevent disasters from happening. Because this is impossible, however, your next priority should be to develop procedures that minimize a disaster's impact. Well-planned and thoroughly documented strategies help reduce the loss of data, time, and money when computer and information systems fail. Proper planning can greatly reduce the trauma of rebuilding and repairing systems after a disaster, and it can help to ensure that rebuilding is successful.

A comprehensive business continuity plan includes detailed provisions for disaster avoidance and prevention, disaster recovery, response, and business resumption. In high-tech fields such as telecommunications and computer networking, the most important element in disaster avoidance is the protection of infrastructure and communications systems against long-term outages. If a company loses its dial tone, for example, customers cannot call in, which can create significant losses.

To ensure the soundness of your disaster avoidance plan, you can increase the amount of installed cables in your system, select the proper equipment, and think through as many "what if?" scenarios as possible. Although it is much easier to plan for disaster avoidance in a new installation, you can plan for it in any existing environment.

One of the best and easiest methods of disaster avoidance is redundancy, which you can build into a system by adding duplicate parts at any or all points. By adding a redundant service entrance cable to create diverse paths, for example, you provide two separate cables for splitting your trunk lines, which offers added protection against cut or damaged cable. A second service entrance cable will cost money, because most local telephone companies are only required to provide one to a building.

If you include an additional service entrance cable as part of your disaster avoidance plan, use fiber-optic cable to carry voice and data services to a building or redundant entrance facility. If you use fiber, you should also use copper cables for redundancy—otherwise, a failure of network electronics could leave your entire building without service. Using both fiber and copper cables provides diversity, and ensures that service can continue through the copper if fiber must be repaired or replaced.

Most multiline telephone systems, such as private branch exchanges (PBX) and key service units (KSU), need electricity to operate. To create redundancy in these systems and avoid disaster, you should first install an uninterruptible power supply (UPS) of adequate size with every telephone system. A UPS operates on batteries and can provide power

8

for 30 minutes to four hours, depending on the unit and the batteries. In addition to UPS systems, you should install power-fail transfer stations and single-line phones that hook directly to the trunk line. These phones do not go through the main telephone system, and do not require power to operate.

You can plan diversity and redundancy in your backbone cables by running more than one and installing them along different paths. Some wide area networks, such as Synchronous Optical Networks (SONET) and Fiber Distributed Data Interface (FDDI), use two-ring topologies that can reroute network traffic between rings when one has a fault. Asynchronous Transfer Mode (ATM) is a mesh-switched topology that works in the same way as SONET and FDDI. Local area networks (LANs) employ active electronics to create redundant power supplies and switching fabric, as well as standby communication paths that automatically become active if the main path fails.

Other aspects of network planning and installation are also critical to disaster avoidance. These methods include grounding, firestopping, and physical connectivity. Another simple way of avoiding disaster is to always lock equipment and doors to critical areas. Finally, you can create redundancy for important network data and applications by "mirroring" part of the network to another building, city, or state.

MANAGING YOUR DOCUMENTATION

The documentation manual provides important information about your network. This information can help you troubleshoot network problems and keep an accurate hardware and software inventory. It can also save you time when making additions, moves, or changes to the network.

Managing Test Results

Test results are a critical part of your documentation. They validate your cable system's performance and provide valuable historical data. Managing test results requires planning because of their potentially large file size—although a text-only, Category 5 test uses less than 1 Kb of disk space, the latest generation of testers can store detailed test data, and could require 48 Kb or more of disk space per test.

The management of test results has become more important in the past few years, with the increase in the number of installations and their size. Use the following basic guidelines to manage test results from cable testers:

- **Standards** — When documenting which test standards to use for testing, be as specific as possible. For example, indicate which test to use, such as TSB-67; the type of cable being tested, such as CAT5E UTP; and the section of cabling being tested, such as a basic link. Ensure that the latest software is loaded into the cable tester, and then select the standard within the tester.

Make sure this standard is recorded in the documentation, along with the cable tester's software version.

- **Cable ID** — Select a labeling scheme and keep it simple. Be sure that the name used to save a cable test matches the label on the patch panel or outlet.

- **Data presentation** — Select the format and media to use for test results. A few options are listed in Table 8-5.

Table 8-5   Format and media choices for test results

Format	Media
Text only	Paper
Text and disk	Floppy disk and paper summary
Text and CD-ROM	CD-ROM and paper summary (preferred)
Graphical	Paper
Graphical and disk	Floppy disk and paper summary
Graphical and CD-ROM	CD-ROM and paper summary (preferred)

The CD-ROM and paper summary options are preferred because you can store more than 10,000 graphical results on one CD. Unlike floppy disks, CDs are not susceptible to electromagnetic sources, so the possibility of losing test results is greatly reduced. Once data is stored on a CD-ROM disk, no one can change or manipulate it. Copies are easy to make.

- **Storing test results** — Most newer cable testers come with a removable memory card and the ability to store thousands of test results. Because these cards are small and easy to lose, you should never store more than one day of test results on one card.

- **Downloading test results** — You should download test results every day, without exception. Like most portable electronic equipment, cable testers are susceptible to theft; losing even one day of test results could be more costly than replacing the tester. Once you download results, review them on the computer and ensure that the correct labeling scheme was used. Make a backup copy of the results and then copy the file to the company server, another computer, or a CD.

- **Files** — Do not store all the results in one file. As with all database programs, files become more difficult to sort and view as they grow larger. A good guideline is to limit file contents to specific areas of the cabling system (for example, one file per rack).

8

Data Management Equipment

An important part of effective management is selecting the right tools for the job. This equipment is briefly described in the following list:

- **Label printers** — These printers range from simple models that require manual keypad input to models that can connect to test tools and print labels after each test is performed.

- **Software solutions** — Use spreadsheet and database software to manage test results, and mapping software that provides a logical view of the network. This software allows you to manage data in a central location, as well as update the data after additions, moves, or changes to the network. You can also use the software in conjunction with test equipment and label printers to provide a complete data management solution. Of course, software applications vary in price and complexity; before choosing software, consider future network growth, licensing limitations, and networking compatibility. Popular mapping applications include Visio, docIT, LAN MapShot, Link Analyst, and NETinventory.

CHAPTER SUMMARY

- Test your cable installation before activating the service to guarantee that the system is working properly. Testing also ensures that all installed components meet the customer's performance specifications, as well as any applicable codes and standards.

- Operational testing includes continuity testing, verification of polarity, and connectivity testing to ensure that there are no shorts or opens. Performance testing ensures that the system complies with all applicable codes and standards. Acceptance testing is designed to prove conformity to specifications and ensure performance based on the customer's measurement criteria.

- Always test UTP cable systems in accordance with the TIA TSB-67 standard, which specifies methods and parameters for testing installed Category 3, 4, and 5 cabling with a hand-held instrument. This standard also defines basic link and channel test configurations for UTP cable. TSB-67 tests that are currently required for Category 5 certification include wire map tests, length tests, attenuation tests, NEXT (near-end crosstalk) tests, and propagation delay tests.

- You must test fiber-optic cable for attenuation to comply with current standards. You should also test for attenuation on all link segments, connectors, adapters, and cable assemblies.

- Even if you only perform new installations, you still need to know how to troubleshoot your system. A successful troubleshooter is logical, methodical, and good at problem solving. Troubleshooting steps include identifying symptoms, identifying the scope of a problem, and recreating the problem.

❐ Many of the tools you use for everyday installation and maintenance are the same ones you use to test cables or troubleshoot problems.

❐ Disaster avoidance is designed to ensure the continuous availability of critical business services in case of disaster. Although you cannot prevent all disasters, you can minimize their effects by planning redundancy and diversity into your telecommunications systems.

❐ The documentation manual provides important information about your network. This information can assist you in troubleshooting network problems, and it provides an accurate hardware and software inventory.

KEY TERMS

attenuation — A measure of a cable's signal loss from end to end. The farther signals travel on a cable, the weaker they become.

attenuation-to-crosstalk ratio (ACR) — The calculated difference between NEXT and attenuation measurements.

bandwidth — The measure of a cable's information-carrying capacity.

baseline — A system's initial state of operation or performance, as quantified by testing. The baseline is used as a basis of comparison for future performance.

basic link — A permanent part of a cable run that includes 90 meters of horizontal cable, the telecommunications outlet, and the first punch-down in the telecommunications room.

business continuity planning — A term that stresses the need for continuous availability of all critical business services. These plans cover all aspects of disaster avoidance, disaster recovery, and business resumption.

certified field tester — A device required to perform ANSI/EIA/TIA tests for certifying compliance of the cabling system. The device tests all parameters required by TSB-67 and TSB-95. It is programmable and highly accurate. A certified field tester is also called a performance tester.

channel — All of the basic link, plus all patch cords and equipment cords.

composite cable — A cable that contains two or more different types of cable within the same jacket.

connectivity — The live connection between two endpoints.

connectivity test — A test to ensure that all terminations are transmitting signals.

continuity — An uninterrupted connection or pathway from the beginning to the end of a cable.

continuity tester — A two-part unit that can test for proper wire mapping, opens, shorts, reversed-pairs, and bad terminations in the cable.

crossed-pair — An error that occurs when one pair of wires is connected to different pins at each end of the cable.

8

delay skew — The measurement of the time between the arrival, at the far end of the cable, of the first signal from one wire pair, and the arrival of subsequent signals from the remaining pairs.

disaster avoidance — Also known as disaster prevention, these measures are employed to prevent, detect, or contain potentially disastrous incidents.

ELFEXT — A test calculation derived by subtracting the attenuation of one cable pair from the FEXT that the pair induces in an adjacent pair.

far-end crosstalk (FEXT) — A test that is similar to the NEXT test, except that the signal is sent from the local end of the cable and the crosstalk is measured from the far end of the cable.

hybrid cable — A fiber-optic cable that has two or more different types of cable within the same jacket.

interconnection adapter — A circuit administration point that provides access to a circuit and mates fiber-optic connectors.

interconnections — Devices used to mate fiber-optic connectors or transition point splices.

jumpers — Devices that connect a power meter to an optical source.

length test — A test to verify that the length of a cable is within the specifications for maximum allowable length.

link segment — The cable, connectors, other connections, and splices between two fiber-optic termination units.

multimeter — A hand-held instrument that performs multiple tests on cable, including ohmmeter function, continuity verification, attenuation measurement, and electrical outlet testing.

near-end crosstalk (NEXT) — A measurement of the signal coupling from one pair of wires to another pair within the same cable.

opens — Breaks in a wire that result in an incomplete circuit and inhibit the continuous flow of transmission signals.

optical time domain reflectometer (OTDR) — A unit very similar to a TDR. An OTDR transmits light waves down the cable being tested, then measures the waves reflected back to determine the cable's length and signal strength.

parameters — Measurement criteria.

polarity test — Confirmation that the positive and negative wires of a cable pair are not crossed.

power meter — A tool that uses an optical light source to measure a cable's signal strength and attenuation. The light source generates light waves along the cable that the power meter detects and measures.

power sum — A measurement that compares the crosstalk effects on all pairs in a cable.

propagation delay — The amount of time it takes a signal to travel from one end of a cable to the other.

return loss — A measurement of the signal that echoes or reflects back into the transmitter. Return loss is usually caused by an impedance mismatch, an imbalance in the cable, or a mismatch in connecting hardware.

reversed-pair — An error that occurs when the two wires of a pair are connected to opposite pins at each end of the cable.

shorts — Unwanted contact between two wires that stops transmission signals.

sniffer — A regular laptop PC equipped with a special NIC and specialized software to analyze network problems.

split-pair — An error that occurs when a wire from one pair is incorrectly connected to a wire from another pair, as if they were a pair.

time domain reflectometer (TDR) — A device that transmits a signal down the cable being tested and gathers information on the signal reflection that is returned. A TDR tests for line impedance, opens, shorts, electrical interference (NEXT), cable distances, and connector or terminator problems.

wavelength — A measure of the color of light, usually expressed in nm.

wire map test — A test that identifies wiring errors and checks connectivity.

8

REVIEW QUESTIONS

1. Which of the following is an important step in cable installation?

   a. firestopping

   b. designing the cable pathways

   c. testing the system

   d. all of the above

2. Which of the following can testing guarantee? (Choose all that apply.)

   a. that the system is fully functioning

   b. that the installed components meet the customer's performance specifications

   c. that the customer will be satisfied with your work

   d. that the system meets all applicable codes and standards

3. What are the three parts of operational testing?

   a. acceptance, continuity, and connectivity

   b. continuity, polarity, and connectivity

   c. polarity, connectivity, and verification

   d. connectivity, continuity, and performance

4. Performance testing is designed to _____.

   a. make sure the system is working

   b. ensure that cables are run properly

   c. ensure that the system complies with all applicable codes and standards

   d. guarantee that the installer is qualified to do the work

5. Acceptance testing demonstrates conformity to whose specifications?

a. the customer's

b. the NEC's

c. the installer's

d. none of the above

6. Which standard applies to testing procedures for compliance of UTP cable systems?

a. ISBN-69

b. ANSI/EIA/TIA-568

c. EIA 10-4

d. TIA TSB-67

7. The two tests for UTP cable systems, as defined by TSB-67, are _____ and _____. (Choose the two that apply.)

a. NEXT

b. basic link

c. operational

d. channel

8. Performing basic link and channel tests is important because workmanship has a direct impact on system performance. True or False?

9. Initial testing at installation provides _____.

a. verification that the system is working properly

b. a performance guide to use as a baseline for future reference

c. a base guideline to use for future reference

d. none of the above

10. Match the test name to its property.

a. wire map

b. length

c. attenuation

d. near-end crosstalk

e. propagation delay

1. measures a cable's signal loss from end to end

2. measures the amount of time it takes a signal to travel from one end of a cable to another

3. identifies wiring errors and checks connectivity

4. measures bandwidth

5. measures signal coupling from one pair of wires to another pair within the same cable

6. verifies that a cable's length is within the maximum allowed

11. The wire map test identifies wiring errors. Match each error with its definition.

    a. shorts

    b. opens

    c. crossed-pair

    d. reversed-pair

    e. split-pair

    1. A wire from one pair is incorrectly connected to wire from another pair, as if they were a pair.

    2. A wire break causes an incomplete signal flow.

    3. Installation of a new piece of equipment overloads a system.

    4. One pair of wires is connected to different pins at each end.

    5. An unwanted connection between two wires stops transmission signals.

    6. Two wires of a pair are connected to opposite pins at each end.

12. If your voice is amplified so loud on a telephone that you cannot hear the other person, the line has unacceptable —————————.

    a. attenuation

    b. shorts

    c. delay skew

    d. near-end crosstalk

8

13. What is the allowable propagation delay for a 100-meter, Category 5 cable at 10 MHz?

    a. 568 nS

    b. 555 nS

    c. 555 GB

    d. 200 nS

14. In addition to recording pass/fail indications, you should always record —————————.

    a. propagation delay time

    b. the length and number of connectors per cable

    c. actual measured values and the frequency of your readings

    d. the quality of tools and materials

15. Which standard defines acceptable loss limits for fiber-optic cable installations?

    a. TSB-99

    b. ANSI/EIA/TIA-656

    c. ISO-568-B3

    d. ANSI/EIA/TIA-568-B.3

16. The tests required for validating a fiber-optic cabling system are
    _____ and _____. (Choose the two that apply.)

    a. bandwidth

    b. near-end crosstalk (NEXT)

    c. wire map

    d. attenuation

17. What are two factors that determine bandwidth?

    a. quality and length of cable

    b. length of cable and pair count

    c. manufacturer and attenuation

    d. cable label and quality of cable

18. Under which circumstances would you perform field testing for bandwidth?
    (Choose all that apply.)

    a. never

    b. when the manufacturer's documentation is unavailable or insufficient

    c. when there is too much attenuation

    d. at the customer's request

19. Attenuation tests do not have to be performed on every link section. True or False?

20. What are the three basic types of link segments?

    a. horizontal, vertical, and backbone

    b. backbone, composite, and vertical

    c. composite, horizontal, and main

    d. horizontal, backbone, and composite

21. When performing certification field tests to ensure compliance with applicable
    standards, your testing equipment must meet which level of accuracy?

    a. level I or level II

    b. level I

    c. level II or level III

    d. level II

22. Which of the following is a key to successful troubleshooting?

    a. being on time and knowledgeable

    b. having the right tools and being methodical

    c. being logical and methodical

    d. being logical and on time

23. When troubleshooting a system that is in service, what should you do first?

    a. Shut down the entire system.

    b. Verify user competency.

    c. Replace the cables and cords.

    d. Identify the scope of the problem.

24. You cannot always prevent disasters, so your next priority should be to
    _____.

    a. control them

    b. minimize their impact

    c. ignore them

    d. talk about them

25. What can you do to ensure that a disaster avoidance plan is sound?

    a. Speculate in "what if?" scenarios.

    b. Increase the number of installed cables.

    c. Select the proper equipment.

    d. all of the above

8

HANDS-ON PROJECTS

Project 8-1

In this exercise, you perform wire map tests on six Category 5 UTP cables. Terminate all cables on one end to a 110-type patch panel. Terminate the other ends on standard, eight-conductor workstation outlet jacks. Each cable has a unique identification number.

1. Run the wire map tests on each cable segment. Record the identification number and the test results for each cable.

2. Using a computer that has Visio installed, create a wire map diagram of each cable. The diagram should include the cable's identification number, a line drawing of its wire mapping, and an indication of whether the cable passed the wire map test. If a cable fails the test, include an explanation of the problem.

3. For any cables that did not pass the test, make necessary repairs and then retest the cable.

4. After repairing and retesting cable, make another diagram in Visio. Indicate the wire mapping you made following the repair, and explain what you did to fix the problem.

Project 8-2

In this exercise, you practice testing Category 5 UTP cable for attenuation, using a TDR and a certified field tester. To perform these tests, you need three segments of Category 5 UTP and RJ-45 connectors. Each segment must have a different length.

1. First, terminate each end of the cable segments with the RJ-45 connectors. Your segment lengths should measure 25 feet, 60 feet, and 100 feet.

2. After terminating the cables, perform attenuation tests on each cable with the TDR. Note the frequency you used and the test results for each cable. Repeat this step using the certified field tester.

3. When you complete the testing, find which pair had the worst performance reading with the TDR, then compare this reading with the specified attenuation values in TSB-67. Repeat this step using the worst performance reading from the certified field tester.

4. Note whether each cable passed or failed the attenuation test. If a cable failed, explain what you think the problem is and how you would fix it.

Project 8-3

In this exercise, you perform attenuation tests on fiber-optic cable using an OTDR. Your instructor will give you four segments of terminated fiber-optic cable, one for each type defined in Table 8-1. Use the OTDR to test each segment in both directions and at both available wavelengths. Record all results.

Project 8-4

This exercise lets you practice computing acceptable link attenuation. In the following scenarios, use Tables 8-2, 8-3, and 8-4 to determine the link attenuation. Remember that a meter equals 1/1000 of a kilometer.

Red Cat Inc.

You need to test the fiber-optic cabling system that you just installed for Red Cat. You have installed a backbone link segment using 62.5/125-μm multimode fiber to connect the main cross-connect and the horizontal cross-connect. The backbone is 215 meters long, has two splices, and is terminated with ST connectors. What is the acceptable link attenuation for this installation?

S. Grey and G. White, Ltd.

Your customer has hired you to install and test a new horizontal link for a recent expansion. The new link is 125 meters from the horizontal cross-connect to an interconnection in the open office area. You used a 24-fiber, 62.5/125-μm multimode fiber. From the interconnection point, you distributed eight multimode cables to modular office furniture outlets, leaving eight spare fibers of the horizontal cable for future use. Each distributed cable is a two-fiber cable that is 22 meters long. All fibers are terminated with ST connectors, except at the outlets, where each is terminated on a Quick-Light ST (QL-ST). What is the acceptable link attenuation for this installation?

Calico Graphics

After purchasing the building next door, Calico Graphics hired you to install new backbone link and horizontal link segments for their expansion. You are ready to test this new installation. The backbone link is a 189-meter length of 62.5/125-μm multimode fiber; it runs from the main cross-connect to the new horizontal cross-connect you installed. The backbone has one splice and uses ST connectors. The horizontal link segment is 19 meters from the horizontal cross-connect to a new interconnection in the open office area. You used a 12-fiber, 62.5/125-μm multimode fiber with ST connectors. From the interconnection point, you distributed five multimode cables to the workstation outlets, leaving two spare fibers. Each distributed cable is a two-fiber cable that is 17 meters long. At the outlets, the fibers are terminated on Quick-Light ST (QL-ST) connectors. What is the acceptable link attenuation for this installation?

Project 8-5

In this exercise, you test some of the troubleshooting techniques you learned in this chapter.

❑ One of your customers has a problem. The customer's system consists of four horizontal cross-connects, each serving a separate group of workstations. All horizontal cables are four-pair, Category 5 UTP; each horizontal cross-connect is linked to the main cross-connect with a copper backbone cable. All the equipment is located at the main cross-connect. The problem is that a workstation in workgroup number 3 cannot log in to the network, and user error is not the cause. All other workstations in this group are working properly. What is your diagnosis of the problem? How would you fix it?

❑ You have just finished testing a new installation. Everything tests well, except for a segment of horizontal cable that connects a group of 10 workstations to the first horizontal cross-connect. The horizontal cable consists of 25 pairs. The problem is that the cable failed continuity and wire map tests on 15 pairs. What is your diagnosis of the problem? What steps would you take to solve it?

Project 8-6

One of your customers wants to implement a disaster avoidance plan, and has asked you to create one. Create an outline of your suggestions for implementing an effective plan. Define the system for which you are designing this plan.

CASE PROJECTS

Case Project 1

Several types of equipment are available for testing both copper and fiber cable. Many of these tools serve multiple purposes, but some serve only one.

1. Make a chart for all the test equipment you can use for copper cable, then do the same for fiber.

2. After you complete these charts, add two columns to each. In these columns, indicate whether each piece of testing equipment is designed for multiple uses or a single use, then list the types of tests each performs.

Case Project 2

Making changes to a system can cause problems. System changes may include the addition of new equipment, such as cabling, connectivity devices, or connection hardware. Other changes include repairs of existing equipment, removal of equipment, or moving equipment. Explain the types of problems these changes can cause and the circumstances that can contribute to these problems. Discuss the pros and cons of reversing a change to restore a system to its previous state.

Case Project 3

Research and explain the changes being considered to UTP cabling standards as a result of improvements to Category 5e, Category 6, and Category 7 cable.

Case Project 4

Make a list of at least five types of problems you might encounter in a telecommunications system, and define the types of symptoms that would identify these problems.

A

BICSI Installer Level I Exam Objectives

I. Industry Orientation

BICSI Objective	Chapter
Divestiture, deregulation, and standards-based guidelines	1
Standards, codes, and regulations	1, 2

II. Structured Premises Cabling Systems

BICSI Objective	Chapter
Entrance facilities, backbone, horizontal, work areas	1, 2, 3, 4, 5, 6
Equipment rooms, telecommunications rooms	1, 2, 3, 4, 5, 6
Cross-connects — main, intermediate, horizontal	1, 2, 3, 4, 5, 6

III. Standards, Codes, and Methodologies

BICSI Objective	Chapter
ANSI/EIA/TIA-568-A, 569-A, 570-A, 606-A, 607	1, 2, 4, 5, 6, 8
EIA/TIA TSB-67, 72, 75, 95	8
ANSI/TIA-526-7, 14A	8
National Electrical Code	1, 2, 7
National Fire Protection Code	2, 7
BICSI *TDMM* and *LAN and Internetworking Design Manual* overview	

IV. Plans and Specifications (Overview)

BICSI Objective	Chapter
Blueprints	
Construction specifications	4, 7

V. Media Characteristics

BICSI Objective	Chapter
Twisted-pair (UTP, ScTP, STP)	1, 2, 3, 5, 6
Color code	5, 6
Categories of cable (3-5+)	1, 5, 6, 8
Coaxial	1, 2, 3, 5
Optical fiber cables (single-mode and multimode)	1, 2, 3, 5, 6

VI. Connectors

BICSI Objective	Chapter
UTP, STP, ScTP, coaxial, optical fiber	3, 5, 6
Connector pin configuration	6
Color codes	5, 6

VII. Transmission Characteristics (Basic)

BICSI Objective	Chapter
AC/DC review	
Analog/digital signals	1, 2, 3, 5, 8
Copper cable media	1, 3, 6, 8
Optical fiber media	1, 3, 6, 8

VIII. Grounding, Bonding, and Electrical Protection

BICSI Objective	Chapter
Basic design	2
Installation	2

IX. Safety

BICSI Objective	Chapter
OSHA	7
Common safety practices	2, 6, 7
Personal protective equipment	2
Hazardous environments	2

X.   Professionalism (Overview)

BICSI Objective	Chapter
Customer relations	8
Communications skills	8
Professional appearance	8

XI.   Preparation for Installation

BICSI Objective	Chapter
Building closets	4, 5, 6
Installing grounding infrastructure	2
Installing support-system infrastructure	2, 4, 5, 6
Preparing work area outlet locations	4, 5, 6

XII.   Pulling Cable

BICSI Objective	Chapter
Pulling backbone and horizontal twisted-pair cable	4, 5
Pulling optical fiber cable	4, 5

XIII.   Firestopping

BICSI Objective	Chapter
Responsibilities	7
Systems	7
New and existing penetrations	7

XIV.   Cable Termination

BICSI Objective	Chapter
Pre-termination functions (forming, dressing, fanning, and labeling cables)	4, 5, 6, 8
Copper cable termination (UTP [Krone, BIX, 110, 66])	4, 5, 6
Copper crimp termination	5, 6
Coaxial cable termination	5, 6

XV. Splicing Cable (Overview)

BICSI Objective	Chapter
Copper	8
Optical fiber	8

XVI. Cable Testing

BICSI Objective	Chapter
Copper cable testing using entry-level testers (VOM and continuity testers)	8
Overview of optical fiber testing	8

XVII. Cable Troubleshooting (Overview)

BICSI Objective	Chapter
Copper cables	8
Optical fiber cables	8

XVIII. Retrofits and System Upgrades

BICSI Objective	Chapter
Overview of identifying active circuits	6, 8
Overview of performing cutovers	
Removal of abandoned cable	

XIX. Miscellaneous Duties (Overview)

BICSI Objective	Chapter
Administrative tasks	Documentation 1 – 8
Documenting results	Documentation 1 – 8
Documenting as-builts	Documentation 1 – 8
Coping with changing technologies	Documentation 1 – 8

Glossary

access floor — A system of removable and interchangeable floor panels that are supported on pedestals, stringers, or both to allow access to the area beneath.

access points — The wireless equivalent of the hubs used in a wired network. Access points broadcast and receive wireless signals to and from surrounding computers via a NIC. Access points also provide the interconnection point between a wireless and wired network.

administrative labeling — The process of identifying every element in a floor plan with a unique name and/or number.

air terminals (lightning rods) — Slender rods installed on a roof at regular intervals to ground lightning current.

alien crosstalk — The interference of signals from one cable with an adjacent cable's transmission.

American Wire Gauge (AWG) — The system used to specify wire size. The greater the wire diameter, the smaller the value is.

ampere — The basic unit for measuring electrical current.

analog — Analog signals are variable voltages that create continuous waves of sound, resulting in inexact transmissions.

annular space — The distance between the penetrating item and the surrounding opening of the penetration.

annunciators — Units that provide graphic displays to pinpoint alarms quickly.

ANSI/EIA/TIA — The three associations involved in developing telecommunications industry standards. Their full names are the American National Standards Institute, Electronic Industries Alliance, and Telecommunications Industry Association, respectively.

antenna discharge unit — The bonding location for the antenna lead-in cable.

ASTM International (formerly the American Society for Testing and Materials) — An independent volunteer group that generates testing standards.

attenuation — A measure of a cable's signal loss from end to end. The farther signals travel on a cable, the weaker they become.

attenuation-to-crosstalk ratio (ACR) — The calculated difference between NEXT and attenuation measurements.

B-wire connectors — Solderless, single-wire splice connections, also known as "beanies."

backboard — A panel used for mounting connecting hardware and equipment.

backbone cable — The cabling that connects one telecommunications room (TR) to another, TRs to equipment rooms, or one building's equipment room to another's.

backbone distribution system — The portion of the premises distribution system that provides connections among entrance facilities, equipment rooms, and telecommunications rooms.

balanced-pair — The twists in cable pairs that help to reduce the effects of crosstalk.

bandwidth — The measure of a cable's information-carrying capacity, which is the difference between the highest and lowest frequencies that the media can transmit.

bare fiber — A fiber that has had all of its primary coatings removed, exposing the glass surface. Bare fiber can be dangerous if you do not follow safety procedures when working with it.

baseband — The transmission of digital signals through direct-current pulses applied to the wire. Baseband requires exclusive use of the wire's capacity, which means that only one signal can be transmitted at a time.

baseline — A system's initial state of operation or performance, as quantified by testing. The baseline is used as a basis of comparison for future performance.

basic link — A permanent part of a cable run that includes 90 meters of horizontal cable, the telecommunications outlet, and the first punch-down in the telecommunications room.

bend radius — The maximum radius that a cable can bend without causing physical or electrical damage or adverse transmission performance.

binder — A colored piece of plastic or string wound around a group of cables for identification.

binder group — A group of 25 twisted pairs in a large-pair-count cable. Each binder group is identified with a uniquely colored binder.

BIX — The trade name of a NORDX/CDT in-building termination and cross-connect system for unshielded twisted-pair (UTP) cables.

BNC (British Naval Connector) and **BNC/T** — The type of connector used on ThinNet (10Base2) cable. The BNC is the connector that goes on the cable. The BNC/T is a T-shaped adapter that connects on one end to the station's network interface card. The bus connects to the other two ends.

bonding — The permanent joining of metallic parts to form an electrically conductive path that will ensure electrical continuity, the capacity to safely conduct current, and the ability to limit differences in potentials between the joined parts.

bonding conductor — A conductor used specifically for bonding.

bonding conductor for telecommunications (BCT) — The conductor that interconnects the building's service equipment (power) ground to the telecommunications grounding system.

bridging clips — Small metal clips used on 66-type punch-down blocks to connect the wires that are terminated on the left and right sides of a block.

Building Industry Consulting Service (BICS) — An organization of telephone company engineers created by AT&T and Bell Canada. BICS works with architects, building contractors, and engineers to design and implement cabling plans for pathways and spaces in commercial buildings.

Building Industry Consulting Services International (BICSI) — A not-for-profit telecommunications organization founded to serve BICS.

bus topology — A single cable that connects all the nodes on a network without intervening connectivity devices.

busbar — A conductor that serves as a common connection point for two or more circuits.

business continuity planning — A term that stresses the need for continuous availability of all critical business services. These plans cover all aspects of disaster avoidance, disaster recovery, and business resumption.

butt set — *See* telephone line tester.

cable — An assembly of one or more insulated conductors within a sheath, constructed to permit use of the conductors singly or in a group.

cable plant — All the cables and termination points in an installation, including work area outlets, patch panels, and punch-down blocks.

cable stripper — A tool that removes a portion of the cable sheath to expose the wires inside.

cable ties — Devices used for securing cables.

cable tray — A device used to route and support telecommunications cable or power cable. It is typically equipped with sides so that cables can be placed within the tray's entire length.

campus environment — A group of related buildings.

Carrier Sense Multiple Access/Collision Detection (CSMA/CD) — An Ethernet protocol that allows nodes to listen for traffic on the network before sending data.

cast-in device — A device that incorporates the sleeving process and firestopping into one simple step.

ceiling zone — A means of distributing horizontal cable from the telecommunications room to the work area.

certified field tester — A device required to perform ANSI/EIA/TIA tests for certifying compliance of the cabling system. The device tests all parameters required by TSB-67 and TSB-95. It is programmable and highly accurate. A certified field tester is also called a performance tester.

channel — All of the basic link, plus all patch cords and equipment cords.

char — A grayish-black crust that forms when organic sealants are burned.

cladding — In fiber-optic cable, a layer of glass around the fibers that acts like a mirror and reflects light back to the core.

clean agents — Electrically nonconductive materials that leave no residue and help protect sensitive electronic equipment.

cleaving — The process of nicking a fiber and then pulling or flexing it to cause a clean break.

coaxial cable — Cable that consists of a central copper core surrounded by an insulator, a braided metal shielding called braiding, and an outer cover called a sheath or jacket.

code — A law designed to protect people and property from hazards, and to ensure the quality of construction.

cold smoke — A nonglowing, smoldering fire.

collars — Usually galvanized steel bands with inlaid intumescent material and adjustable mounting tabs for attachment to a wall or floor assembly.

composite cable — A cable that contains two or more different types of cable within the same jacket.

conductors — Copper or aluminum cables that interconnect various system components. Wires through which a current of electricity flows.

conduit — A rigid or flexible, metallic or nonmetallic pipe through which cables can be pulled.

connectivity — The live connection between two endpoints.

connectivity test — A test to ensure that all terminations are transmitting signals.

connector — A piece of hardware that connects the cable to the network device.

consolidation point — An interconnection point or transition point for horizontal cabling.

containment system — The fire protection system responsible for reducing the rapid spread of fire and toxic fumes from their point of origin.

continuity — An uninterrupted connection or pathway from the beginning to the end of a cable.

continuity tester — A two-part unit that can test for proper wire mapping, opens, shorts, reversed-pairs, and bad terminations in the cable.

conventions — Common practices or methods that help make procedures easier to follow and remember.

core hitch — Hardware that connects vertical cable to a winch.

crimp tool — A tool that creates a secure, permanent contact between a modular plug and a cable.

cross-connect — A group of wall- or rack-mounted connection points used to mechanically terminate and administer building wiring. It is also the point in a network where a circuit is connected from one facility to another by cabling between the equipment.

crossed-pair — An error that occurs when one pair of wires is connected to different pins at each end of the cable.

crosstalk — The infringement of the signal from one wire pair on another wire pair's signal.

cut sheet — A document, usually in tabular form, that lists each cable run.

data transmission — The sending of signals generated by voltage over a designated path.

decibel (dB) — A measurement unit of signal strength or of a sound's intensity.

delay skew — The measurement of the time between the arrival, at the far end of the cable, of the first signal from one wire pair, and the arrival of subsequent signals from the remaining pairs.

demarcation point (demarc) — The point at which control or ownership of the communications facilities changes from the Telco equipment to the customer's equipment.

dense wave division multiplexing (DWDM) — The combination and transmission of multiple signals simultaneously at different wavelengths on the same fiber.

detection system — The fire protection system responsible for providing early warning signals of fire.

digital — Digital signals are precise voltages that create pulses with specific values called bits, resulting in more precise transmissions.

directory services — The database and network services that store and provide access to network resources and security information.

disaster avoidance — Also known as disaster prevention, these measures are employed to prevent, detect, or contain potentially disastrous incidents.

distribution duct — The duct that carries the cable from the feeder duct to a specific floor area in an underfloor duct system.

distribution field — The connecting hardware that provides the link between the cross-connect and the telecommunications outlet.

draftstopping — Installing barriers that block the spread of fire within the large concealed spaces of flooring, attics, and crawlspaces.

dressing — Placing cables into a neat and symmetrical pattern for proper alignment and positioning for termination.

earth grounding — An electrical connection to the earth obtained by a grounding electrode system.

effective ground — An electrical connection to a low-resistance ground that permits current to discharge without the buildup of hazardous voltages on the telecommunications cabling.

electromagnetic interference (EMI) — Noise generated when stray electromagnetic fields induce currents in electrical conductors.

ELFEXT — A test calculation derived by subtracting the attenuation of one cable pair from the FEXT that the pair induces in an adjacent pair.

entrance room (facility) — An entrance to a building for both public and private network service cables.

equipment grounding — An electrical connection of the non-current-carrying metal parts of equipment raceways and other enclosures to the grounding electrode system.

equipment room — An enclosed space for housing equipment, cable terminations, and cross-connects.

error-checking algorithm — The process used in a frame to check for errors in data transmission.

Ethernet — A networking technology originally developed by Xerox and improved by Digital Equipment Corporation, Intel, and Xerox. Used on most LANs.

extinguishant — The substance used to put out a fire.

extinguishing foam — A highly effective combination of water, a foaming agent, and air, used to extinguish Class A and Class B fires.

far-end crosstalk (FEXT) — A test that is similar to the NEXT test, except that the signal is sent from the local end of the cable and the crosstalk is measured from the far end of the cable.

fault current — *See* foreign electrical voltage.

feeder duct — In cellular and underfloor duct systems, the main duct used to bring cable from telecommunications rooms to distribution ducts or cells.

Fiber Distributed Data Interface (FDDI) — In a ring topology, this interface contains two rings: a primary ring and a secondary ring. The secondary ring provides fault tolerance (redundancy) and backup if the primary ring fails.

fiber-optic cable — Cable that contains one or more glass fibers in its core. Data is transmitted by converting electrical signals at the sending end into optical signals, which are then transmitted through the central fibers via a pulsing light sent from a laser or light-emitting diode (LED), and reconverted into electrical signals at the receiving end.

fire block — Fire-resistant material designed to form a barrier in walls and under raised or access floors.

fire control panels — Devices that provide supervision and coordination among the various elements of a fire detection system.

fire pillow — A specially treated glass cloth filled with a mixture of mineral fiber and reactive expansion agents. Fire pillows expand when exposed to heat, and then harden to provide a complete and durable seal.

fire resistance rating (fire rating) — A rating that determines the ability of a wall or floor to withstand fire and continue to perform its structural function, as determined by the ASTM E-119 standard.

fire seals — Small pieces of rubberlike, flexible, fire-retardant material that adhere tightly to cable trays, conduits, and cables, allowing them to move within the penetration.

fire separation — A type of construction assembly that acts as a barrier against the spread of fire.

fire-rated foam — A one-component polyurethane foam that expands to fill and seal gaps around single and multiple penetrations that have limited access.

fireblocking — Installing barriers that block the spread of fire within the concealed small spaces of stud walls, at soffits and drop ceilings, and at the top and bottom of stair stringers.

firestopping — A method of passive fire protection that helps contain fire and toxic gases to the area of origin by sealing around penetrations and construction joints in fire-rated floors and walls.

firewall — A type of fire protection that subdivides a building or separates adjoining buildings.

flexible conduit — A type of conduit, usually made of flexible metal that allows it to be bent in different directions without distorting it. Flexible conduit is normally used to connect rigid pathways to other pathways that may not join in exact alignment.

foreign electrical voltage — Any voltage (current) imposed on a system that is not supplied from the central office, telephone equipment, or the system itself. This unwanted voltage is also known as fault current.

FT rating — The combination of an F rating (the number of hours that a fire-resistant barrier can withstand fire before allowing the flames to pass through an opening) and a T rating (the number of hours it takes temperatures on the non-fire side of a fire-rated assembly to exceed 325°F above the ambient temperature). The FT rating is always the lower of the two measurements.

fusing — The process of aligning and then heating fibers.

fusion splicing — A splicing method that uses a machine to precisely align two fiber ends and weld them together using heat or an electric arc. The resulting continuous connection between the fibers enables light transmissions with losses as low as 0.1 dB.

ground — A conducting connection, whether accidental or intentional, between an electrical circuit or equipment and the earth, or to some other conducting body that serves in place of the earth. Grounding is the backbone of effective protection for all telecommunications systems.

ground fault — Current misdirected from the hot (or neutral) lead to a ground wire, box, or conductor.

ground system — A system of hardware and wiring that provides an electrical path from a specified location to an earth-ground point.

ground terminations (ground rods) — Metal rods driven into the earth to guide lightning current harmlessly to ground.

grounding conductor — A conductor used to connect electrical equipment to the grounding electrode and a building's main grounding busbar.

grounding electrode — A conductor that provides a low-resistance, direct connection to the earth.

grounding electrode system — One or more grounding electrodes bonded to form a single, reliable ground for a building, tower, or similar structure.

hazardous (classified) locations — A location where fire or explosion hazards may exist due to flammable gases or vapors, flammable liquids, combustible dust, or ignitable fibers.

hertz (Hz) — The unit for measuring a range of frequencies.

horizontal cabling — The portion of a structured cabling system that connects the telecommunications room and the work area, and includes the cabling from the work area telecommunications outlet/connector to the horizontal cross-connect (floor distributor) in the telecommunications room. It may be installed in either a horizontal or vertical plane.

horizontal cross-connect (HC) — A method of connecting horizontal cabling to intrabuilding backbone cabling or equipment cable by using connection hardware and jumpers or patch cords.

hub — A multiport repeater containing one port that connects to a network's backbone and multiple ports that connect to a group of workstations. Hubs regenerate digital signals.

hybrid cable — A telecommunications cable that contains two or more types of conductors, such as UTP and optical-fiber cable.

impact tool — A tool that provides torque and impact for connecting wires to both 66-type and 110-type punch-down blocks.

impedance — The measurement of a conductor's opposition, or resistance, to the flow of alternating current.

index matching gel — Material inside a mechanical splice that helps to couple the light from one fiber to another.

inductive amplifier (tracer) — A tool used to find and identify cables by locating the sound emitted by a tone generator.

insulated — Coated with dielectric material that physically separates wires and prevents conduction between them.

insulation displacement connector (IDC) — Connecting hardware with receptacles that house small pieces of metal capable of piercing a wire's insulation when it is inserted with an impact insertion tool thus making it unnecessary to strip the insulation away from the wire to ensure a proper connection.

interbuilding — Refers to connections between one building and other outlying buildings.

interbuilding backbone — A backbone network that provides communications between buildings.

interconnection adapter — A circuit administration point that provides access to a circuit and mates fiber-optic connectors.

interconnections — Devices used to mate fiber-optic connectors or transition point splices.

intermediate cross-connect (IC) — A cross-connection between first- and second-level backbone.

intrabuilding — Refers to connections within the same building, usually on different floors.

intrabuilding backbone — A backbone network that provides communications within a building.

intumescent — Designed to expand at a predetermined temperature range.

J-hook — A J-shaped supporting device for horizontal cables that is attached to building structures. Horizontal cables are laid in the niche formed by the J for support.

jumper(s) — An unjacketed grouping of twisted pairs used between connection hardware to cross-connect backbones, equipment, and horizontal cabling.

junction boxes — Openings in the ductwork that provide access to the duct system for installing and servicing cable.

ladder cable tray — A tray with two side rails connected by individual transverse members. The tray looks very much like a ladder.

latency — The delay between entering commands on your computer and their acceptance by the server.

lead-in — The part of the antenna cable that enters a building and continues inside to the final connection.

length test — A test to verify that the length of a cable is within the specifications for maximum allowable length.

lightning rods — Slender rods installed on a roof at regular intervals to ground lightning current.

link segment — The cable, connectors, other connections, and splices between two fiber-optic termination units.

local area network (LAN) — A network of computers and other devices confined to a single building, or even one office.

logical topology — The method used to communicate between devices.

loose cables — Cables that are run in the ceiling without the use of conduits.

mA (milliampere) — A measure of a unit of electrical current, equal to 1/1000 of an ampere.

made and other electrodes — Any electrode not specified in NEC Article 250H, but defined in NEC Article 250, section 83, subsections b-d. These electrodes include rod and pipe electrodes, plate electrodes, and metal underground systems such as piping systems.

main cross-connect (MC) — The primary connection and flexibility point for intrabuilding backbone cabling and equipment cables.

main distribution frame — A steel-bar framework that usually holds the phone company's central office protective devices and serves as the major cross-connect point for the central office lines and the customer's wiring. It is also used to interconnect loop cable pairs and line-equipment terminals on a switching system.

main telecommunications room — The main equipment room or main cross-connect for the interconnection of entrance cables, first-level backbone cables, and equipment cables.

mechanical splicing — A splicing method that uses simple alignment devices to hold two fiber ends together precisely, enabling light to pass between the fibers with losses as low as 0.3 dB.

medium — A means of transmitting signals, usually via cable. The plural form of the word is *media*.

megabit — One million bits of data.

megabits per second (Mbps) — A measurement of a network's data rate based on the network's physical characteristics.

mesh topology — A system in which all nodes and devices share many redundant interconnections.

mineral wool batt insulation — Nonflammable, noncombustible insulation made from spun rock or slag.

mortar — A gypsum-based, fire-resistant material that expands when activated by water and sets to form an excellent seal.

multimeter — A hand-held instrument that performs multiple tests on cable, including ohmmeter function, continuity verification, attenuation measurement, and electrical outlet testing.

multimode fiber — Fiber that carries up to hundreds of thousands of modes of light simultaneously.

National Electrical Code (NEC) — The most comprehensive book on electrical safety code in the United States, written and administered by the NFPA.

National Electrical Manufacturers Association (NEMA) — A standards association that focuses on electrical power and grounding.

National Fire Protection Association (NFPA) — The association that writes and administers the NEC.

near-end crosstalk (NEXT) — A measurement of the signal coupling from one pair of wires to another pair within the same cable.

network interface — *See* demarcation point.

network interface card (NIC) — The device that enables a workstation to connect to the network and communicate with other computers.

network interface device — Equipment used to terminate cable at the demarc.

nonintumescent sealant — An acrylic-based or silicone-based sealant that remains flexible when cured to allow movement.

ohm — A measurement of resistance.

Open Systems Interconnection (OSI) model — A model for understanding and developing computer-to-computer communication. It divides network architecture into seven layers.

opens — Breaks in a wire that result in an incomplete circuit and inhibit the continuous flow of transmission signals.

optical time domain reflectometer (OTDR) — A unit very similar to a TDR. An OTDR transmits light waves down the cable being tested, then measures the waves reflected back to determine the cable's length and signal strength.

parameters — Measurement criteria.

passive system — A nonmechanical, nonelectrical fire containment system that requires no human intervention or moving parts.

patch cable — A relatively short section of cable (3 to 50 feet) with connectors at both ends that connect network devices to data jacks, or horizontal cables to the horizontal cross-connect.

patch cord — A length of cable with connectors on one or both ends that join telecommunications circuits and links at the cross-connect.

pathway — A sequence of connections for network devices or networks on an internetwork. Also, a pathway is the vertical and horizontal route of the telecommunications cable.

peer-to-peer — A means of networking computers using a single cable.

penetration — A void or hole in a building's construction through which pipes, conduits, and cable trays may pass.

physical topology — The physical layout of the network, including the configuration of the cables and devices.

Plastic Insulated Conductor (PIC) cable — Twisted-pair cable designed to ease cable-pair identification.

plenum — A chamber to which one or more air ducts are connected to form part of an air distribution system. Cables installed in an air distribution system require a higher fire rating.

point of entrance — The point at which cabling emerges through an exterior wall, through a floor, or from a conduit. It can also be the point where the local service provider's cabling ends and the customer's cabling begins.

polarity test — Confirmation that the positive and negative wires of a cable pair are not crossed.

polyvinyl chloride (PVC) — Material found in the insulation of most wire and cable, and in most plastic conduit.

potentials — Measured voltages.

power meter — A tool that uses an optical light source to measure a cable's signal strength and attenuation. The light source generates light waves along the cable that the power meter detects and measures.

power sum — A measurement that compares the crosstalk effects on all pairs in a cable.

power winch — A piece of equipment that provides pulling force for raising vertical cables.

power-limited applications — Applications with a circuit that limit power (generally to 50 volts and under) to the external wiring in the event of an overload condition.

premises distribution system — A generic term that includes both backbone and horizontal cabling and all their components.

private branch exchange (PBX) — A large telephone system that switches calls among users on local lines while allowing all users to share a certain amount of external lines.

propagation delay — The amount of time it takes a signal to travel from one end of a cable to the other.

protector — Fuses that protect lines, cables, facilities, and equipment from abnormally high voltages or currents, lightning, and power surges.

protocols — The rules that a network uses to transfer data.

pull boxes — Openings in the duct system that provide access for pulling cables.

punch-down block — A solid plastic block with imbedded metal connectors, for terminating wires from larger cables (more than six pairs).

punch-down tool — *See* impact tool.

putty — A nonhardening, noncuring firestopping product that expands when heated.

raceway — Any enclosed channel designed for holding wires, cables, or busbars.

radio frequency interference (RFI) — Waves that emanate from electrical devices or cables carrying electricity. RFI can also be caused by a strong broadcast signal from a radio or television station.

redundancy — The practice of installing and using multiple systems for protection against system failure.

reel and sheave block — Equipment that provides a means of applying a break at the reel or sheave when raising or lowering cable through vertical pathways.

refractive index — The measure of a material's ability to bend light.

regulation — A local authority's ability to enforce codes and standards to regulate the building and construction industry.

repeater — A connectivity device that regenerates and amplifies an analog or digital signal.

return loss — A measurement of the signal that echoes or reflects back into the transmitter. Return loss is usually caused by an impedance mismatch, an imbalance in the cable, or a mismatch in connecting hardware.

reversed-pair — An error that occurs when the two wires of a pair are connected to opposite pins at each end of the cable.

ring — One of the wires in a pair, in twisted-pair cabling. The ring is connected to the DC negative wire (–48 volts) that carries the signal.

ring topology — In this system, each node is connected to the two nearest nodes so that the entire network forms a circle. Data is transmitted in one direction around the ring. Each node receives every transmission; when passing on a transmission, the node acts as a repeater, a device that regenerates signals.

riser cable — Main distribution cable segments that run between floors or sections of a building. This cable is more correctly known as backbone cable.

RJ-45 connectors — The 8-pin connectors used with twisted-pair cable.

SC connector — One of the most popular connectors made for fiber-optic cable.

scalability — Growth ability and potential.

sealant — Material used to seal openings around penetrations and construction joints.

service loops — Extra wire that is stored in a wall, ceiling, or floor, and used to repair damaged cable, repair installation errors, or assist in the moving, changing, or addition of devices.

service provider (SP) — A company that provides telecommunications service to a building.

sheath — A protective covering over a conductor assembly that may include one or more metallic members, strength members, or jackets.

sheave — A curved apparatus used to guide vertical cable into the sleeve.

shoe — A curved plastic apparatus that guides cables and protects them from corner abrasions during cable pulling.

shorts — Unwanted contact between two wires that stops transmission signals.

signal bounce — A phenomenon in which data signals travel endlessly between the two ends of the network.

single-mode fiber — Fiber that carries a single mode of light to transmit data from one end of a cable to another.

sleeve — A short section of conduit, either metallic or nonmetallic, that lines an opening in the wall or floor for cables to pass through.

sleeving — The insertion of a durable cylindrical device through a penetration so that another pipe can be inserted through it.

sneak current — A foreign voltage that is too low to make an overvoltage protector operate.

sniffer — A regular laptop PC equipped with a special NIC and specialized software to analyze network problems.

solid bottom cable tray — A tray with a solid bottom and longitudinal side rails.

span — The length between two cabling support points. In an aerial plant, the span is the space between two poles or building connection points.

spine cable tray — An open tray with a central rigid spine and cable support ribs along the tray's length at 90° angles.

splice boxes — Openings in the underfloor duct system that provide access for making connections in the cable.

splice enclosure — A box, case, or cabinet, usually made of steel or metal, that houses and protects cable splices.

splicing — The joining of two or more segments of wire to create one continuous wire.

split-pair — An error that occurs when a wire from one pair is incorrectly connected to a wire from another pair, as if they were a pair.

sprinklers — Devices that apply water directly onto flames and heat to cool combustion and prevent ignition of adjacent combustible materials.

ST connector — One of the most popular connectors made for fiber-optic cable.

standard — A document of specifications that guarantee a minimum level of performance.

star topology — In this system, every node is connected through a central device, such as a hub. Any physical cable on a star topology connects to only two devices, so a cabling problem will affect only two nodes at most. All nodes transmit data to the hub, which then retransmits the data to the segment that contains the destination node.

structured cabling — A method for uniform, enterprise-wide, multivendor cabling specified by ANSI/EIA/TIA-568.

suppression system — The fire protection system responsible for extinguishing fires.

surge — A rapid rise in current or voltage, usually followed by a fall back to a normal level. Also referred to as a transient.

surge arresters (suppressors) — Devices that are installed in conjunction with a lightning protection system to protect electrical wiring and electronic systems.

telecommunications outlet/connector — The location in the work area that is terminated with a jack for plugging in telecommunications equipment.

telecommunications service — The cabling and services available from a local service provider.

telephone line tester (butt set) — A tool used for testing lines, jacks, and circuits. It can easily connect to the metal terminals on punch-down blocks, to screw terminals, and directly to a cable pair.

terminal strip — A piece of metal with attached screws that allow wires to be connected. Terminal strips are usually found in small-system network interface devices.

termination — The act of connecting a cable or wire to connecting hardware.

terminator — A resistor at the end of a bus network that stops signals after they reach their destination.

throughput — The amount of data that a cable can transmit during a given period of time.

time domain reflectometer (TDR) — A device that transmits a signal down the cable being tested and gathers information on the signal reflection that is returned. A TDR tests for line impedance, opens, shorts, electrical interference (NEXT), cable distances, and connector or terminator problems.

tip — One of the wires in a pair, in twisted-pair cabling. The tip is connected to the positive side of a battery, which is the telephone industry's equivalent of a ground in a standard electrical circuit.

Token Ring — A networking technology developed by IBM. It employs a ring topology using a token to allow data transmission.

tone generator (toner) — A device that connects to one end of a pair of wires, then sends a sound throughout the cable so it can be located and identified on the other end.

topology — The physical layout of a computer network.

transient — A rapid rise in current or voltage, usually followed by a fall back to a normal level. Also referred to as a surge.

trench duct — A flat, metal duct that is divided into sections to provide separate compartments for different services.

twist ratio — The number of twists per meter or foot in twisted-pair cable.

twisted-pair cable — The most common form of cabling used on LANs. Each pair has a different number of twists per inch, depending on the grade, to help eliminate interference.

Underwriters Laboratories — A U.S.-based independent testing laboratory that creates safety tests and standards for electrical equipment.

utility column — An enclosed pathway that extends from the ceiling to furniture or to the floor, and guides electrical wiring, telecommunications cable, or both.

vampire tap — A connector that pierces a hole in a ThickNet cable.

ventilated channel cable tray — A channel section with a one-piece bottom that is no more than 150 mm wide.

ventilated trough cable tray — A tray with a ventilated bottom and side rails.

wavelength — A measure of the color of light, usually expressed in nm.

wire map test — A test that identifies wiring errors and checks connectivity.

wireless — Technology that transmits signals through the atmosphere.

work area — An area where users operate workstations or PCs.

work area cables — The modular cords that connect the telecommunications outlet to the network interface card (NIC) in the work area.

work area outlet — *See* telecommunications outlet/connector.

workstation — A computer intended for individual use.

wrap strips — Long strips of intumescent material, usually 1 or 2 inches wide, that are wrapped around a penetration a certain number of times.

zero tolerance — A term for a system that allows no margin for error.

zone cabling — Cabling that runs from the telecommunications room to the open office area, using a consolidation point or multiuser telecommunications outlet.

Index